Dictionary of International Human Rights Law

John S. Gibson

The Scarecrow Press, Inc.
Lanham, Md., & London

SCARECROW PRESS, INC.

Published in the United States of America
by Scarecrow Press, Inc.
4720 Boston Way
Lanham, Maryland 20706

4 Pleydell Gardens, Folkestone
Kent CT20 2DN, England

British Cataloguing-in-Publication Information Available

Library of Congress Cataloging-in-Publication Data

Gibson, John S. 1926–
Dictionary of international human rights law / John S. Gibson.
p. cm.
Includes bibliographical references.
1. Human rights—Dictionaries. I. Title.
K3239.3.G53 1996 341.4.′.81′03—dc20 95-47066 CIP

ISBN 0-8108-3118-X

∞ ™ The paper used in this publication meets the minimum requirements of American National Standard for Information Sciences—Permanence of Paper for Printed Library Materials, ANSI Z39.48–1984.
Manufactured in the United States of America.

With great respect and admiration, this book is dedicated to Professor Theo van Boven, professor of international law, University of Limburg, Maastricht, The Netherlands.

Contents

Preface

The *Dictionary of International Human Rights Law* is designed to provide the reader with the sources, definitions, landmarks, and cross references for sixty-four rights in international treaties and four "declared" rights as well.

Human rights include civil, legal, political, economic, social, and cultural rights of people everywhere. Constitutions and constitutional systems of the world's states provide for rights for their citizens and others in their jurisdictions. Almost all human rights are now incorporated into international treaties.

A right as such is an entitlement with the title derived from one or more sources and always with some limitation on the entitlement. In the United States Declaration of Independence, life is an entitlement or a right. Its source is in natural law which has been defined as "right reason" in the late eighteenth-century meaning of natural law. Others may find different sources for the right to life. However, the main source of right to life for most of humanity is in Article 6 of the International Covenant on Civil and Political Rights which states that "every human being has the inherent right to life." The first paragraph in the Preamble to the Covenant proclaims the "inalienable rights of all members of the human family." "Inherent" and "inalienable" are majestic doctrines of eighteenth-century natural law. Irrespective of other definitions of "inherent" and "inalienable," the fact remains that the right to life is in the Covenant, the Covenant is a treaty, and a treaty is the prime source of international law for all of us on this small planet.

Limitations on rights include not transgressing on the rights of others and obeying the requirements of the political community, usually the state. In this sense, rights and duties are sides of the same coin. No one has absolute entitlement, and therefore almost no right is absolute. Duty to respect the rights of others and obligation to the community at large are not always prominent when we extol our rights. On the other hand, there are historical and contemporary problems in preventing obligation to duty and limitations on rights from irreparably damaging the rights themselves.

A right is often an ideal, and the realities of any political community often place barriers to the attainment of the ideal. Some rights, such as the right to life, should fuse the ideal with the reality. Others, such as the right to health, may depend largely on resources available to achieve the right. Our commitment to human rights must seek to move the reality toward the ideal with full awareness of the challenges to this commitment in time and place.

The first section of the *Dictionary of International Human Rights Law* has eleven "Issues and Contexts" that relate to most of the rights in the dictionary. The five parts of the second section set forth the rights themselves: Civil and Political; Legal; Economic, Social, and Cultural; Collective; and Declaratory. The introduction to the second section explains the organization for each right's entries and provides a catalogue of the international conventions, treaties, declarations, and other sources of human rights. Each of the five parts has a brief introduction as well. The "landmarks" section for each right provides a brief historical background for that right.

A dictionary is a resource for those with varying requirements for a reference. Entries are therefore bound to be repetitious with respect to some basic sources, such as the English Magna Carta of 1215 for legal rights. A dictionary is not for casual reading but rather a compilation of general or specific entries, usually serving an ad hoc purpose. The entries in the dictionary are based upon treaties and other international instruments, some of which are cited in the resource volumes in the bibliography.

Professor Theo van Boven, former Director of the United Nations Division of Human Rights, recently registrar of the International Court on War Crimes in Former Yugoslavia, and perhaps the most distinguished scholar and international public servant in the cause of human rights, was largely responsible for my undertaking the authorship of the *Dictionary of International Human Rights Law*. In the preface of his own dictionary, Dr. Samuel Johnson wrote that "to have attempted much is always laudable, even when the enterprise is above the strength that undertakes it." It would be presumptuous for me to claim any comparison to either Dr. Johnson or his historic dictionary. However, I am in full agreement with the sentiment expressed by Dr. Johnson and at least hope that my own modest enterprise contributes to the cause of rights for humans.

Abbreviations for Principal Human Rights Treaties and Declarations*

ACR	American Convention on Human Rights, 1978
AFR	African Charter on Human and Peoples' Rights, 1986
ASEAN	Declaration on the Basic Duties of Association of Southeast Asian Nations (ASEAN) Peoples and Governments, 1983
ECR	European Convention for the Protection of Human Rights and Fundamental Freedoms, 1953
ESCR	International Covenant on Economic, Social, and Cultural Rights, 1976
ICPR	International Covenant on Civil and Political Rights, 1976
ISLAM	Cairo Declaration on Human Rights in Islam, 1990
UDHR	Universal Declaration of Human Rights, 1948
*	Dates indicate when covenants and conventions entered into force

Abbreviations for Organizations and Other Agencies Cited in the Dictionary

CEDAW	Committee on the Elimination of Discrimination Against Women
CSCE	Conference on Security and Cooperation in Europe
FAO	Food and Agricultural Organization
IFAD	International Fund for Agricultural Development
ICJ	International Court of Justice
IHRL	International Human Rights Law
IO	International Organizations
ILO	International Labor Organization
NIEO	New International Economic Order
OAS	Organization of American States
UNCTAD	United Nations Conference on Trade and Development
UNDP	United Nations Development Program
UNESCO	United Nations Educational, Scientific, and Cultural Organization
WHO	World Health Organization
WIPO	World Intellectual Property Organization

Note: See directory, pages 39–41, for a catalogue of citations used in entries in the dictionary.

Issues and Contexts

Twelve issues and contexts in international human rights law provide an introduction to and broader perspective for the entries on the specific rights in the dictionary. They include in the following:

A. Sources of Rights
B. Universality of Rights
C. Categories and Priorities of Rights
D. Conflicts of Rights
E. Limitations on Rights
F. Interpretation of Rights
G. Implementation of Rights
H. Compliance with Rights
I. States and Rights
J. International Organizations and Rights
K. Time Frames and Rights
L. Perspectives on Rights

The two prime human rights covenants are the United Nations Covenant on International Civil and Political Rights (ICPR) and the Covenant on Economic and Social Rights (ESCR). Both treaties were adopted by the General Assembly in 1966 and entered into force in 1976. The civil, political, legal, economic, social, and cultural rights in the dictionary are those in these covenants, along with several in the dictionary's collective rights. Consult the directory in part 2 of the dictionary for references on rights and for all the human rights treaties which are cited in the entries for rights. IHRL is international human rights law.

A "State Party" is a state which has signed and ratified a human rights treaty such as the ICPR. States Parties are committed to incorporate the rights in the treaty into their own national or "municipal" law. They are also obliged to comply with all provisions of the human rights treaty. States Parties jointly administer the treaty. They serve on the "treaty body" or the committee responsible for compliance with the treaty and for protection and enhancement of the rights in the treaty.

A. Sources of Rights

The sources of IHRL may be classified under the sources of international law in Article 38 of the Statute of the International Court of Justice (ICJ). They include treaties, international custom and usages, and principles of law. Judicial decisions, teachings of highly qualified publicists (jurists and scholars), and *ex aequo et bono*, or judgment in justice and fairness, are secondary. Declarations, General Assembly resolutions, and diplomatic papers and records, among others, may be evidences of international law.

Treaty law is firm or "hard" law. Custom and principles are less firm but significant sources of law in the absence of treaty law. Judicial decisions are secondary sources under Article 38. However, decisions by the European Court of Human Rights are very firm law and are binding on States Parties to the 1950 European Convention for the Protection of Human Rights and Fundamental Freedoms (ECR). Teaching and writings by prominent jurists and scholars and *ex aequo et bono* are "softer" law. Firm or hard law in general is law that is relied on in adjudication in courts, largely because it is writing in terms of treaties, legislation, contracts, and other firm sources of law. The other sources, not having this firm foundation, are considered less reliable and thus are "softer" law.

Declarations and resolutions such as those by the General Assembly are evidences of law but rarely sources. However, one could argue that yearly resolutions by the Assembly on a specific subject such as violations of human rights in Southern Africa take on the status of customary law because of constant usage. A right may have two or more sources. The right to life in Article 6 of the United Nations Covenant on Civil and Political Rights (ICPR) is based on natural law but is also in the treaty law of the Covenant.

1. Treaty Law

The two prime United Nations human rights treaties are the ICPR and the Covenant on Economic, Social, and Cultural Rights (ESCR). Other universal treaties (including charters, conventions, covenants, and statutes), regional treaties (ECR), and protocols to treaties (Protocol to the 1969 American Convention on Human Rights) comprise the principal body of international human rights treaty law.

The 1969 Vienna Convention on the Law of Treaties is the central source of international law on treaties. Part II of the Convention, "Observance, Application, and Interpretation of Treaties," is of particular importance with respect to the binding nature of treaties. Article 26 of the Convention states that "every treaty in force is binding on the parties to it and must be performed by them in good faith."

2. International Custom

Custom is "evidence of a general practice accepted by law" in Article 38 of the Statute of the ICJ. The Universal Declaration of Human Rights of December 10, 1948 (UDHR) is generally accepted as IHRL because of extensive and near-universal usage of most of its provisions, its citation in international human rights treaties and by international and national judges, its incorporation into constitutions of many states, and other evidences of states' acceptance of the Declaration as IHRL. Most treaty law has origins in custom and principles which, when translated into treaties, become firmer law.

3. Principles

a. Religious Principles

For hundreds of millions of people, natural law as a principle is derived from the eternal law of God. This is the source of natural law for St. Thomas Aquinas's *summa theologica* of the 1260s and also for the Roman Catholic Church. In the Islamic world, the Shari'ah is Islamic law emanating from the Revealed Books of God. In the American Declaration of Independence of 1776, "all men . . . are endowed by their Creator with certain unalienable rights . . ." Other references in the Declaration to a deity include Supreme Judge, Nature's God, and divine Providence. It is left largely to the reader to identify these sources of law.

b. Philosophic Principles

For many, natural law is philosophy and not religion. The UDHR and the two prime treaties are based on doctrines of natural law, including "inherent dignity and inalienable rights of all members of the human family." For many, Confucius, Marx, and others provide principles which serve as sources for human rights. In the American Convention on Human Rights "the essential rights of man . . . are based on attributes of the human personality." In the African Charter on Human and Peoples' Rights "fundamental human rights stem from the attributes of human beings . . ."

4. Judicial Decisions

Judicial decisions are hard law if treaties provide that courts and decisions by courts are to be binding on states signing and ratifying the treaties. This is the case for judicial decisions by the European Court of Human Rights. This also applies to the Inter-American Court of Human Rights and the International Court of Justice when states accept the compulsory jurisdiction of the Court under Article 36 of the Court's Statute. Of course states are obliged to abide by the decisions of their own courts on international and national human rights according to their constitutional law. International judicial bodies usually have the authority to interpret IHRL and may have the option to deliver advisory opinions on IHRL as well.

Quasi-judicial decisions are those made by an organ established by states and incorporated into treaties to monitor and oversee compliance by States Parties to the treaties. An example is the Human Rights Committee of the ICPR which is the "treaty body" engaged in monitoring and supervising compliance of States Parties to the provisions of the ICPR. The Human Rights Committee has made many decisions over twenty years on issues involving State Parties' compliance or noncompliance with their obligations under the ICPR. This monitoring and surveillance authority is also vested in treaty bodies of five other human rights conventions, such as the Committee Against Torture in the 1984 Convention Against Torture.

5. Publicists

Article 38 of the ICJ Statute includes "the teachings of the most highly qualified publicists of the various nations." The writings of Hugo Grotius, John Locke, Emerich de Vattel, Francisco de Vitoria, and other great scholars and jurists provide compelling evidence on the theory, substance, and interpretations of IHRL.

6. Combinations of Sources

As observed above, there are many ways in which sources of law may be combined. A major example of multiple sources is the Martens Clause in the four 1949 Geneva Conventions on International Humanitarian Law negotiated under the aegis of the International Committee of the Red Cross. States are obliged to conform to the "principles of the law of nations, as they result from the usages established among civilized peoples, from the laws of humanity, and the dictates of public conscience."

The Martens Clause, furthermore, is a provision in international treaties, the principal sources of international law.

B. Universality of Rights

Human rights are universal. The ICPR's rights are for "All peoples. . ." (Article 1) and "Every human being" or "everyone" in most articles. The ESCR refer to "States Parties" in guaranteeing rights but states ratifying the ESCR include all areas and regions of the world. The UDHR for the most part refers to "everyone." President Franklin D. Roosevelt's "Four Freedoms" of January 6, 1941, which launched the incorporation of "human rights and fundamental freedoms" in the United Nations Charter, declared the first three freedoms to apply "everywhere in the world" and the fourth, "Freedom from Fear," to be honored "anywhere in the world." The origins, negotiating history, and provisions of the UDHR and the two prime Covenants emphatically intend universality and not geographical, cultural, or any kind of relativity.

An argument might be made that some rights such as civil, legal, and political are essentially "Western," as they evolved from philosophic and, to some extent, Christian religious principles. It might be contended that "inherent dignity and equal and inalienable rights of all members of the human family" in the Preamble to ICPR and ESCR is a Western statement of natural law. However, these principles are incorporated into the two prime treaties and ratified by the vast majority of states.

In signing and ratifying the treaty, a state accepts its provisions unless it adds a reservation or statement providing a different interpretation. States Parties to the two prime treaties have not challenged the treaties' natural law sources. Further, two of the three major authors of the UDHR who devised the basic natural law source of the Declaration were from Lebanon (Charles Malik) and China (P. C. Chang). The first draft of the UDHR was based on rights proposals from Panama. ESCR, also based on the sources of inherent and inalienable rights, includes economic and social rights which are supported by most by African, Asian, Islamic, and other nations.

There are, of course, some regional treaties for rights such as conventions in Europe, the Americas, and Africa and declarations for Islamic and Southeast Asia peoples. Some of these treaties emphasize their regional values. The 1950 European Convention in its Preamble hails the "common heritage of political traditions and ideals, freedom and the rule of law. . ." of its member states. The 1990 Cairo Declaration on Human Rights in Islam states that all rights therein "are subject to the Islamic Shari'ah (law)." The 1986 African Charter is concerned with Human Rights and Peoples' Rights. However, regional conventions, by the rights they enumerate and protect, reflect on the whole a universal consensus on human rights rather than individual versions of rights or exclusions of the basic civil, political, and legal rights in ICPR.

Naturally there will be relativism of varying degrees in a state's interpretation and policy with respect to human rights. Culture and national laws in many states discriminate against women. In many states ethnocentrism recognizes higher status for certain ethnic, religious, racial, and national groups and their members to the detriment and discriminatory treatment of others. Childrens' rights and safety are bleak in many nations. Economic disparities in most nations impair the ideal of equality, often in the administration of justice. Economic deprivation also reduces the capacity of states to achieve the economic and social rights in ESCR, which require significant economic resources. Some states which have not abolished the death penalty are accused of too many exceptions to the right to life in Article 6, ICPR. Many states declare that national emergency or public order necessitate significant limitations on the exercise of human rights in their jurisdictions.

Each year there is ample testimony and evidence submitted to the Commission on Human Rights about conditions in most countries that impair achievement of rights and protection of rights for their peoples. It is widely recognized that the full achievement of rights enshrined in international treaty law is in the distant future. It is also recognized that relativism in many nations, if within acceptable limits, is a natural expression of diversity in a enormously pluralistic world. However, the pursuit of the goal and tangible evidence by states of that pursuit will move achievement of rights toward the vision of the Universal Declaration of 1948. No departure is permissible from universality of the right of humans to life—free of torture, unusual punishment, and slavery—and to enjoy basic judicial guarantees as provided in Article 4 of ICPR.

C. Categories and Priorities of Rights

The basic categories of human rights with an example of each are as follows:

1. Civil (right of assembly)
2. Legal (due process of law)
3. Political (right of petition to governance)
4. Economic (right to work)
5. Social (right to health)
6. Cultural (right to take part in cultural life)
7. Collective (peoples' right of self-determination)
8. Declaratory (right of development)
9. For all categories (right of nondiscrimination)

1, 2, and 3 are in ICPR; 4, 5, and 6 are in ESCR; and 7 , 8, and 9 combine civil, legal, economic, and social rights.

The above list suggests a ranking of rights in terms of importance. This is true to some extent. The civil, legal, and political rights in ICPR preceded the other rights in their evolution and especially in their enumeration in the late eighteenth-century United States and French Declarations. The ICPR rights are firmer international law. The ICPR includes provisions for States Parties to ensure people in their jurisdiction enjoyment of these rights, for people alleging State Party violation of these rights to have a remedy in law, and for States Parties to enforce such remedies when granted. Most ICPR rights are incorporated in the national law of states and do not require economic resources for their implementation and enforcement. Also, Article 4 of ICPR identifies civil and legal rights that may not be waived or derogated, especially right to life; freedom from torture, cruel or unusual punishment, and slavery; and some basic judicial rights as well. Freedom from discrimination and right to due process of law must be added to firm law or *jus cogens*. Another important civil right is the right against genocide as set forth in the 1948 Genocide Treaty.

Economic, social, and cultural rights in ESCR emerged in the nineteenth century, and many entered the legal systems of some states in the late nineteenth and twentieth centuries. The right to work and rights associated with work were guaranteed and protected by the International Labor Organization and ILO conventions. Most other economic and social rights did not become international human rights until the advent of the United Nations in 1945, the UDHR in 1948, and especially the ESCR in 1966. Most of these rights are limited to States Parties to ESCR, while the ICPR introduces each right as applying to individuals. To be enjoyed by people, most of these rights require economic resources. The right to health in Article 12-1 of ESCR is a goal. Implementation of or means to the goal are outlined in Article 12-2. Article 2 of ESCR sets forth procedures for the implementation of ESCR which are much more detailed and conditional than implementation of ICPR rights in Article 2 of ICPR. It is important to remember that in the Preambles to both the ICPR and the ESCR, each set of rights depends upon the other.

Collective rights may be firm law, such as rights for refugees under the 1951 Convention, or softer law, such as the right to "Self-determination of Peoples." Declaratory rights are based on General Assembly declarations and are evolving toward treaty rights.

Priorities of rights will always be debated. Each individual and each society may have its own priorities. To a hungry person, the right to food will have a higher priority than the right to assembly. The civil right to life in #6, ICPR, is paralleled with the economic and social right to an adequate standard of living in #11-1, ESCR.

D. Conflicts of Rights

Another perspective on priorities of rights is when one right conflicts with another. Someone, usually an authoritative official in government such as a judge, must give one right priority over another. Some examples using IHRL are as follows.

1. Right of expression through speech (ICPR #19-1) vs. right of a government to maintain public order if government considers a speech inflamatory and likely to incite violence (ICPR #19-3-b).

2. Right to fair and public hearing for a person accused of distributing pornographic material (ICPR #14-1) vs. right of government to ban the press from hearing on grounds of offense to public morals (ICPR #14-1).

3. Right of a seventeen-year-old person found guilty of homicide not to be sentenced to death (ICPR #6-5) vs. the right of a government under its own laws to impose the death penalty on a person under eighteen years of age convicted of homicide.

4. Right of person to publish an article which may defame another person (ICPR #19-1) vs. the right of the latter person to protection of his/her reputation (ICPR #19-3-a).

5. Right of a person through freedom of association (ICPR #22-1) to organize a group to overthrow a government vs. the right of the government to forbid association on the grounds of national security (ICPR #22-2).

6. Right of person to engage in prayer in public school (ICPR #18-1) vs. right of government to forbid school prayer on grounds of separation

of church and state as prescribed by its law and also violating rights of others (ICPR #18-3).

7. Right of a person to have access to "highest attainable standard of physical and mental health" (ESCR #12-1) vs. right of government to allocate resources as it wishes with little concern for resources for health care (ESCR #12-2 as interpreted by the government under ESCR #2).

8. The right of police officers in a community to organize a trade union (ESCR #8-1) vs. the right of the government to prevent such organization (ESCR #8-2).

The above conflicts of rights were derived from actual cases before the European Court of Human Rights and the Human Rights Committee of the ICPR. Many other examples of conflicts of rights on the international level as in ECR and ACR illustrate similar conflicts at national levels. In the United States, a protracted conflict subject to much jurisprudence is that of the right to life of a fetus vs. freedom of choice for the woman carrying the fetus to abort. IHRL has also dealt with this conflict of rights and the key issue, when does life begin?

E. Limitations on Rights

A right is not absolute. There are three principal limitations on rights: the requirements of the society, respect for the rights of others, and judgment giving priority to one right over another if there is a conflict between rights. Other limitations may include an authoritative interpretation, usually judicial, of a right and its limitations and the decision of a person to place limitations on the exercise of his or her own rights.

With one exception, there are no specific limitations on the rights in the United States Constitution and its first ten Amendments. The exception is in the Fifth Amendment which permits "private property to be taken for public use" but only with "just compensation" (government right of eminent domain). As no right is absolute, however, limitations have been placed on these rights by presidential orders, legislation, and judicial decisions, especially by the Supreme Court.

In Article 4 of the French Declaration of the Rights of Man and the Citizen of August 26, 1789, a person's rights are limited by the right to enjoy the "same rights (by) all other individuals." In Article 5, legislation may "forbid only those actions (rights) which are harmful to society." Basic freedom to hold opinions, "including religious ones," is cited in Article 10, "provided that the manifestation of these does not disturb the public order established by legislation." The right to "speak, write and publish freely" is protected in Article 11, provided that a person "must answer for any abuse of such freedom. . ." In Article 17, "no individual may be deprived of (property) unless some public necessity, legally certified as such, clearly requires it. . ." This is the right of eminent domain as in the Fifth Amendment to the United States Constitution.

At the San Francisco United Nations Conference in the spring of 1945, the Panamanian draft for a "Declaration of Essential Human Rights" stated in #18 that "in the exercise of his rights, everyone is limited by the rights of others and by the just requirements of the democratic state." This wording, while not included in the United Nations Charter, was slightly modified and incorporated into the official draft for the 1948 Universal Declaration of Human Rights. This draft was expanded to become Article 29-2 of the Declaration. "In the exercise of his rights and freedoms, everyone shall be subject only to such limitations as are determined by law solely for the purpose of securing due recognition and respect for the rights and freedoms of others and of meeting the just requirements of morality, public order and the general welfare in a democratic society."

Rights are also limited by the determination of states of "just requirements" of their societies. In Article 4 of ICPR, the States Parties to the Covenant may derogate or waive their obligations to protect rights under the Covenant "in time of public emergency which threatens the life of the nation . . ." However, limitations on the state's "right of derogation" in Article 4 refer to specific Articles on rights from which no derogation may be made. They include right to life (#6), immunity from torture and unusual punishment (#7), freedom from slavery (Paragraph 8, Articles 1 and 2), not to be imprisoned for inability to fulfill a contract (#11), protection from *ex post facto* law (#15), right as a person before the law (#16), and freedom of religion (#18). However, right to life is limited by capital punishment as set forth in #6 and freedom of religion in #18 is indeed limited in #18-3.

Rights in six articles in ICPR have specific limitations. They include movement in territory (#12-2), public hearing and trial (#14-1), thought and religion (#18-3), expression (#19-3), assembly (#21), and association (#22). Expression is also limited by #20-1 which forbids war propaganda. The grounds for limitation by states in addition to "public emergency" in #4-1 include the following: national security, public order (and ordre public in French), public health, public morals, public safety, and prejudicing the interest of justice. All of these Articles except

#14 include the limitation on exercise of rights in the "protection of the rights and freedoms of others" (#22-2).

Similar limitations are included in all treaties on human rights. The European Convention for the Protection of Human Rights and Fundamental Freedoms has more extensive limitations than ICPR, such as limitations on the right of privacy (#8) and expression (#10 includes "prevention of the disclosure of information received in confidence"). The freedom of expression in #13 of the American Convention on Human Rights is limited in part by questionable public entertainments, and the Islamic Shari'ah or law places limitations on all rights in the 1990 Cairo Declaration of Human Rights.

Limitations on rights, especially those in the ICPR, often depend upon interpretation of such words as "public emergency" in #4 and morals, public order, or national security in a democratic society in #14-1 and other ICPR articles. The "Siracusa Principles on the Limitation and Derogation Provisions of the ICPR" were formulated by a group of thirty-one distinguished experts on IHRL at a conference in Siracusa, Italy, in April and May 1984. The Principles interpret the limitations provisions in the ICPR, including democratic society, public order, public health, public morals, national security, public safety, rights and freedoms of others, and restrictions on a public trial. Particular attention is focused on narrowing states' rights to declare a public emergency in ICPR #4. The Principles also review rights which may not be derogated, especially the right to life. The Siracusa Principles are designed to guide states and judicial authorities, especially courts, toward specific interpretations of limitations on state authority and enhancing states' protection of the rights in the ICPR (*Encyclopedia of Human Rights,* pp. 198–202, and Freedom of the Individual under Law, part 2, directory).

In some human rights treaties, the requirement of peoples' duties to merit rights may also be viewed as a limitation on rights. There was much debate on this issue at the United States Constitutional Convention in the summer of 1787. Rights are not accompanied by any duties in the Constitution and in its first ten Amendments. The French Declaration of the Rights of Man and the Citizen of August 26, 1789, however, calls for rights and duties in its Preamble, the duty to ensure the rights of others to enjoy their liberties and other duties in various articles.

The authors of the Universal Declaration of Human Rights of December 10, 1948, devoted considerable time and deliberation to the question of duties, especially since the Soviet Union had long held that any rights granted by the state required commensurate duties to society and the state. The Soviet delegates were firm on this issue in Declaration debates. Agreement was finally reached on what became the first paragraph of Article 29: "Everyone has duties to the community in which alone the free and full development of his personality is possible." This was a compromise between delegates from the socialist and the non-socialist nations. It relates duties to the social nature of the person and precedes Article 29, paragraph 2, of the Declaration which limits rights in terms of those of others and the requirements of the "democratic society."

Duties are not emphasized in the ICPR, ESCR, and ECR with the exception of the person's duty not to infringe on the rights of others or present a threat to the public order (which are also limitations on rights). The 1948 American Declaration of the Rights and Duties of Man is replete with duties. The Preamble states that "the fulfillment of duty by each individual is a prerequisite to the rights of all. Rights and duties are interrelated in every social and political activity of man. While rights exalt individual liberty, duties express the dignity of that liberty." Articles 29 through 38 begin with "It is the duty of every person. . ." The November 22, 1969, American Convention on Human Rights, however, only mentions duties in Article 32, entitled "Relationship between Duties and Rights." Paragraph 1 states, "Every person has responsibilities to his family, his community, and mankind," and paragraph 2 repeats the limitations of rights of others and the "just demands of the general welfare. . ."

The African Charter on Human and Peoples' Rights of October 23, 1986, declares in the Preamble that "the enjoyment of rights and freedoms also implies the performance of duties on the part of everyone. . ." Chapter II is entitled "Duties," with eight specific duties for individuals set forth in Article 29. The Declaration of the Basic Duties of ASEAN Peoples and Governments of December 9, 1983, clearly emphasizes state duties to protect rights. Item f in the Universal Islamic Declaration of Human Rights of 1981 asserts that "our duties and obligations have priority over our rights. . ." The requirement of a human duty to deserve most human rights merits much examination and consideration.

F. Interpretation of Rights

Each state through its constitutional processes interprets the meaning, application, limitations, and conflicts of the manifold rights enjoyed by the people under its jurisdiction. Interpretation is undertaken by the executive, legislative, and/or judicial organs of government depending upon the state's written or unwritten constitution. Examples include interpretation by the United States Supreme Court and the Parliament of the United Kingdom.

Criteria used by states for interpretation of rights include provisions in constitutions and constitutional documents, the original intent of authors of the constitution, construction or plain meaning of the right, the context provided by the contemporary use of the right, and priorities between the meaning of one right and that of another in case of conflict of rights. Further, the executive organ or authority of a state may have or assume authority to interpret a right as it wishes, as well as placing limitations on rights through an interpretation and declaration of public emergency or the demands of national security.

As treaties are the prime source for IHRL, interpretation of words in treaties, as we have observed, is of great significance. When states ratify treaties such as the ICPR, they often include their own reservations and understandings of specific rights, words, and provisions. The United States attached many reservations and understandings when it ratified the ICPR in 1992, including its own interpretations of these provisions. The 1969 Vienna Convention on the Law of Treaties is of paramount importance on these issues, especially Section 3 of Part III, "Interpretation of Treaties." A long-term objective is more consensus between and among states and increased uniformity with respect to limitations on and interpretation of rights in IHRL.

There is no specific authority for interpretation in ICPR. The Human Rights Committee of the ICPR, established in Article 28 of Part IV, was not specifically authorized by the Covenant to interpret the rights in the ICPR. However, the Committee has found it necessary to engage in interpretation in making decisions about communications presented to it which contain petitions for a redress of a grievance upon allegation of violation of rights by a state and/or non-state actors. The Committee may receive such petitions if states voluntarily accept authority by the Committee to receive petitions under Articles 41 and 42 with respect to violations by other states and under the First Optional Protocol for individual petitions against state violations.

Treaty bodies in five other human rights conventions, such as the Committee Against Torture in the Convention Against Torture, also by necessity make interpretations as they make judgments with respect to communications and petitions alleging violations. The "1503 Procedure" under the United Nations Commission for Human Rights, which enables people complaining of a "consistent pattern of gross and reliably attested violations of human rights and fundamental freedoms" to petition to the Commission for a due process procedure, has led to interpretations of rights.

The European Court of Human Rights under the European Convention of Human Rights has had well over forty years of judgment authority on human rights issues brought before it through Convention procedures. It makes judgments on hundreds of cases each year. Although each case is discrete and distinct, the Court's decisions and interpretations of rights including intent in the Convention, meaning in its current context, and limitations and conflicts of rights, have entered into the mainstream of national and international human rights law. Under #45 of the Convention, the Court's jurisdiction extends "to all cases concerning the interpretation and application" of the European Convention. Further, the Court's decisions on and interpretations of rights in the Convention are binding on States Parties to the Convention when they declare their recognition of the Court's compulsory jurisdiction under #46 of the Convention.

For instance, a case in the Netherlands turned on whether an assembly and specific activities of protesters at a public meeting was or was not a threat to public order. The case came before the courts in the Netherlands, which decided that the right of the state and its definition of public order did not prevail over the rights and activities of the protestors. The case was appealed by the Netherlands and finally came before the European Court in Strasbourg. The Court, in defining the "right to freedom of peaceful assembly" in Article 11-1 of the Convention, interpreted "peaceful" and "assembly" in such a manner as to conclude that the protest was not peaceful and that the assembly was of such a nature as to disturb public order. It reversed the decision of the Netherlands court and decided in favor of the Netherlands' right to limit this right of assembly on the grounds that the protesters' activities violated the requirements for public order.

Courts and lawyers in the Netherlands, in appraising the decision in this case, adjusted to this ruling and interpretation which became a more definitive statement on the limits of peaceful assembly. Further, judicial systems and lawyers in other States Parties to the Convention reviewed this decision which they consider binding if and when a similar case arises in their jurisdictions. In brief, the European Court has evolved into a major organ for the interpretation of international human rights law, largely because of the authority delegated to it by States Parties to the

Convention, especially under #45 and 46. The Inter-American Court of Human Rights of the American Convention on Human Rights also has delegated to it by States Parties the authority of interpretation and application of the Convention in #62. The Court is progressively adding to the body of interpretation of human rights through its decisions and advisory opinions.

"Original intent" of the authors of human rights conventions as a guide to interpretation may enlighten jurists. However, "original intent" is less important than the contemporary context of the right. "Original intent" for many rights runs deep into history, such as the right of "property" and the freedom of "religion." These and many other rights evolved in historical stages far different from the contemporary context which must necessarily temper their interpretation. In any event, words of the human rights treaties must be defined in order to apply the law, and definitions of many terms inevitably trigger debate and dispute. The definition of the state's right to declare "public emergency" and "national security" are vivid examples. Jurisprudence in the United States demonstrates the continuing process of interpretation of human rights as jurists and others seek to reconcile an individual right with the rights of society at large.

G. Implementation of Rights

Implementation of human rights is the elevating of the right in a treaty or other source in law to the realization of its enjoyment by humans. A right in a treaty is an ideal unless it is implemented as a law. Mode One of implementation of human rights is by the state, which under its treaty commitments elevates the treaty right into its own law. Mode Two is implementation by an international legal authority such as the European Court of Human Rights which has authority delegated to it by States Parties to the European Convention to make decisions which States Parties consider binding on their national law.

In Mode One, implementation includes States Parties to human rights treaties incorporating or "domesticating" the rights in the treaties into their own national or "municipal" law. Article 2-2 of the ICPR requires States Parties to "adopt such legislative or other measures as may be necessary to give effect to the rights recognized in the present Covenant." Implementation includes compliance which under #40 of ICPR means states reporting to the Human Rights Committee "on the measures they have adopted to give effect to the rights recognized herein and on the progress made in the enjoyment of those rights." Implementation includes surveillance and monitoring of states' compliance, which is also a responsibility of the Human Rights Committee in #40 of ICPR.

Implementation includes the right of due process for individuals and/or groups of people who contend that the state in whose jurisdiction they are located is not providing and/or protecting their right to enjoy human rights under treaty law. Due process is provided for in the UN Commission on Human Rights 1503 Procedure cited above in interpretation of human rights, in procedures for states' complaints against other states (#41 and #42, ICPR), and procedures for individuals' complaints against states in the First Optional Protocol to ICPR, cited above in "Interpretation."

The Human Rights Committee, through procedures under #41 and #42, ICPR, and in the First Optional Protocol, has demonstrated its capacity through friendly procedures and diplomacy to bring about measures of compliance by states for the implementation of human rights in their jurisdictions. Treaty bodies under other human rights conventions, such as the Committee Against Torture under the Convention Against Torture, have also had considerable experience in advancing state compliance. Working Parties and Special Rapporteurs under the Commission on Human Rights, such as the Special Rapporteur on Torture, have compiled impressive records of surveillance, monitoring, and gaining compliance of states with their obligations under human rights treaties. The annual reports to the Commission and the General Assembly by their Working Parties and Special Rapporteurs, as well as reports by the Human Rights Committee and other treaty bodies to the General Assembly of the United Nations, provide abundant evidence of United Nations procedures for implementation of human rights.

Mode Two of implementation is by international organs such as the European Court of Human Rights and the Inter-American Court of Human Rights. Mode Two implementation depends on states' delegating authority to the courts of the conventions which have jurisdiction over the highest national courts of States Parties in specific and delegated areas of authority. Parenthetically, the Court of the European Union is an example of such a higher court. The European record is nearly perfect on States Parties' implementation of decisions and interpretations of law by the European Court of Human Rights under the 1950 European Convention and Protocols to the Convention. States found in Court decisions not to be in conformity with the provisions of the European Convention are obliged to alter their laws to bring them into harmony with those decisions. A European jurisprudence on human rights law has thus developed which has increasing global authority with respect to interpretation and implementation of IHRL.

H. Compliance with Rights

A state is obliged by its commitments in a human rights treaty to comply with the provisions of the treaty in good faith under the 1969 Vienna Convention on Treaties. Peaceful measures, especially negotiation, are extensively used to bring about compliance by a state with alleged violations of human rights in its jurisdiction. If those measures do not succeed, enforcement may be used to compel a state found to be in violation to undertake compliance or to be subjected to sanctions or other punishment. In Article 2-3, ICPR, each State Party ensures that a person whose rights have been violated "shall have an effective remedy" and to have the claim of violation "determined by competent judicial, administrative or legislative authorities. . ." Further, the State Party shall "ensure that the competent authorities shall enforce such remedies when granted." The 1950 European Convention on Human Rights in the last paragraph of the Preamble to the Convention declares that the European countries are taking "the first steps for collective enforcement of certain Rights stated in the Universal Declaration (of Human Rights)."

Chapter VI of the United Nations Charter is concerned with peaceful settlement of disputes through measures designed to prevent a dispute proceeding to a threat or breach of international peace and security. Chapter VII of the Charter includes thirteen articles concerned with enforcement action if and when peaceful measures fail to prevent action in violation of the Charter. Procedures in IHRL for compliance and/or enforcement include most of the measures in Chapter VI and VII of the Charter.

Negotiation in #33 of Chapter VI is the prime peaceful measure. The Working Parties and Special Rapporteurs of the Human Rights Commission constantly use negotiation in seeking to persuade governments in violation, such as the use of state torture, to cease illegal practices and return to the protection of human rights. The Human Rights Committee of the ICPR and treaty bodies in other human rights conventions rely primarily on negotiation and other modes of peaceful settlement in #33 for bringing about compliance to human rights law by states considered in violation.

The Human Rights Commissions of the European and American Conventions on Human Rights use negotiation and other diplomatic measures in seeking to reconcile differences between parties in legal disputes on human rights before a case is permitted to go on to the Court of Human Rights for judicial determination and decision. Officials of the International Committee of the Red Cross have long used peaceful means of persuasion for compliance with respect to states considered in violation of the international humanitarian law of the four Geneva Conventions of 1949.

There is no doubt whatever that these peaceful means have secured compliance for protection of human rights for people in many countries and with respect to many kinds of rights. However, it is impossible to measure statistically such success, given the confidential nature of peaceful means for resolution of human rights violations. And, of course, diplomacy and other peaceful means never guarantee a successful outcome. Article 33 also includes judicial settlement under pacific settlement of disputes. The European Court and the Inter-American Court of Human Rights are emphatic with respect to requiring parties before the Courts to comply with decisions by these courts.

If peaceful means fail to bring about state and other actor compliance with IHRL, recourse may be taken to other measures, short of sanctions, including public condemnation of states for human rights violations. Such condemnations by the UN Commission on Human Rights and other organs are often effective. They severely impair the prestige and credibility of a state, which often goes to great lengths to avoid such a public criticism. Coercive diplomacy and other pressures on the state in violation, such as the threat or actual expulsion of the state from the United Nations, may also produce reversal of policy and compliance.

Human rights violation may be considered so severe by the Security Council as to be a threat to or breach of the international peace and security guaranteed under Chapter VII of the United Nations Charter. The sequence of measures for enforcement in Chapter VII proceed from pressure for compliance to possible uses of force. A determination by the Security Council under #39 of a state's violation of IHRL as a threat to or breach of the peace may, under #40, be preceded by measures for compliance before more specific measures of enforcement are taken. If compliance fails, the Council, under #41, may threaten or apply sanctions short of force to compel the state in violation to comply. If the threat or actual sanctions do not produce compliance, the Council, under #42, may take military action "to maintain or restore international peace and security."

An array of sanctions is available under #41 to the Security Council "to give effect to its decisions." They may include withholding of economic assistance, freezing of assets, partial or complete interruption of communications, embargoes and quarantines, trade restrictions, and severance of diplomatic relations. Partial or actual use of force under #42 may include threats of force, military embargoes or blockades, no-fly zones, and military intervention by land, sea, or air. These measures may be imposed under the authorization of the Security Council by member states, regional organizations, or United Nations forces. In recent years, some human rights violations, such as those by Iraq, have been considered threats to the peace under Chapter VII. This determination has given the Security Council a significant role in enforcement for human rights violations and commanding states' compliance with their obligations to protect human rights.

I. States and Rights

We still live in a world of sovereign states which have sovereign equality (#2-1, UN Charter), possess immunity for their territorial integrity and political independence (#2-4), and are legally protected from United Nations intervention into their domestic jurisdictions (#2-7). However, legal sovereign equality does not protect small and insecure states from influence by powerful states. Further, the five permanent members of the Security Council in #23 of the UN Charter have significant authority over other UN members, especially in voting rights in the Security Council. Territorial independence and political integrity continue to be vital to state sovereignty. On the other hand, immunity for domestic jurisdiction under #2-7 has been progressively diluted by the requirements of international security and well-being in the past several decades.

Some 185 states, as members of the United Nations, represent an enormous variety in size and location of territory, population, doctrines and structures of governance, history, culture, economic capability and resources, and perspectives on their relations between and among each other. Each has the same goal of security and well-being for its central interests, but the differences between and among states determine how each defines its security and well-being and what each requires to pursue those goals. The United States, in the Preamble to its 1787 Constitution, declares that the people "establish justice, secure domestic tranquility, provide for the common defense, promote the general welfare, and secure the blessings of liberty"—goals for security and well-being.

All states subscribe to the 1948 Universal Declaration of Human Rights and its goals and specific rights. About 120 states adhere through their ratification of the ICPR to the words of the Preamble with respect to the inherent dignity and equal and inalienable rights of all members of the human family. In Article 25 they also endorse in principle their commitment to basic democratic structures and processes of governance which provide the most sound basis for the enhancement and protection of human rights. It may therefore be said that the majority of the world's states define their goals of well-being in human rights within the general framework of the IHRL of the Declaration and the ICPR. One-hundred-fifteen states have ratified the ESCR, further evidence of a growing of consensus on human rights and well-being.

Governments of states pursue national policy as a means to their goals. Human rights policies are developed within the executive or administrative branches of government, although some such as the United States must include the legislature as an important actor in human rights policy. The top leader of the state, whether president, prime minister, king, or chairman, has the basic responsibility for defining and pursuing human rights policy which is generally developed by the foreign ministry of the state.

Of principal importance is the state's human rights policy in the United Nations and other international organizations where international human rights policy is pursued and negotiations lead to IHRL. Officials with human rights policy authority develop state policy under the overall direction of top leadership and pursue that policy through their delegations to international organizations. The state's policy and votes in the UN Commission on Human Rights at its annual six-week meetings in Geneva are of key importance. Beyond Geneva is the state's human rights policy in all areas of the world through its bilateral and multilateral relations with other nations.

There is often inconsistency between a state's avowed support for the goals of IHRL and its policy with another nation which is in obvious violation of some dimension of IHRL. An example is arbitrary arrest and punishment of political dissenters by State Y. State X may overlook these human rights violations by State Y if State X chooses to place a higher priority on security or trade relations with State Y. This example of selective human rights policy may well impair the difficult task of advancing consistency in international protection and enhancement of hu-

K. Time Frames and Rights

The context of time is of major importance in appraising a human right. The context of 1776 in the United States Declaration of Independence provides an important case study. "We hold these truths to be self-evident: that all men are created equal; that they are endowed by their Creator, with certain unalienable rights; that among these are life, liberty, and the pursuit of happiness. . ." Some of these words are timeless. "Self-evident" is an obvious fact, fortified by reason. "Equal" is a term used abundantly and in many ways in ICPR and other human rights treaties. "Creator" is not any one God but rather in the Declaration's words "the laws of nature and . . . nature's God. . ." "Rights" are "unalienable" because they are inherent in humans. The rights of "life, liberty, and the pursuit of happiness" are fundamental and are the foundations and source for other rights. "Life, liberty, and property" are enshrined in the Fifth and Fourteenth Amendments to the Constitution. These words are indispensible to the United States constitutional system and are confirmed in IHRL.

However, only "man" is the beneficiary of this structure of rights. Man in 1776 was limited to the white, educated, propertied male over the age of twenty-one. Then, throughout most of history, and in many societies today the principal beneficiaries of human rights are the dominant male elites who define personal qualities and possessions for human rights, uniformly their own, and deny those rights to others who are not in their privileged domain.

In time in the United States and many other democracies, the property requirement for "men" was diminished and then abolished. In the Fourteenth Amendment to the United States Constitution of 1868, the word became "person" whom no state may "deprive" of "life, liberty or property without due process of the law, nor deny to any person within its jurisdiction the equal protection of the laws." However, consider the time between 1868 and the Nineteenth Amendment of 1919 confirming the right of women to vote, the granting in 1924 of citizenship to all Native (or indigenous) Americans, and the Civil Rights Acts of 1964 and 1965, which in law elevated all United States citizens, irrespective of color, to the rights proclaimed and enjoyed by the 1776 "men."

The "equal protection of the laws" is a right no "State of the United States" may deny to any citizen. Consider the decades between 1868 and the Supreme Court decision in *Brown v. Board of Education of Topeka* (1954) that finally held that states providing "separate but equal" public education were denying "equal protection of the laws." But the Supreme Court has no enforcement authority. Through the lower courts and civil rights lawyers, school desegregation in many towns, cities, and states was gradually gained in spite of hollow rhetoric and determined neglect from political branches of government. It took twenty years in Boston for the major school desegregation Federal Court order of 1974.

Words proclaiming rights may take long periods of time to become reality for many humans. When one reads the Magna Carta of June 15, 1215, the magnificent words ring forth, placing limits on arbitrary rule and providing protection for the King's subjects. Of capital importance is the classic protection of "legal judgment . . . by the law of the land," which became "due process of the law" in the next century. Many centuries passed before the ideals were translated into law and rights for increasing numbers of people. The Charter was violated and ignored by many monarchs over those centuries, but its standards were indestructable and its words cited over and over again in legislation, statutes, and court decisions as the prime means to give reality to human rights. Consider how long it took for the First Amendment freedom of the press to be relieved of countless restrictions and limitations, as evidenced by the Supreme Court cases of *Near v. Minnesota* in 1931 and *New York Times v. Sullivan,* 1963.

One can review the annual *United States Country Reports on Human Rights* with critiques on human rights practices in most of the world's states. However, United States standards for judgments differ substantially from conditions in many nations which lack the human rights traditions and abundant resources of the United States. Many of these countries in Africa, Asia, and the Americas are progressing through stages of political, economic, and social development in a temporal context that does not permit enjoyment of many of the civil, political, legal, economic, and social rights often taken for granted in Western industrialized democracies.

It is impossible for many such nations to leap over the centuries from their colonial histories to develop modern conditions permitting extensive enjoyment of all kinds of rights. These nations have an obligation, on the other hand, to honor the civil, legal, and political rights they voluntarily accepted when they signed human rights treaties, especially the ICPR. This category of rights does not require extensive resources but does demand commitment and determination for their realization. At the same time, these nations merit a huge measure of assistance from the privileged nations to advance their economic and social rights and well-being.

How should time treat deposed government officials who inflicted severe human rights violations on people when they were in power? Should a new government arrest them and take them to court for their crimes? Or, should their acts be viewed with impunity? In the cause of "national reconciliation," should such officials be given amnesty or be pardoned by the new government?

In Argentina, some officials of the military government (1976–1983) were tried by the successor government for certified human rights crimes, especially enforced disappearances of thousands of people. Many were found guilty and sent to prison for their crimes. However, a later government released them on the altar of national reconciliation. In Chile, human rights violations by government officials between 1973 and 1988 were generally viewed with impunity by the successor government.

"Crimes against Humanity" by leading officials of the German government between 1933 and 1945 were included in the indictment in the 1945–46 Nuremberg trials. Since that time, human rights crimes by officials of governments which have been succeeded by new governments have rarely been subjected to adjudication or punishment. Victims and their families have demanded justice. Others, however, have called for reconciliation and for time to heal "old grievances." Can "time," however, really wash over such crimes including those certified to have been committed in former Yugoslavia?

The rights we study in the progression of history state the ideal which requires sacrifice and dedication to be translated into reality, often over long periods of time. Further, many humans deprived of rights look around them and see another world of enjoyment of rights. This was true for many years of the peoples under domination in the former Soviet Union and Eastern European nations. While dining in East Berlin in 1966, the author and his wife met two women in Cafe Bucharest. We could not communicate well but on a map showed them that we would be in Paris the next day. They tugged at their chins and indicated they would have long beards before they saw Paris. We always hoped time permitted them to see the City of Lights.

Time can also reverse the reality of deprivation of human rights in a short span. Anne Frank met a cruel death about the end of March 1945. She never could have imagined that the Nazi war criminals would be indicted for their unparalleled crimes in less than five months. May the 1990s mark an era when time can bury the inhumanity of human rights violations throughout the world, but not the memory of them.

L. Perspectives on Rights

International human rights cover so many areas of human and public concern that it is impossible to do justice to all the dimensions of their impact on over 5.5 billion people on our small planet. The World Conference on Human Rights held in Vienna from June 14 to 25, 1993, concluded with the *Vienna Declaration and Program of Action.* In only twenty-eight pages, the *Declaration* is a broad sweep of historical, contemporary, and controversial issues with respect to human rights containing many recommendations for fulfilling the promise of human rights in the 1948 Universal Declaration. Following are some of its themes.

1. Progressive Problems

a. The *Declaration* in Section I-28 rightly "expresses its dismay" at the massive violations of human rights today, "especially in the form of genocide, 'ethnic cleansing,' and systematic rape of women in war situations, creating mass exodus of refugees and displaced persons. . ." In I-29, the *Declaration* "expresses grave concern" (about these violations) "in disregard of standards as contained in international human rights instruments and international humanitarian law and about the lack of significant and effective remedies for the victims." The *Declaration* in Section I-30 cites the continuation of gross and systematic violations of human rights, documented each year in reports to the United Nations Commission on Human Rights by its experts in the field throughout the world.

b. Another progressive problem was the data presented at the June 1994 World Conference on Population and Development on global population growth and projections for the twenty-first century. The world's population has more than doubled since the 1948 Universal Declaration of Human Rights, with over 5.5 billion humans today and a projection of close to 8 billion by 2015. About 225,000 births take place each twenty-four hours, over 80 million each year. The resources and environments essential to any adequate standard of living as a right in Article 11 of the ESCR are simply not available for some two billion people, let alone the accompanying problems of the enjoyment of civil, legal, and political rights for all.

2. Progressive Achievements

a. The gains in the protection and enhancement of human rights for hundreds of millions of peoples in the former Soviet bloc and in the Republic of South Africa are hailed, irrespective of the chaos and disasters of such massive accommodation to change. The same is true for Palestinians in the Middle East as well. The global landscape of democracy as a way of life and a way of governance gives every promise of progressive expansion as the most essential ingredient for the protection and enhancement of human rights.

b. The *Declaration* cites many achievements in recent years and presents a multitude of recommendations in all areas of human rights. Of particular importance is the recommendation in Section II, 13-16, for the strengthening of the United Nations Centre for Human Rights, which is the global engine for the progressive development of IHRL. Also, Part D of Section II declares in #78 that "human rights education, training and public information [are] essential for the promotion and achievement of stable and harmonious relations among communities. . ." All peoples, especially those who are illiterate or semi-illiterate, must be informed about the human rights they possess and can protect and improve through a variety of protection mechanisms. Training of police and military officials in human rights law, which they must guarantee to all they encounter, is likewise of high priority in protecting peoples' rights. On this point, #10-2-i of the 1983 ASEAN Declaration of the Basic Duties of ASEAN Peoples and Governments requires "continuously educating and training police, para-military, military and other investigative personnel to inculcate knowledge of and respect for human rights. . ."

3. Technology

The progressive advancement of technology impacts on human rights in many ways. Means of massive military annihilation are constantly being developed despite the end of the Cold War. Often overlooked is #26 of the United Nations Charter, which calls for "the least diversion for armaments of the world's human and economic resources. . ."

Life creation with sperm implantation and fertilization techniques is juxtaposed with advancing biotechnical means of abortion, presenting issues on the right to life and related rights for deserved debate. Medical technology for prolonging and also for curtailing life are also issues of controversy in rights for humans. Technology for sustaining and enhancing life in economically and environmentally deprived areas and for enriching the quality of life everywhere are welcomed and encouraged.

4. Déjà Vu

The desecration of human rights continues throughout the world as recorded by United Nations agencies, nongovernmental organizations such as Amnesty International, and the daily media. Nowhere are violations of humans more tragically prominent and verified than in the former Yugoslavia where "ethnic cleansing" and other mutilations of men, women, and children occur and recur every day. The International Criminal Tribunal for Former Yugoslavia, established by the Security Council in a resolution of May 25, 1993, and located in The Hague in the Netherlands, has issued indictments of Bosnian Serb leaders and others for genocide, crimes against humanity, war crimes, and other violations of human rights. Modelled to some extent on the Nuremberg War Crimes Charter, indictments, and Tribunal of 1945 and 1946, the Hague Tribunal will soon try the alleged perpetrators for their overwhelming violence against their former fellow citizens of Yugoslavia. The former Yugoslavia, Rwanda, Cambodia, and other territories where suffering from continuation of human abuse and denial of human rights takes place forces all of us never to be satisfied with the current condition of international human rights law.

5. Eleanor Roosevelt

This prime personage who engineered the 1948 Universal Declaration of Human Rights through the United Nations once asked and answered a most significant question. "Where, after all, do universal rights begin? In small places, close to home—so close and so small that they cannot be seen on any map of the world. Yet they ARE the world of the individual person: the neighborhood he lives in; the school or college he attends; the factory, farm, or office where he works. Such are places where every man, woman, and child seeks justice, equal opportunity, equal dignity without discrimination. Unless these rights have meaning there, they have little meaning anywhere." This, perhaps, is the best perspective of all on international human rights.

The Dictionary

The five categories of rights in the dictionary are Civil and Political; Legal; Economic, Social, and Cultural; Collective; and Declaratory. The rights are listed at the end of this introduction as well as in the directory which is a catalogue of the primary resources cited in the dictionary along with abbreviations used for the entry on each right.

Civil and Political Rights are set forth in the United Nations Covenant of Civil and Political Rights of December 16, 1966 (ICPR). The dictionary begins with Civil Rights, which includes the one political right article in ICPR.

Legal Rights are included in the Covenant on Civil and Political Rights (ICPR) but merit a discrete section of the dictionary.

Economic, Social, and Cultural Rights are included in the Covenant on these rights of December 16, 1966 (ESCR). ICPR and ESCR are termed the "prime covenants" as they are the two principal universal human rights treaties. Along with the 1948 Universal Declaration of Human Rights, they comprise the "International Bill of Human Rights."

Collective Rights are those for categories of people such as aliens and minorities and also for individuals who are included in the category or the collectivity.

Declaratory Rights are the subject of declarations and resolutions of the General Assembly of the United Nations and other sources which are not based on treaty law but declare the existence of a right. An example is the 1986 General Assembly resolution, the Declaration on the Right to Development. Most rights under treaty law were originally declaratory rights. Many of the contemporary declaratory rights may become treaty rights, such as those for disabled persons and indigenous peoples.

Outline for Each Entry

Each entry for each right has five parts:

The Right
Other Sources of the Right
Expanded Definition of the Right
Landmarks in the Evolution of the Right
Cross References to Other Similar Rights

I. The Right. The dictionary entries for Civil, Political, and Legal Rights (parts 1 and 2) cite ICPR as the basic treaty and therefore international law on these rights. The ICPR is the most widely ratified treaty on civil, political, and legal rights. It reflects nearly universal consensus on these rights irrespective of variations in interpretations of specific rights states may incorporate in any reservations or understandings they may attach upon their ratification of the Covenant. The ICPR also represents States Parties' obligations to incorporate these rights in their constitutional and legal systems. A legal right in the Covenant may be more brief or extensive than legal rights in other conventions such as the European Convention on Fundamental Freedoms and Human Rights of 1950. Rights of other conventions are cited in the entry for each right, enabling the reader to make the necessary comparisons.

The dictionary entries for Economic, Social, and Cultural Rights (part 3) cite the ESCR as the basic treaty and international legal authority on these rights. The ESCR was authored by representatives of states from all regions and cultures of the international community. The authors of both prime Covenants state in the Preambles to each Covenant that each set of rights "can only be achieved" if the other set of rights is also enjoyed by all humans as well. Other human rights treaties dealing with this set of rights, such as the Convention Against Racial Discrimination, will also be cited.

A typical citation will be the right, the treaty (Covenant on Civil and Political Rights), and the article of the treaty (Article 3). Subsequent citations will use the abbreviation for the treaty (ICPR for Covenant on Civil and Political Rights) and "#" rather than "Article," e.g., ICPR #6.

II. Other Sources of the Right. The other principal sources for each right are organized in the following manner.

The first section includes treaty sources which reflect firm foundations for international law. Of considerable importance, therefore, are the European Convention on Fundamental Freedoms and Rights, November 4, 1950 (ECR); American Convention on Human Rights, November 22, 1969 (ACR); African Charter on Human and Peoples' Rights, October 23, 1986 (AFR); International Labor Organization Conventions (ILO) where applicable; other principal UN human rights conventions including those on race, women, children, torture, and refugees; and other international treaties where appropriate.

Second are declarations on human rights which are not legally binding as treaties but provide strong evidence of customary IHRL. Of particular importance is the Universal Declaration of Human Rights, December 10, 1948 (UDHR). Other declarations include the European Social Charter, 1961 (Eur. Charter); the Declaration on the Conference on Security and Cooperation in Europe, 1975 (CSCE); Cairo Declaration on Human Rights in Islam, 1990 (ISLAM 1990); the Declaration on Basic Duties of ASEAN Peoples and Governments, 1983 (ASEAN); the Declaration on Social Progress and Development, 1969 (Dec Social Progress); and the Declaration on the Human Rights of Individuals who are not Nationals of the Country in which They Live, 1985 (Dec on Non-Nationals).

Third are other sources such as annual reports of Special Rapporteurs of the UN Commission on Human Rights (e.g., on torture); relevant resolutions of the General Assembly; and reports of treaty bodies under specific treaties such as the Human Rights Committee of ICPR. The Geneva Conventions of 1949 and the Geneva Protocols of 1977 on international humanitarian law for victims of armed force are not included in "Other Sources."

III. Expanded Definition of the Right. This section for each entry expands on the definition of the right. However, the definition of any right, such as freedom of speech, is tempered by the definition of the right by each State Party to the ICPR or ESCR (see F. Interpretation of Rights, Issues and Contexts). The constitution of each state as well as its legislation, statutes, codes of law, and judicial decisions will have much to say about the state's definition. In addition, the State Party may enter a reservation or understanding about a right when it ratifies a human rights treaty that will illuminate how it defines the right.

Further, the Human Rights Committee of the ICPR, the treaty bodies of other human rights conventions such as the Committee Against Torture of the Convention Against Torture, and the commissions and courts of the ECR and the ACR all participate in defining rights in the course of their due process responsibilities. The Court of the ECR in particular has had a profound influence on interpretation of civil and legal rights for its European members. It would be impossible for the dictionary to draw upon all of these sources in providing the reader with the many perspectives on rights definitions and interpretations.

This may suggest that a definition of freedom of speech at the international level, for example, would be impossible. The opposite is the case, however. There is a high level of consistency on rights' definitions as each international body, such as the Human Rights Committee or the European Court of Human Rights, is very mindful of interpretations of other bodies and evolving agreement on rights' definitions, including limitations on rights. As states incorporate international rights into their own national legal systems, such as the international definition of torture, transnational definitions that advance levels of uniformity in definitions in the global human rights constitutional system are developing (See transnational definition of torture in Issues and Contexts). However, as always, in the world of sovereign states with historical and cultural human diversity, law as an expression of that diversity should and never will be absolutely uniform.

IV. Landmarks in the Evolution of the Right. The evolution of each of the diverse human rights in the dictionary appropriately requires study of volumes of history on how rights for humans developed from the very beginnings of civilization. Rights for humans began when people in primitive family and then social groupings recognized that some deference to others was essential for their mutual security and well-being. Rights of groups and then individuals grew as political communities emerged and as theology and philosophy began to deal with humans, how they become human, and how they can become more human.

Civilizations in Africa, Asia, the Americas, Greece, Rome, and Europe all contributed to the mainstream of what eventually became rights for humans. The rights in UDHR and then in ICPR and ESCR evolved largely out of Western civilization. However, people from all civilizations authored human rights under the United Nations umbrella, and nations representing all civilizations have signed and ratified the two prime human rights treaties.

In the domain of civil, political, and legal rights, the English Magna Carta of June 15, 1215, is the most important landmark in the historical foundation of human rights. The English struggle and sacrifices for rights, especially in the seventeenth century, confirmed the idea of an inherent set of rights of life, liberty, and property. Rights for Englishmen were transferred to Englishmen in the American colonies who, like the Barons of 1215 facing King John, declared and won rights against their arbitrary English monarch, George III, in 1776.

The English Bill of Rights of 1689, the United States Declaration of Independence of 1776, and the American Constitution of 1787 with its

Bill of Rights of 1791 are landmarks of enormous magnitude for civil, political, and legal rights. France joined this march toward internationally recognized human rights with its Declaration of the Rights of Man and the Citizen of 1789. With the incorporation of the rights in the Declaration in the Napoleonic Code of Law of 1806 and the Code flowing into the legal systems of most of the world's states, rights for humans gradually became protected and enhanced. Wars, the inhumanity of people to other peoples, and other human deprivations continued to be and still are realities throughout the world. With Allied victory in 1945, the establishment of the United Nations and then the Universal Declaration of Human Rights of 1948, however, international law began to make major strides in all areas of human rights.

Where appropriate, the dictionary touches on some of these landmarks. One dimension of a landmark is not included in dictionary: that is the "travaux preparatoires" or the negotiating history for each right. The history of the negotiations of the Universal Declaration and the ICPR and ESCR, including the intent of authors of the Declaration and Covenants, is vital to a full understanding of the crafting of each word of each right. The serious reader is constrained to explore the travaux preparatoires to gain insight on each right, although one must always realize that the negotiating history is political as well as legal diplomacy. The student of the United States Constitutional Convention or the United Nations Charter well understands this.

Citations in Landmarks of some English and American colonial documents are in archaic English with spelling that is rather out of date today. Article 2 of the Massachusetts Body of Liberties of December 10, 1641, for instance, includes this important right: "every person within this Jurisdiction, whether Inhabitant or forreiner, shall enjoy the same justice and law, that is generall for the plantation, which we constitute and execute one towards another without partialitie or delay." Equal protection of the law is now an international human right under Article 26 of the ICPR and other treaties as well.

V. Cross References to Other Similar Rights. Each right is accompanied by citations of other rights which relate to it. Rights are naturally interrelated to each other, and often each contributes to an understanding of others. **Due Process** in legal rights is inclusive of most of the other legal rights. **Asylum** is associated with **Nationality** and **Refugees**, and

Religion, **Thought**, and **Conscience** is a natural cluster. Studies, resources, declarations, reports, documents and other sources are included in cross references. The index to the dictionary supplements cross references.

A final note is in order on dictionary entries. Most rights in the covenants and conventions refer to the male with ample use of he, him, and his. The 1989 Convention on the Rights of the Child and 1990 Convention on Migrant Workers remedy this shortcoming with he or she, and his or her. Where only he, him, and/or his is used in a treaty, let us assume that the intention is to include she, her, and hers as well.

The Five Categories of Human Rights

I. Civil and Political Rights (p. 42)
   - Assembly
   - Association
   - Asylum
   - Child
   - Dignity, Honor, Reputation
   - Discrimination
   - Life
   - Name
   - Nationality
   - Political and Public Service
   - Press
   - Property
   - Religion
   - Speech
   - Territory, Movement in
   - Women

II. Legal Rights (p. 86)
   - Appeal
   - Arrest
   - Bail
   - Compensation
   - Contract Inability
   - Courts/Tribunals
   - Death Penalty
   - Detention
   - Double Jeopardy
   - Due Process
   - Equal Protection of the Law
   - Ex Post Facto Law
   - Habeas Corpus
   - Innocence Presumption
   - Judgment and Sentencing
   - Juvenile Due Process
   - Legal Assistance

Person before the Law
Privacy
Punishment
Security of Person
Self-Incrimination
Torture
Trial
Trial Procedure

III. Economic, Social, and Cultural Rights (p. 135)
Author
Culture
Education
Family
Food
Health
Science
Social Security
Standard of Living
Work, Right to
Work, Conditions
Work, Trade Unions
Work, Trade Union Rights

IV. Collective Rights (p. 170)
Aliens
Apartheid
Genocide
Migrant Workers
Minorities
Refugees
Peoples, Self-Determination
Peoples, Natural Resources
Slavery
Stateless

V. Declaratory Rights (p. 201)
Development
Disabled Persons
Indigenous Peoples
Mercenaries

Directory

This is a catalogue of the primary resources for entries in the dictionary. The treaty, declaration, or other resource is listed below with its formal name, followed by the code or abbreviation used in dictionary entries. Other primary resources not listed below will be cited in specific entries by their full titles. Ian Brownlie's *Basic Documents on Human Rights* (Oxford: Clarendon Press, 1992, Third Edition) is recommended as an excellent source for most conventions and declarations cited in the dictionary.

A. Treaties (Covenants, Conventions, Charters, Constitutions)
   1. Two Prime United Nations Human Rights Covenants
      a. International Covenant on Civil and Political Rights (1966)—ICPR; the two Protocols to the ICPR will also be cited
      b. International Covenant on Economic, Social, and Cultural Rights (1966)—ESCR
   2. Principal United Nations Human Rights Conventions
      a. Convention on the Prevention and Punishment of the Crime of Genocide (1948)—Genocide Convention
      b. International Convention on the Elimination of All Forms of Racial Discrimination (1966)—Convention on Racism
      c. International Convention on the Suppression and Punishment of the Crime of Apartheid (1973)—Convention on Apartheid
      d. International Convention on the Elimination of All Forms of Discrimination Against Women (1979)—Convention on Women
      e. Convention Against Torture and Other Cruel, Inhuman, or Degrading Treatment (1984)—Convention on Torture
      f. Convention on the Rights of the Child (1989)—Convention on Child
   3. Other United Nations Human Rights Conventions
      a. Convention Relating to the Status of Refugees (1951)—Convention on Refugees (also, Protocol, 1967)
      b. Convention on Political Rights of Women (1953)—Convention on Women's Political Rights
      c. Convention Relating to the Status of Stateless Persons (1954)—Convention on Stateless
      d. International Convention on the Protection of the Rights of All

Migrant Workers and Their Families (1990)—Convention on Migratory Workers

4. Specialized Agencies
   a. International Labor Organization Constitution (1919)—ILO Declaration of Philadelphia (1944)
   b. ILO Conventions
   c. United Nations Educational, Scientific, and Cultural Organization Constitution (1945)—UNESCO
   d. UNESCO Convention Against Discrimination in Education (1960)—UNESCO Convention on Education
5. Regional Conventions
   a. European Convention for the Protection of Human Rights and Fundamental Freedoms (1950)—ECR; Protocols to ECR will be cited
   b. American Convention on Human Rights (1969)—ACR; the 1988 Protocol will be cited
   c. African Charter on Human and Peoples' Rights (1986)—AFR

B. Declarations
   1. Universal Declaration of Human Rights (1948)—UDHR
   2. Declaration on the Granting of Independence to Colonial Countries and Peoples (1960)—Dec on Independence
   3. European Social Charter (1961)—Eur. Charter
   4. Declaration on Social Progress and Development (1969)—Dec Social Progress
   5. Declaration on the Establishment of a New International Economic Order (1974)—NIEO Dec
   6. Programme of Action on the Establishment of a New International Economic Order (1974)—NIEO Program
   7. Charter of the Economic Rights and Duties of States (1974)—Charter, Rights and Duties
   8. Standard Minimum Rules for the Treatment of Prisoners (1957, 1977)—Std. Rules, Prisoners
   9. Conference on Security and Cooperation in Europe: Final Act (1975)—CSCE. Also, follow-up conferences and declarations
   10. Cairo Declaration on Human Rights in ISLAM (1990)
   11. Declaration on the Elimination of All Forms of Intolerence and of Discrimination Based on Religion or Belief (1981)—Dec on Religion
   12. Declaration on the Basic Duties of ASEAN Peoples and Gov-

ernments (1983)—ASEAN (Association of Southeast Asian Nations)

13. Declaration on the Human Rights of Individuals who are not Nationals of the Country in which They Live (1985)—Dec on Non-Nationals

Other Primary Resources

1. General Assembly Resolutions
2. Reports, UN Human Rights Working Groups and Rapporteurs
3. Resolutions, other organizations (e.g., UNESCO)
4. *Black's Law Dictionary*. 5th ed. St. Paul, Minnesota: West Publishing Company, 1979.
5. Perry, Richard L., ed. *Sources of Our Liberties*. Chicago: American Bar Foundation, 1978.

I

Civil and Political Rights

Introduction

International human rights law with respect to civil and political rights seeks to enhance and protect the historical civil and political rights that are fundamental to the security and well-being of humans everywhere. These rights are firmly established in the Covenant on Civil and Political Rights (ICPR) which was approved by the General Assembly on December 16, 1966, and entered into force on March 23, 1976.

The title of the Covenant on Civil and Political Rights does not include the word "legal" and thus places specific legal rights under civil rights. One can argue the distinction between the two. The dictionary, however, has separated these two sets of rights, because legal rights deal with due process of the law in substance and procedure while civil rights are largely substantative, such as the right to life and the freedom of religion. One exception is Article 25 which is concerned with political rights and public service and is the only direct provision for political rights in ICPR. Article 25 is explicitly democratic in substance and procedure, but many other civil rights in ICPR, such as association, assembly, press, and speech, are indispensible to the realization of democratic political rights.

The historical roots of each right in ICPR as described briefly in the Landmarks section for each entry represent centuries of development and sacrifice for the rights enjoyed by many humans today but denied to many more. History is not distinguished on the rights of others such as women and children. Controversy abounds on conflicts between civil rights and the rights of the community at large such as "national security" and "public order." Civil rights such as the right to life continue to be debated and interpreted differently by individuals and governing authorities as well as the judiciary. No one argues that these rights are clear, precise, or devoid of debate and contention.

Part IV of the ICPR provides for the monitoring of States Parties' compliance with the obligations they accepted in ratifying the Covenant. The Human Rights Committee is established in Article 28 to supervise and administer this section of the ICPR which deals with implementation of the Covenant. Under Article 40, States Parties "undertake to submit reports on measures they have adopted which give effect to the rights recognized herein and on the progress made in the enjoyment of those rights." The Committee of Eighteen experts has met many times for almost twenty years to monitor states' compliance to Covenant provisions and to facilitate states meeting their treaty commitments under the procedures established in Article 40.

Article 41 of ICPR provides for States Parties voluntarily recognizing the Committee's competence to receive communications from one state alleging noncompliance to the ICPR by another state. The First Optional Protocol to ICPR provides for states voluntarily recognizing the rights of individuals to submit complaints of a state's not recognizing or protecting civil, legal, or political rights of an individual under the jurisdiction of that state to the Committee. Articles 41–45 of ICPR provide for extensive measures of due process for the Human Rights Committee to utilize when dealing with state complaints. Articles 1–7 of the First Optional Protocol set forth Committee due process for individual complaints. The Second Optional Protocol of ICPR of December 15, 1989, as as its objective the abolition of the death penalty. The annual reports of the Human Rights Committee, as well as volumes of Committee reports on its deliberations and decisions, provide a wealth of authoritative material on interpretation and implementation of IHRL.

Assembly

I. The Right. The right of peaceful assembly shall be recognized. No restrictions may be placed on the exercise of this right other than those imposed in conformity with the law and which are necessary in a democratic society in the interests of national security, public safety, public order (ordre public), the protection of public health or morals, or the protection of the rights and freedoms of others. Covenant on Civil and Political Rights, Article 21.

II. Other Sources. ECR. #11-1; ACR, #15; AFR, #11, Convention on Racial Discrimination, #5 (d) (ix);

UDHR, #20.

III. Expanded Definition. "The concourse or meeting together of a considerable number of persons at the same place" (Black, 106). As a civil right, assembly is essential to people gathering together to discuss civil and political issues or to gain agreement on some specific course of civil or political action. However, if and when assembly is viewed by the state as a threat to its security and well-being or when it is considered by others as a threat to or violation of their rights, an assembly and its participants may be accused of violation of law. Treaty affirmations of the right of assembly are accompanied by broad restrictions which are more specifically defined by each State Party to the treaties. *See also* restrictions placed on right of assembly by states ratifying ICPR, especially European states members of ECR.

IV. Landmarks. The broadening of participation by people in governance in England and the American colonies in the seventeenth century by necessity required peaceful assembly of people for discussion of issues and for choosing "such deputies for the General Court" and giving "advise (and) vote . . . in Civil Assembly . . ." as stated in Section 70 of the Massachusetts Body of Liberties of December 10, 1641. Assembly for the right of petition and "freedom of speech and debates or proceedings in parliament" are implied in the 1689 English Bill of Rights of December 16, 1689.

In the American colonies, this basic political right is confirmed in the Declaration and Resolves of the First Continental Congress of October 14, 1774, in Resolution 8: "That they have the right peaceably to assemble, consider of their grievances and petition the king; and that all prosecutions, prohibitory proclamations, and commitments, for the same, are illegal." Compare Resolution 8 with the more democratically oriented (and post–Declaration of Independence) Article XVI of the Constitution of Pennsylvania of August 16, 1776: "That the people have a right to assemble together, to consult for their common good, to instruct their representatives, and to apply to the legislature for redress of grievances, by address, petition, or remonstrance." Other state constitutions followed, as did the First Amendment to the United States Constitution of December 15, 1791: "Congress shall make no law . . . abridging . . . the right of the people peaceably to assemble . . ." The right to assembly is certainly implied in the French Declaration of the Rights of Man and the Citizen of August 26, 1789. The Declaration has been incorporated in subsequent French Constitutions including the most recent, 1958. The Declaration was also absorbed into the French Civil Code of 1804 and therefore into the constitutional systems of all nations embracing the civil code of law.

V. Cross References. *See* Association, Political, and Speech (Civil and Political Rights) and Due Process (Legal Rights).

Association

I. The Right. (1) Everyone shall have the right to freedom of association with others, including the right to form and join trade unions for the protection of his interests. (2) No restrictions may be placed on the exercise of this right other than those which are prescribed by law and which are necessary in a democratic society in the interests of national security, public safety, public order (ordre public), the protection of public health or morals, or the protection of the rights and freedoms of others. This article shall not prevent the imposition of lawful restrictions on members of the armed forces and of the police in the exercise of this right. (3) Nothing in this article shall authorize States Parties to the International Labor Organization Convention of 1948 concerning Freedom of Association and Protection of the Right to Organize to take legislative measures which would prejudice, or to apply the law in such a manner as to prejudice, the guarantees provided for in that Convention. Covenant on Civil and Political Rights, Article 22.

II. Other Sources. ESCR, #8-1 (a); ECR, #11-1; ACR, #16; AFR, #10-1, 2; Convention on Child, #15; ILO Constitution Preamble and Conventions

#87, 1948, #98, 1949, #135, 1971, #141, 1975, #151, 1978, and #154, 1981; Convention on Apartheid, #2-c; Convention on Racism, #5 (d) (ix); Convention on Refugees, #15; and Convention on Stateless, #15;

UDHR, #20-1, #23-4; UDHR, #20-1, 2; ILO Declaration, 1944, Preamble.

III. Expanded Definition. An association is a voluntary grouping of people participating in a common purpose and generally in pursuit of a common goal. "Purposes" as cited in ACR, #16-1, include "ideological, religious, political, economic, labor, social, cultural, sports, or other purposes." The right to associate for the purposes of a trade union is prominent in ICPR, #22-1 and 3. However, any "association," such as a political party, a political interest group, a religious organization (however extensive or small), and others may have implications and concerns for a state governance which may view association as a threat to its interpretation of state security and well-being. Therefore, all treaty provisions on association are tempered by exceptions as determined by the state or by a threat of association to the rights and freedoms of others.

IV. Landmarks. Throughout history, associations of all kinds have bound people together in the pursuit of common interests and goals. The central issue for civil and political rights is the extent to which an association is viewed by governing officials of the political community as a threat to its security and well-being, including the venerable condition of public order. Religious associations in particular were viewed as threats to that order, such as the Christians to the Roman Empire for some two hundred years and the long history of political persecution of all kinds of religious groups and associations, especially Jewish.

The emergence of economic and social rights which came into prominence during the French Revolution, accompanied by the so-called Industrial Revolution, led to many demands by the disadvantaged for collectively to pursue and gain modest economic and social rights. Early in the nineteenth century, factory workers in particular began to join forces to press for improved conditions at the workplace. This demand for association into a union of workers, especially in England, the United States, and Western Europe, was resisted by employers and factory owners who were supported by state officials. Strikes and other measures by the workers, some early judicial decisions, and more enlightened politics and government led to the right to form unions and eventually to bargain collectively. Only in the twentieth century, however, did trade unions gain full rights of unfettered association.

Associations generally have full rights and privileges except those deemed seditious or destructive in ultimate objectives by governments. Associations of this nature, especially those considered as criminal or terrorist in nature, were and condemned and pursued by all governments.

V. Cross References. *See* Assembly, Political, and Religion (Civil Rights and Political Rights); Due Process (Legal Rights); Work (Right to, Conditions, Trade Unions, and Trade Union Rights in Economic, Social, and Cultural Rights); and most Collective Rights.

Asylum

I. The Right. Every person has the right to seek and to be granted asylum in a foreign territory, in accordance with legislation of the state and international conventions, in the event he is being pursued for political offenses or related common crimes. American Convention on Human Rights, Article 22, paragraph 7.

Every individual shall have the right, when persecuted, to seek and obtain asylum in other countries in accordance with laws of those countries and international conventions. African Charter on Human and Peoples' Rights, Article 12, para 3. ". . . any individual enjoying the right of asylum under Article 12 of the present Charter shall not engage in subversive activities against his country of origin or any other State party to the present Charter; (and) their territories shall not be used as bases for subversive or terrorist activities against the people of any other State party to the present Charter." AFR, Article 23, para 2 (a) & (b).

II. Other Sources. Convention on Refugees, #31, 32, 33; Convention on Stateless, #31;

UDHR, #14-1, 2; Declaration on Territorial Asylum, General Assembly Resolution 2312 (XXII), 1967; (a) ISLAM, #12; Principles of International Cooperation in the Detention, Arrest, Extradition, and Punishment of Persons Guilty of War Crimes and Crimes Against Humanity, General Assembly Resolution 3074 (XXVIII), 1973, #7.

III. Expanded Definition. Asylum is a sanctuary, or place of refuge and protection, where criminals and debtors found shelter and from which they could not be taken without sacrilege (Black, 114). In international law, asylum is the sanctuary provided by one state to a person who has left the state of his nationality or other state for reasons acceptable to the state granting asylum. The recipient must adhere to the law of the receiving state and not use that territory as a basis of any action considered illegal by the receiving state. There is no legal obligation by a state to provide asylum, and there are many and varied conditions the asylum-granting state may require for a person to gain asylum.

Because of protracted disagreement on conditions among states negotiating the ICPR, the right of asylum was not incorporated into that Covenant or into the ECR. The United Nations devoted approximately twenty-five years to negotiating a draft convention on Territorial Asylum but did not succeed.

In the past forty years, however, asylum often has been granted by a state to a person who can demonstrate a "well-founded fear of being persecuted for reasons of race, religion, nationality, membership of a particular social group or political opinion, (who) is outside the country of his nationality and is unable or, owing to such fear, is unwilling to avail himself of the protection of that country or . . . is unwilling to return to it." (Convention Relating to the Status of Refugees, 1951, Article 1-A (2).

Asylum is often granted, in particular, to people fleeing the country of their nationality for political reasons but is not granted to people accused of criminal activity. Most states have treaties of extradition with most other states which provide for the return of the person accused of a crime to the country of his or her departure. In all cases, the right of asylum is a right granted or not granted by the receiving state, unless a treaty obligation of that state defines conditions of asylum and of extradition to which the receiving state is obliged to adhere.

IV. Landmarks. People fleeing their native countries and seeking a protected sanctuary in another country frequently occurs in history. However, the country receiving the person seeking asylum has always had the right to grant or refuse asylum. The person in flight may have left his country of origin for a number of reasons, some or many of which may not be acceptable to the receiving country. The person seeking asylum may cause political risks to the receiving country if asylum is granted, especially if a grant of asylum is viewed by the country of departure as an unfriendly act. People have often sought relief by gaining entry to the embassy of a third party in the receiving country and asking for asylum. Asylum has usually been denied to fleeing criminals but also quite often to those who are political refugees from another state. The patterns of asylum over history are fairly consistent, but asylum was never considered a right in any manner parallel with other human rights.

Asylum is closely interrelated with policy and law on refugees, which gained considerable maturity under the League of Nations (*see* Refugees, Collective Rights). The 1928 Havana Convention on Asylum was the first major treaty to codify the standard procedures for asylum. Refugee law was consolidated in the 1951 Convention on the Status of Refugees which defined a refugee and, for many states, the valid conditions for granting asylum (*see* III above). The granting of asylum is not specifically mentioned in this Convention, its Protocol of 1967, or the Convention on Statelessness (*see* II, above). However, under these conventions, a State Party may not expel a refugee except for specific reasons and thus by inference must provide asylum, at least on a temporary basis.

V. Cross References. *See* Territory, Movement in, and Political (Civil and Political Rights); Due Process, and Equal Protection of the Law (Legal Rights); and Aliens, Migrant Workers, and Refugees (Collective Rights).

Child

I. The Right. Every child shall have, without any discrimination as to race, color, sex, language, religion, national or social origin, property, or birth, the right to such measures of protection as are required by his or her status as a minor, on the part of his or her family, society, and State. Covenant on Civil and Political Rights, Article 24-1.

II. Other Sources. Convention on the Rights of the Child; ESCR, #10-3; ECR, #5-1 (d); ACR, #19 & 17-5; ACR 1988 Protocol, #16; AFR, #18-3; Convention on Women, #16 (d), (e), (f);

UDHR, #25-2; Dec on Religion, #5; European Social Charter, #7 & 17; ISLAM, #7; ASEAN, #5-10; Dec Social Progress, #4.

III. Expanded Definition. The basic right of the child is to be protected as a person who is not able to protect himself or herself in society. Protection is to be provided by the family and/or other organs of society without any discrimination whatever so that all children will have the basic right to be free from want and fear.

The Convention on the Rights of the Child states in #1 that "a child means every human being below the age of eighteen years unless, under the law applicable to the child, majority is attained earlier." Child rights are extensive as set forth in the Preamble and the articles of the CRC.

A child is a person below the age of eighteen, but an important question in international and national laws of States Parties is when the life of a child actually begins. ACR, #4-1, declares that the right to life "shall be protected by law and, in general, from the moment of conception." ISLAM (1990) states in #7 that child rights begin "as of the moment of birth . . ." CRC is silent on the lower limit, although much debate on this point is in the negotiating history of CRC. The International Labor Organization Minimum Age Convention of 1973 qualifies minimum age in accordance to the types of work that different categories of employment require of the employee.

In the laws of States Parties, "the law applicable to the child" with respect to when the life of the child begins depends on national law and even subnational law, such as state law in the United States. Nearly all national law, however, at least protects the rights of women who are carrying children, as well as the rights of women per se.

The definition of the rights of the child will vary with respect to the laws of States Parties and their reservations to CRC upon ratification. For example, the right of the child to be heard and freedom of expression (#12 and 13, CRC) and similar rights may not be acceptable in states which tend to place restraints on many kinds of child rights or freedoms. Legal rights and protection against discrimination and exploitation as well as right of due process of the law in #40 CRC are the most important rights of the child.

IV. Landmarks. Throughout history, the child had few if any rights in most cultures. The parents and guardians of children generally had broad rights and few responsibilities in dealing with their children. Prior to the nineteenth century, most Western states had some laws dealing with issues of children, including those on custody and guardianship, some protection for orphans, unwanted, and illegitimate children, and the estates of minors. However, it was not until the early 1800s, with rising tides of liberalism and industrialization, that some states began to legislate for modest protection of children. Nineteenth-century English literature, especially Charles Dickens's *Bleak House,* chronicles the plight and legal deprivation of children, in particular those in conjested urban environments.

Child labor was an early concern with the rise of public education. As early as 1802 in England, the Health and Morals of Apprentices Act placed limits on the child's workday in cotton mills to twelve hours and limited night work. The Factory Act of 1833 extended regulation of child labor, and some Eastern states in the United States followed suit.

School attendance laws in England began with legislation in 1834 and the comprehensive law of the 1870 Elementary Education Act. Education in the United States was a state constitutional responsibility, but public education laws grew rapidly in the nineteenth century. Children's rights to be protected from exploitation and to receive free and public education were accompanied by legislation to protect the child from harsh and abusive treatment, whether in the home or not. The English Offenses Against the Person Statute of 1861 and subsequent legislation in many Western states emphasized state concern and obligations with respect to younger citizens.

At the international level, the first International Labor Conference meeting in Berlin in 1890 expressed concerns for more legislation to deal with child labor. The 1900 International Association for Labor Legislation in Basel, Switzerland, also pressed for such legislation as the international labor movement gained recognition and influence. This led to the creation of the International Labor Organization at the Paris Peace Conference in 1919 and considerable strides in child rights by the ILO. The ILO's Constitution of 1919 sought in its Preamble improvement in "the protection of children, young persons and women" through international conventions and due process for allegations of violations of these conventions.

Article 23 (c) of the League of Nations Covenant "entrusted the League with general supervision over the execution of agreements in regard to traffic in women and children." The 1921 League treaty prohibiting traffic of women and children launched the international legal protection of children to a limited extent. The League Assembly established a Child Welfare Committee which raised the consciousness of international legal concern for children. The 1924 Geneva Declaration on the Rights of the Child added to the proclamation of juvenile rights and was signed by some fifty states which accepted commitments to translate many Convention rights into national legislation.

The United Nations, after 1945, moved rapidly to extend the work of the League in children's rights and welfare. The General Assembly established the United Nations International Children's Emergency Fund (UNICEF) in a resolution on December 11, 1946. The Commission on

Human Rights, under direction from its parent Economic and Social Council, over many years drafted the Declaration on the Rights of the Child which was approved by the General Assembly on November 20, 1959. More time and difficult negotiations finally led to the Convention on the Rights of the Child of November 20, 1989. The widely ratified Convention's Committee on the Rights of the Child has legal authority for monitoring State Party compliance with the Convention and for its implementation and due process as well.

V. Cross References. *See* Discrimination, Name, Nationality, Religion, and Women (Civil and Political Rights); Due Process and Juvenile Due Process (Legal Rights); Education and Family (Economic, Social, and Cultural Rights); and Aliens, Migrant Workers, Minorities, Refugees, Disabled Persons, and Indigenous Peoples (Collective and Declaratory Rights).

Each year the General Assembly passes resolutions on many facets of child rights and well-being. The Assembly proclaimed 1979 as the Year of the Child. The World Summit on Children in September 1990 was attended by sixty heads of state. It approved the Declaration on Survival, Protection, and Development of Children along with a plan of action for the 1990s which was signed by 136 states. In September 1990 the United Nations Commission on Human Rights appointed Mr. Vitit Muntarbhorn as Special Rapporteur to consider matters relating to the sale of children, child prostitution, and child pornography in response to widespread exploitation of children in many nations.

Child rights are also the responsibility of many United Nations Specialized Agencies, especially the United Nations Children's Fund (UNICEF) and the International Labor Organization. Others include the Food and Agricultural Organization and other food organizations, the World Health Organization, the United Nations Development Program, and many others.

Dignity, Honor, Reputation

I. The Right. No one shall be subjected to . . . unlawful attacks on his honor and reputation. Everyone has the right to the protection of the law against such interference or attacks. Covenant on Civil and Political Rights, Article 17, paragraphs 1 and 2. All persons deprived of their liberty shall be treated with humanity and with respect for the inherent dignity of the human person. CPR, #10-1. *See also* #19-3-a, CPR, with respect to expression.

II. Other Sources. ACR, #11-1, 2, & 3 and #14-1, 2 & 3; AFR, #5; UDHR, #12 and Preamble; ISLAM, #4; Declaration on the Rights of Disabled Persons (1975), #3.

III. Expanded Definition. Dignity, honor, and reputation are core attributes of the human person and reflect the integrity of the person, demanding protection against any unlawful attacks from any source. It is of special importance that the first paragraphs of the Preambles to ICPR and ESCR declare that the rights in these Covenants "derive from the inherent dignity of the human person," which establishes the majestic identity of human rights and human dignity.

Provisions in human rights treaties enhance the definition of dignity, honor, and reputation. Article 5 of AFR is eloquent: "Each individual shall have the right to the respect of the dignity inherent in a human being." Article 4 of ISLAM (1990) states that "every human being is entitled to inviolability and the protection of his good name and honour during his life and after his death . . ."

Dignity, honor, and reputation must be protected against libel and slander in particular. Libel is that which is written or printed, and published, calculated to injure the character or reputation of another by bringing him into ridicule, hatred, or contempt (Black, 1103). Slander is oral defamation, the speaking of false words concerning another, whereby injury results to his reputation (Black, 1634).

A key word in ICPR, #17-1, is "unlawful." It is for due process of the law to determine whether a libel, slander, or any other injury to dignity, honor, and reputation is indeed unlawful. In particular, due process often must deal with conflicts between libel and slander on the one hand and the rights of freedom of speech and the press on the other. In ACR "anyone injured by inaccurate or offensive statements . . . has the right to reply or to make a correction" (#14-1), and the media has a special responsibility to "protect honor and reputation . . ." (#14-3). Further, unlike many laws of states, international human rights law provides for compensation to the person unjustly accused of violation of law and/or judgment by a tribunal if and when there is a "miscarriage of justice . . ." (*see* Compensation, Legal Rights).

IV. Landmarks. Both common and civil law have protected people against damage to their dignity, honor, and reputation by others. The Magna Carta of June 15, 1215, states in Article 39 that "no free man shall . . . in any way be destroyed . . ." and destruction certainly can come from an attack on honor and integrity. Article 1 of the Massachusetts Body of Liberties of December 10, 1641, in expanding upon #39 of Magna Carta, declares that "no mans honour or good name shall be stayned . . ." A person's honor is not necessarily protected from damage by the state itself if the state declares an overriding interest or necessity in attacking dignity, honor, or reputation as alleged by the victim. The civil and criminal codes of all nations must be examined for landmarks in law and judicial decisions in national treatment of attack on dignity, honor, and reputation. Libel and slander are not mentioned in human rights treaties. However, the language is clear with respect to "unlawful attacks" on honor and reputation, and ACR is unique in its "right of reply." Right of compensation from the state for "miscarriages of justice" is a significant contribution of international human rights law to dignity, honor, and reputation.

V. Cross References. *See* Discrimination, Life, Name, and Property (Civil and Political Rights); Compensation, Due Process, Privacy, Person before the Law, and Security of Person (Legal Rights); and Author (Economic, Social, and Cultural Rights).

Discrimination

I. The Right. All persons are equal before the law and are entitled without any discrimination to equal protection of the law. In this respect, the law shall prohibit any discrimination and guarantee to all persons equal and effective protection against discrimination on any ground such as race, colour, sex, language, religion, political or other opinion, national or social origin, property, birth, or other status. Covenant on Civil and Political Rights, Article 26. Any advocacy of national, racial, or religious hatred that constitutes incitement to discrimination, hostility, or violence shall be prohibited by law. ICPR, #20-2. Nondiscrimination in public emergency. ICPR, #4-1.

II. Other Sources. ESCR, #2-2; ECR, #14; ACR, #1-1, #24, and #13-5 (against incitement to discrimination); AFR, #2; Convention on Racism;

Convention on Women, #1; Convention on Child, #2-1 and ICPR #24-1 on Child; ILO Convention on Discrimination (Employment and Occupation, No. 111, 1958); Convention Against Discrimination in Education (UNESCO, 1960, and Recommendation and Protocol, 1962); and Genocide Convention, #II;

UDHR, #7; UNESCO Declaration on Race and Racial Prejudice, 1978; ISLAM (1990), #5 (a) for marriage (however, *see* #1 with respect to "All men are equal . . ."); Dec Social Progress, #1; Dec on Disabled Persons, Principle #3; Eur. Charter, Preamble, Paragraph 3; Charter of Paris, 1990, Principle One, Paragraph 5; and others. Of interest is the Lusaka Manifesto on Southern Africa, 1969, which proscribes any "racialist majority government . . . of deliberate and permanent discrimination between its citizens on grounds of racial origin." This is to apply to the then present situation and to future governments and to any later reversal of discrimination.

III. Expanded Definition. The UNESCO Convention Against Discrimination in Education in Article 1 defines discrimination as "any distinction, exclusion, limitation or preference which, being based on race, colour, sex, language, religion, political or other opinion, national or social origin, economic condition or birth, has the purpose or effect of nullifying or impairing equality of treatment . . ." *See also* Convention on Racial Discrimination, #1, and ILO Discrimination Convention, No. 111, 1958, #1, for parallel definitions. Discrimination is the purposeful and illegal denial of equality in any of its dimensions. ICPR also includes the guarantee of "effective protection against discrimination," which includes an "effective remedy" for this violation of law (ICPR, #2-3). ICPR also prohibits by law "Incitement to discrimination" (#20-2) which may contend with freedom of expression (ICPR, #19), which, in turn, has its own restrictions (#19-3). A comprehensive definition of discrimination necessitates analysis of provisions and language in all human rights treaties and declarations, including the categories of grounds of discrimination.

IV. Landmarks. Equality for humans is first stated in the United States Declaration of Independence of July 4, 1776, with the "self-evident truth" that "all men are created equal . . ." The French Declaration of the Rights of Man and the Citizen of August 26, 1789, in Article 1 states that "in respect of their rights men are born and remain free and equal." Both declarations refer only to men and the use of "equal" in both is hardly a dedicated commitment to nondiscriminatory or nonarbitrary treatment of humans. However, both comprise a start toward the concept of equality, which is also a beginning to nondiscriminatory treatment of humans.

Equality in Legal Rights, especially equal protection of the law, grew in the nineteenth century. However, equality in most areas such as race, gender, national origin, and economic status were and are endemic in all nations. At the international level, the League of Nations Covenant was silent on human equality and nondiscrimination. United States President Woodrow Wilson had wanted to include a clause in the Covenant providing for religious liberty. This might have succeeded had it not been for a Japanese proposal for equality of nations including race and nationality. The Japanese recommendation on racial equality was unacceptable to the European powers and both proposals were therefore silently and diplomatically abandoned.

The United Nations Charter of June 26, 1945, states in Article 1-3 and four other Articles that the United Nations should advance human rights for all "without distinction as to race, sex, language or religion . . ." These words first appear in the Big Four Amendments to the draft Charter on May 4, 1945, at the San Francisco Conference. As incorporated into the Charter, this code of nondiscrimination became the beacon for the early and progressive development of human rights law by the United Nations.

V. Cross References. *See* introduction to Legal Rights as well as Compensation, Due Process, and Equal Protection of the Law. Provisions on prohibition of discrimination are in all treaties and declarations cited above in Other Sources and are integral to the responsibilities and operations of the Special Rapporteurs and Working Parties in the human rights machinery under the aegis of the Commission on Human Rights and the Subcommission. *See also* General Assembly annual resolutions on discrimination in many areas including Res. 48/91, December 20, 1993, Third Decade to Combat Racism and Racial Discrimination, 1993–2003. *See also* UN Human Rights Commission appointment of Special Rapporteur on Contemporary Forms of Racism, Racial Discrimination, Xenophobia and Related Intolerance, 1993.

Life

I. The Right. Every human being has the inherent right to life. This right shall be protected by law. No one shall be arbitrarily deprived of his life. Covenant on Civil and Political Rights, Article 6, para I.

II. Other Sources. ECR, #2-1; ACR, #4-1; AFR, #4 and #20; ISLAM (1990), #2-a; Convention on Child, #6; Genocide Convention, #2; Convention on Apartheid, #2;

UDHR, #3.

III. Expanded Definition. The right to life is the most fundamental human right and the foundation of all human rights. As such, it must be protected by the law of the state or jurisdiction in which the person is living or located. This is a positive obligation of the state, because there shall be no arbitrary deprivation of life by any state or person. Prohibition of arbitrary deprivation of life also implies right of due process for the person in the event of any threat of arbitrary deprivation of life. ICPR, #4-2, states that there shall be no derogation from #6 (right to life), although #6, paragraphs 2, 4, 5, and 6 are concerned with the death penalty as an exception to right to life (*see* Death Penalty, Legal Rights).

The sources of right to life vary. ICPR affirms the "inherent right," which has roots in historical natural law. ECR, ACR, and AFR are silent on sources. ISLAM, #2-1, states that "life is a God-given gift. . ."

The commencement of "life" is a subject of contention. ICPR, ECR, and AFR are silent on this point. ACR states in #4-1 that the right to life "shall be protected by law and, in general, from the moment of conception." There is jurisprudence on the extent to which "in general" modifies "moment of conception." ISLAM states in #7 that every child has rights "as of the moment of birth," which suggests that life begins at that moment. It is of interest that the Constitution of Virginia of June 12, 1776, states in Section 1 that "men . . . have certain inherent rights . . . when they enter into a state of society . . . namely, the enjoyment of life . . ." Presumably one enters "society" only upon birth. Contemporary medical science and technology are also deeply involved in this issue in terms of capability to produce the fetus through a variety of fertilization techniques. Further, such science and technology have the capability of prolonging some physical life beyond the functioning and/or life of the brain. Jurisprudence must deal with these contentious issues that relate to the definition of life.

IV. Landmarks. "Thou shall not kill," Exodus XX-13, is an early affirmation of the right to life. The body of natural law, from its origins in Greece and its absorption by Roman law and the Christian Church, gradually flowed into Western philosophy and governance. Life, however, was always compromised throughout history and remains so today with the proclaimed right of states to engage in massive uses of force and also to deal with life and death with the dubious justification of state sovereignty. The Hague Convention of 1907 on the laws of war declared its intention was to "diminish the evils of war, so far as military requirements permit . . ." This waiver on the right to life is woven in all human rights treaties, often in terms of "national security" or "public emergency" (#14-1 & #4-1, ICPR).

The Magna Carta of June 15, 1215, stated in #39 that "no free man shall . . . in any way be destroyed . . . except by legal judgment of his peers or by the law of the land." In due course, the Magna Carta and other English statutes and laws affirmed the right of a person to protection against arbitrary rule. It was in the American colony of Massachusetts, however, that "life" was added to the proscription in the 1215 Magna Carta. In Article One of the Massachusetts Body of Liberties of December 10, 1641, it states, "No man's life shall be taken away . . . unlesse it be by vertue or equitie of some express law of the Country . . ." Other colonies followed Massachusetts's right to life.

Natural law philosophy led to the affirmation of the inherent right to life in the writings of Hugo Grotius (1583–1625) and John Locke (1632–1704), who was particularly eloquent in his proclamation of the inherent rights of life, liberty, and property. Natural law philosophy enveloped the American statesmen in the eighteenth century, especially Thomas Jefferson, who penned the United States Declaration of Independence in late June 1776. The emphatic "self-evident truth" that all men are endowed with the rights of "Life, Liberty and the pursuit of Happiness" was Jefferson's historic contribution to the universal "inherent right to life" of ICPR. Affirmation that there shall be no deprivation of "life, liberty, or property, without due process of law," is in the Fifth Amendment to the Constitution and the Fourteenth Amendment of 1868.

The French Declaration of the Rights of Man and the Citizen of August 26, 1789, does not include the "right to life" among the "natural and imprescriptible rights of man" in #2. However, the right may certainly be inferred from the Declaration's Articles and abundant rights protecting the person. The universal right to life was enshrined in #3 of the UDHR of December 10, 1948, and then entered into the international treaty law in #6 of the ICPR.

V. Cross References. *See* Death Penalty, Due Process, Person before the Law, and Security of Person (Legal Rights) and Apartheid and Genocide (Collective Rights).

Name

I. The Right. Every child shall be registered immediately after birth and shall have a name. Covenant on Civil and Political Rights, Article 24, paragraph 2.

II. Other Sources. ACR, #18; Covenant on the Rights of the Child, #7-1, 2.

III. Expanded Definition. A name provides identity for the newly born child, especially if the name includes the "surnames of his parents or that of one of them" (ACR, #18). A name provides a distinct designation for the person with human rights and entitlements to those rights. The law of the state where the child is born may "regulate the manner in which this right shall be ensured for all by use of assumed names if necessary" (ACR, #18).

IV. Landmarks. In the world's past and present cultures people have had names since the beginning of recorded history with many and varied designations. The dehumanization of millions of people under the Hitler regime from 1933 to 1945 led to the inclusion of name along with nationality in ICPR, #24.

V. Cross References. Child, Discrimination, and Nationality (Civil and Political Rights); Due Process and Person before the Law, (Legal Rights); and Family (Economic, Social, and Cultural Rights).

Nationality

I. The Right. Every child has a right to acquire a nationality. Covenant on Civil and Political Rights, Article 24, para 3.

II. Other Sources. ACR, #20-1, 2, 3; Convention on the Rights of the Child, #7-1; Convention on Racism, 5-d (iii); Convention on Women, #9-1, 2; Convention on Refugees, #1-2 (in definition of refugee); Convention on the Nationality of Married Women, 1958; Convention on the Reduction of Statelessness (1954), #1, ff;
UDHR, #15-1, 2.

III. Expanded Definition. Nationality is that quality or character that arises from the fact of a person's belonging to a nation or state.

Nationality determines the political status of the individual, especially with reference to allegiance; domicile determines his civil status (Black, 1222). A national may be a citizen of the state, depending on the constitutional requirements of the state for citizenship and for entitlement to full civil, legal, and political rights. All citizens are nationals, but not all nationals are citizens—e.g., a United States corporation as a person before the law is a national. Nationality is a contractual obligation with the national's allegiance to the state in return for state protection of the national.

ICPR provides for a child to have a "right to acquire a nationality," while ACR states in #20-1 that "every person has the right to a nationality." Clearly the word "acquire" in ICPR moderates the "right" which is automatic in ACR. The Convention on the Rights of a Child #7-1 also tempers the right with the word "acquire." "Acquire" thus refers to a condition or process to secure the right which would be determined by the state in which the person is born or resides. Under the law of the child, the upper limit of "child" is eighteen years of age. Under ICPR, therefore, the right does not exist to a person eighteen or over, unlike the broader "person" in ACR. In any event, international law recognizes the right of each state to determine the constitutional provisions for nationality and citizenship which may be supplemented by a state's adherence to a treaty with provisions for nationality and citizenship such as the conventions cited in II, above.

IV. Landmarks. Citizenship is rooted in ancient political communities, especially Rome, while "national" emerged only with the rise of the nation-state in the late eighteenth century. However, it was and is the law of each state that determines who is or is not a citizen and/or national.

The right to nationality in UDHR of December 10, 1948, is the first statement on this right in international law. It evolved in the drafting of the Declaration, largely as a response to the massive denationalization of millions of people by the Hitler regime from 1933 to 1945. Further, the millions of stateless peoples during and after World War II led to the determination to equate nationality with basic human rights. There remains in the mid-1990s, however, considerable ambiguity on the right of nationality with the more than forty million refugees and internally displaced people throughout the world. The right to nationality also concerns minorities, indigenous peoples, migrants, and others.

V. Cross References. Asylum, Child, Discrimination (especially on grounds of nationality), Territory, Movement in, Name, Political and

Public Service, and Women (Civil and Political Rights); Due Process, Person before the Law, and Security of Person (Legal Rights); Family (Economic, Social, and Cultural Rights); Aliens, Migrant Workers, Minorities, Refugees, Stateless, and Indigenous Peoples (Collective and Declaratory Rights).

Political and Public Service

I. The Right. Every citizen shall have the right and the opportunity, without any of the distinctions mentioned in article 2 (of ICPR) and without unreasonable restrictions: (a) To take part in the conduct of public affairs, directly or through freely chosen representatives; (b) To vote and to be elected at genuine periodic elections which shall be by universal and equal suffrage and shall be held by secret ballot, guaranteeing the free expression of the will of the electors; (c) To have access, on general terms of equality, to public service in his country. Covenant on Civil and Political Rights, Article 25 (#2-1 mandates rights "without distinction . . .").

II. Other Sources. ECR, Preamble, paras 4 and 5, and Protocol One, #3; ACR, #23; AFR, #13; Convention on Political Rights of Women, 1953; Convention on Racism, #5 (c); Convention on Women, #7, 8. *See also* treaties which prohibit political discrimination (Discrimination, Civil and Political Rights);

UDHR, #21; Dec Social Progress, #5 (c) and #18; Declaration on Disabled Persons, #4.

See also Declaration on Democratic Values (by the seven major industrial democracies, June 8, 1984) and Charter of Paris for a New Europe: A New Era of Democracy, Peace and Unity, CSCE States, 1990.

III. Expanded Definition. Governance by consent of the governed, the means for the governed to convey their consent, and the governing authorities under the same law as the governed are the essence of political democracy. Political democracy, in turn, requires many other civil rights such as freedom of religion, speech, press, and assembly, and legal rights such as due process and equal protection of the law. "Fundamental Freedoms . . . are best maintained on the one hand by an effective political democracy and on the other by a common understanding and observance of Human Rights upon which they depend" (ECR, Preamble, paragraph

4). The right of public service, as well as service in the political branches of government, is another guarantee of governance of, by, and for the people.

Article 25, ICPR, has many provisions for political rights and public service. They include the following: access or the right of direct participation, as in a New England town meeting, and/or indirect participation by elected representatives, such as the Lok Sahba (House of the People) of India; Choice of Representatives or the right to vote freely, in genuine and periodic or regular elections with universal and equal suffrage on a secret ballot; and Universal Suffrage or the right to vote with no discrimination based on race, color, sex, language, religion, political or other opinion, national or social origin, property, birth, or other status (#2, ICPR).

ICPR also states that the political right should be "without unreasonable restrictions," which permits the State Party to place reasonable restrictions on the political right. ECR in #16 provides for "restrictions on the political activity of aliens." Article #23-3, ACR, lists seven possible restrictions on the political right and public service, only one of which, language, conflicts with ICPR, #2.

The political and public affairs right is not transferable from one jurisdiction or state to another. It is the only right in the covenants and conventions which is limited to the "citizen" of the State Party and not a right of "everyone" or "each person." Each state has full authority and independence to define citizenship in the state.

The ICPR and ECR refer often to the "democratic society" (ICPR, #14-1, #21, #22-1; ECR, #8-2, #9-2, and #11-2. *See also* Dec on Non-Nationals, #5-2, and "free society" in ESCR, #13-1). In the diplomatic negotiations on the UDHR, a proposal was made to refer to the "democratic state." However, some delegations felt that a democratic state may be so in name only and not one necessarily willing to guarantee or protect human rights and democratic processes as already developed in what became UDHR #21. A "democratic society" was proposed as expressive of democracy as a way of life, and thus this term was placed in #29 of UDHR.

IV. Landmarks. Political democracy in many forms has deep roots in history. The democracy of Athens and some other Greek city-states in the fifth century provided the first major arena in which democracy (although restricted to elite male citizens) flourished. The early Norman kings in England, beginning with Henry I in 1100, began to negotiate with their own elites for reciprocal rights which led, in part, to the contractual structure of the Magna Carta of June 15, 1215, between King John and his Barons.

As legal and civil rights began to congeal in England, more demands by elites for the right to be consulted and to give consent for monarchial wars and financial needs led to the first Parliaments in the thirteenth century. In his Writ of Summons of the "Model Parliament" in 1295, King Edward I declared, "What touches all should be approved by all and it is clear that the common dangers should be met by measures agreed upon in common." This equation moved with glacial speed toward the stronger Parliaments of the seventeenth century, accompanied by the affirmation of rights in the Magna Carta, the due process of the law, the right of habeus corpus, and the English Bill of Rights of 1689. This pageant of events was the indispensible historical foundation for the contract between the governed and governing officials in the writings of John Locke (1632–1704) and Thomas Jefferson (1743–1826).

Patterns of representative government varied in the American colonies which, as in England, were governed by white males of property. Colonial governments developed their own representative political processes. New England town meetings with very direct democracy arose in the seventeenth century and remain very vigorous today. Beyond local government, colonial charters moved toward representative government. In Article II of the Frame of Government for Pennsylvania of April 25, 1682, for instance, "freemen" shall gather and "shall chuse out of themselves seventy-two persons of most note for their wisdom, virtue and ability . . . and act as the provincial Council of the said province."

The First Continental Congress in a Resolve of October 26, 1775, hailed representative government: ". . . the first grand right, is that of the people having a share in their own government, by their representatives chosen by themselves, and in consequence of being ruled by laws which they themselves approve, not by edicts of men, over whom they have no control."

The United States Constitution of 1787 did not establish a political democracy. It is important to note, however, that the First Amendment to the Constitution of December 15, 1791, provided for the right of people "to petition the government for a redress of grievances." The right of petition by the ruled to the rulers was confirmed in Article 61 of the Magna Carta and was threaded throughout English and American statutory law after that time. It is a firm legal foundation for political democracy and, incidentally, for rights of political interest groups to "petition" officials in government for whatever purposes they seek, redress of grievances or not.

Article 6 of the French Declaration of the Rights of Man and the Citizen of August 26, 1789, is of great interest in comparing its contents to #25 of ICPR. "Legislation is the expression of the general will. All citizens have a right to participate in shaping it, either in person, or through their representatives. It must be the same for all, whether it punishes or it protects. Since all citizens are equal in its eyes, all are equally eligible for all positions, posts and public employments in accordance with their abilities and with no other distinctions than those provided by their virtues and their talents."

The genius of the authors of the Constitution enabled their successors to graft political democracy on the elitist republican form of government of the Constitution. Political democracy grew and thrived in the nineteenth century and became more universal in the twentieth, especially with the Nineteenth Amendment to the Constitution on women's suffrage of August 18, 1920. United States President Woodrow Wilson saw World War I as a battle between "selfish and autocratic power" and "the really free and self-governed peoples of the world" in his April 2, 1917, address to Congress calling for a declaration of war against Germany.

Wilson viewed the war as one to make "the world safe for democracy." Others, however, saw democracy's inability to prevail against the German and Japanese tyranny of "autocratic power" in the 1920s and 1930s. The allied nations defeated those tyrannies in 1945, and the United Nations sought again to universalize political democracy in #21 of the UDHR.

V. Cross References. Political democracy and public service involve nearly all the civil rights in the dictionary. *See* Equal Protection of the Law and Person before the Law (Legal Rights) and Peoples, Self-Determination (Collective Rights). *See also* the Resolution of the Organization of American States (OAS), 1080, June 1991, requiring that each member of the OAS be a "representative democracy." *See also* OAS amendment of its Charter of December 12, 1992, allowing suspension of a member by two-thirds vote in the General Assembly if that state's "democratically constituted government has been overthrown by force."

Press

I. The Right. (1) Everyone shall have the right to hold opinions without interference. (2) Everyone shall have the right to freedom of expression: this right shall include freedom to seek, receive, and impart information and ideas of all kinds, regardless of frontiers, either orally, in writing or in print, in the form of art, or through any other media of his choice. (3) The exercise of these rights provided for in paragraph 2 of this Article carries with its special duties and responsibilities. It may therefore be subject to certain restrictions, but these shall only be such as are provided by law and are necessary: (a) For respect of the rights and reputations of others (b) For the protection of national security or public order (ordre public) or of public health or morals. Covenant on Civil and Political Rights, Article 19. (1) Any propaganda for war shall be prohibited by law. (2) Any advocacy of national, racial, or religious hatred that constitutes incitement to discrimination, hostility, or violence shall be prohibited by law. CPR, Article 20.

II. Other Sources. ECR, #10; ACR, #13 and #14; AFR, #9; Convention on Racism, #4 and #5-d-(viii): Convention on Child, #13; Convention on the International Right of Correction (1962); Constitution, UNESCO, #1-2-(d). Also all conventions with provisions prohibiting discrimination on ground of expression (*See* Discrimination, Civil and Political Rights).

UDHR, #19; ISLAM, #22; ASEAN, #7 (Mass Communications Media); Dec on Non-National, #5-e; Declaration on Mass Media, UNESCO, (1978); Declaration on Race and Racial Prejudice, UNESCO, (1978), #5-3.

III. Expanded Definition. Freedom of speech and freedom of the press are linked throughout the evolution of human rights as they are in #19 ICPR, in the First Amendment to the United States Constitution, and in all provisions of treaties of international human rights law. However, each has its own origins and distinctive nature in law. Each stems from a person's privately held opinions, which may be conveyed by that person's overt expression of opinions in speech, publication, writing, art, or other medium, including electronic media of all kinds. Paragraphs 1 and 2 of #19, ICPR, thus suggest an extensive right: (1) to seek information and ideas of all kinds, (2) to receive information and ideas of all kinds, (3) to impart information and ideas of all kinds, and (4) to do so without limits of frontiers of any jurisdiction, especially the State Party to the ICPR seeking and receiving information essential to forming opinions in addition to those otherwise held by the person which may be conveyed by the press.

However, Paragraph 3 of #19, ICPR, places limitations on freedom of speech. Those limitations must be provided for in the law of the state in order (1) to protect the rights of others, (2) to protect the reputations of others, (3) to protect national security, (4) to protect public order (ordre public), and (5) to protect public health or morals.

Each of these limitations is extensive in scope and is subject to the determination and interpretation of States Parties to ICPR. Each applies to the seeking, receiving, and imparting of ideas and information as noted above. In addition, Article 20, ICPR, contains additional limitations on freedom of expression through the press with such words as "propaganda," "hatred," "incitement," and others. These are significant restrictions as interpreted and applied by a State Party or an international authority such as the ICPR Human Rights Committee or a human rights court.

Further, ECR, ACR, and especially the Convention on Racial Discrimination have more stringent restrictions on the right to freedom of expression, especially #4 of the Convention on Racism. Article 14, ACR, also provides for a "right of reply" for anyone who claims injury by "inaccurate or offensive statements or ideas disseminated to the public in generally legally regulated media of communication . . ." This right is also confirmed in the United Nations Convention on the International Right of Correction, August 24, 1962. In brief, the right of expression is compromised by the right of the state to limit a person's opinions through expression by the press on many grounds.

IV. Landmarks. Book burning has for ages been a tool of those who seek to repress the written word as harmful to their interests. Julius Caesar gravely damaged the great library at Alexandria in 46 B.C., with over 700,000 volumes and manuscripts destroyed in raging flames. In the New Testament, Acts 19:19 describes book burning, and the three centuries of the Inquisition were ones of vast censorship. In fact, the right to print freely in any form, and thus to read, was very limited in nearly every society.

With the invention of printing from moveable type by Johann Gutenberg in Strasbourg around 1436, human communication through the printed word vastly accelerated the exchange of information, ideas, and opinion among people at all levels of society. In short order, political and religious authority, which usually monopolized information, was challenged by the printed word. In time, authority responded with attempts to curtail what it considered a threat to its version of security and well-being. Kings and their governments feared publications they considered seditious, and the Roman Catholic Church published its own *Index Liborum,* a list of publications forbidden because they were considered contrary to the Faith.

Around 1566, the Elizabethan government in England began to control the press through licensing, with rules and ordinances for "those professing the art, trade, or mystery of printing, or selling books." The rules became more stringent, especially against religious opposition. In 1586, the Court of the Star Chamber confined printing to London, Oxford, or Cambridge, and no books were to be printed "contrary to any statute or royal order." James I (1566–1625) and Parliament continued these controls, which were accompanied by wide powers of the government to search and seize unlicensed books.

Change came with the abolition of the Star Chamber in 1964 and the realization that the task of attempted government surveillance over all publishers, including those of unlicensed books, was nearly impossible. Of great importance as well was John Milton's famous *Areopagitica* in 1644, which was a stirring plea for abolishing the licensing of the printed word. Laws were gradually relaxed, and the licensing legislation was allowed to expire by 1695. However, many restrictions remained, especially with respect to allegations of seditious libel and any incitement to rebellion.

The press was likewise very limited in the American colonies, until the celebrated trial of New York newspaper publisher John Peter Zenger in 1735. Accused of libel, Zenger and his attorney, Andrew Hamilton, proved to the jury that Zenger did publish the truth in his criticism of government policy. The truth, in turn, surmounted the New York claim to control of the press. A press increasingly more free from government regulation grew in the colonies. The First Continental Congress in 1774 hailed "the freedom of the press (in the) advancement of truth" and the Constitution of Virginia of June 12, 1776, pioneered the right, declaring in Section 12 that "freedom of the press is one of the great bulwarks of liberty and can never be restrained." Subsequent state constitutions hailed freedom of the press along with freedom of speech. The Massachusetts Constitution of October 25, 1780, held that "the liberty of the press is essential to the security of freedom."

The United States Constitution is silent on the press. This was soon remedied, however, with the First Amendment of December 15, 1791, which declared, "Congress shall make no law . . . abridging the freedom of speech, or of the press . . . " The French Declaration of the Rights of Man and the Citizen of August 26, 1789, affirmed in Article 11 "the free communication of thoughts or opinions being one of the most precious rights of man; every citizen may speak, write and publish freely, save that he answer for abuse of such freedom according to cases established by legislation." All states in varying degree have legislated on what they consider to be abuses of the full freedom of the press as publication in variance to what the state considers essential to its security and well-being. The restrictions on the press contained in human rights treaties are ample evidence of the venerable contention between the right of a free press and the rights of the state.

V. Cross References. See Discrimination, Dignity, Property, Speech, and Political (Civil and Political Rights); Due Process and Privacy (Legal Rights); and Author and Culture (Economic, Social, and Cultural Rights).

See also "Freedom of Opinion and Expression," *United Nations Action,* pp. 112–21 for General Assembly resolutions and draft conventions on freedom of information. The Assembly in 1987 endorsed the United Nations Educational, Scientific, and Cultural Organization's policy and program for a "New World Information and Communication Order." The NWICO was authored and promoted by the developing nations to eliminate what they considered to be imbalances and inequities in global information flows due to the near monopoly of the press held by the Western nations. By 1995, however, this "New Order" has been quietly retired as UNESCO has turned to other approaches to advance what it states as the "right to communicate."

Property

I. The Right. Every natural or legal person is entitled to the peaceful enjoyment of his possessions. No one shall be deprived of his possessions except in the public interest and subject to the conditions provided for by law and by the general principles of international law.

The preceeding provisions shall not, however, in any way impair the right of a State to enforce such laws as it deems necessary to control the use of property in accordance with the general interest or to secure the payment of taxes or other contributions or penalties. European Convention for the Protection of Human Rights and Fundamental Freedoms, Protocol One, Article 1, March 20, 1952.

II. Other Sources. ACR, #21; AFR, #14 and 13-3; Convention on Racism (1966), #5 (d); Convention on Women (1979), #16-1 (h); Convention on Refugees, #13 and 14; Convention on Stateless, #13; Convention on Apartheid, #II (d); Convention on Migratory Workers, #15; ILO Conventions on property rights of workers; Convention establishing World Intellectual Property Organization (1967); Paris Convention for Protection of Industrial Property (1983). Also all conventions with provisions prohibiting discrimination on grounds of property (*see* Discrimination, Civil and Political Rights).

UDHR, #17; ISLAM, #5; Dec Social Progress, #6-2; Declaration on Disabled Persons, #13; and Dec Non-Nationals, #5-2-(d).

See also "The Right of Everyone to Own Property Alone as Well as in Association with Others," Luis Valencia Rodriguez, Independent Expert on Property Rights, UN Commission on Human Rights, December 1992. There is no provision on property in ICPR.

III. Expanded Definition. ". . . in the strict legal sense, [property is] an aggregate of rights which are guaranteed and protected by the government" (Black, 1095).

Property is a term used popularly to refer to a thing owned by a person, but used more accurately in law to refer to a scheme of relationships, recognized or established by government, between individuals with respect to an object. The object may be tangible, such as land, or completely the creature of law, such as patent or copyright. Since the objects of property and the protected relationships vary among societies and over time, it is difficult to find a least common denominator of property. *Encyclopaedia Britannica,* vol. 18, p. 631 (1967).

"The tie between man and property is often not merely of economic interest; the basis of attachment is of the nature of the sentiment, a complex set of emotional considerations centering in the object. Thus to the [New Zealand indigenous] Maori, his tribal land is his greatest treasure . . ." Ibid., p. 585.

Property rights are never absolute, as is stated in ECR Protocol I, above, and in all treaties with provisions on the right of property. They may not be used against the public interest of the state or to impair the rights of others. Further, property may be taken by the state in the public interest and for a public purpose, usually with fair, adequate, and prompt compensation. This is the right of the state to eminent domain. There may be no compensation if the property endangers public welfare or the rights of others as determined by the state. In any event, one may not be arbitrarily deprived of his or her property (UDHR, #17-2). If so, the person has the right of remedy and due process of the law.

In brief, property is often viewed in its material dimension in terms of personal possessions, real estate, financial assets, contracts, and other visible moveable or immoveable objects. Property also includes "intellectual property," such as rights to "literary, artistic and scientific works; performances of performing artists, programs and broadcasts; inventions in all fields of human endeavor; scientific discoveries, industrial designs; trade marks, service marks and commercial names and designations; and protection against unfair competition . . ." *See* Convention Establishing World Intellectual Property Organization, II, above.

Land as property and rights of indigenous people to land as well as others who may not possess specific title to land are substantial areas of concern and often confrontation, especially in developing nations. Land rights of Native Americans in North America have been the subject of much litigation in the past decades. Land for the "right of development" and right to natural resources in #1, ICPR, and ESCR have become frontier issues in human rights law.

IV. Landmarks. Property in its many forms has always been regulated by the political community. Property rights were well defined in Roman law, and much of the terminology of real property has roots in Latin. Feudal law in Europe was complex and detailed in the reciprocities of rights and duties of feudal actors. This was especially the case with the dominant role of the monarch, who usually enjoyed absolute ownership, at least in theory.

William I (1027–1087) after his conquest of England in 1066 began to alter the continental structure of feudalism with commanding personal control over his subordinates in return for their loyalty and support. His successors, beginning with Henry I (1068–1135), broadened the contractual relationship between monarchs and their elite subjects.

A more extensive contract was forced on King John by the English Barons in the Magna Carta of June 15, 1215. The "Great Charter" had many concerns with the rights of property, including "land, castles, and franchises or (one's) right" in Article 52. It declared in Article 28 that "[no authority] shall take anyone's grain or other chattels, without immediately paying for them in money . . ." In Article 39, "no free man shall be . . . dispossessed . . . except by the legal judgment of his peers or by the law of the land." In brief, property is a right. If it is taken by an official for state purposes, it must be by what we now call the due process of the law, and compensation must be extended to the property owner. The basic law of property in III, above, was in place by 1215, irrespective of the ebbs and tides of abuses of property rights in history.

The Massachusetts Body of Liberties of December 10, 1641, confirms this equation of Article 1: ". . . no mans goods or estaite shall be taken away from him unlesse it be by vertue . . . of some express law . . ." With the flow of natural law and natural rights theory in the seventeenth century, "property" became a natural right. This was a central proposition of John Locke (1632–1704), who held that property and liberty were inextricably related and that property was both of the person as well in his material possessions. This dimension of Locke's philosophy is expressed well in Chapter I, Section A, Article I of the 1777 Constitution of Vermont. ". . . all men are born equally free and independent, and have certain natural, inherent and unalienable rights, amongst which are the enjoying and defending life and liberty; acquiring, possessing and protecting property, and pursuing and obtaining happiness and safety." These words are also incorporated in Article I, paragraph II of the 1784 Constitution of New Hampshire.

James Madison (1751–1836) included both dimensions of property in his authorship of the Fifth Amendment to the Constitution of the United States of December 15, 1791: "[no person shall] be deprived of life, liberty, or property, without due process of law; nor shall private property be taken for public use without just compensation." On the inherent right of property, Madison wrote as follows: ". . . a man has property in his opinions and the free communication of them. He has property of peculiar value in his religious opinions, and in the profession and practices dictated by them. He has property very dear to him in the safety and liberty of his person. . . . In a word, as a man is said to have a right to his property, he may be equally said to have property in his rights." "Life, liberty, and property" are also rights that the United States must protect under the Fourteenth Amendment of 1868.

Eminent domain, the Fifth Amendment right of the state to take property for public use with compensation, was, in theory, in the Magna Carta as well as in fact in a number of state constitutions of the 1770s and 1780s. The French Declaration of the Rights of Man and the Citizen of August 26, 1789, also includes property among the natural rights of man in Article 1. Article 17 of the French Declaration is equally important. It states, "Since property is an inviolable and sacred right, no individual may be deprived of it unless some public necessity, legally certified as such, clearly requires it; and subject always to a just and previously determined compensation."

All states recognize the right of property in its material dimensions, but most states do not consider property a natural right as the jurisprudence of most states is not based on natural law. All states regulate the use of property, including the right of the state to take ownership of property for a public purpose, usually with compensation. Therefore there is no disagreement on Article 17 of UDHR of December 10, 1948: "everyone has the right to own property as well as in association with others (including communal property)" and "no one shall be arbitrarily deprived of his property." Property as a right is not in ICPR and ESCR because of failure in the negotiations of these covenants to reach agreement on the right to compensation. However, many rights in ICPR and ESCR such as dignity, privacy, name, and author's rights are property rights in the terms of James Madison's definition of the right of property.

V. Cross References. Dignity, Life, Territory, Movement in, and Name (Civil and Political Rights); Due Process, Privacy, and Security of Person (Legal Rights); Author and Culture (Economic, Social, and Cultural Rights); Aliens, Migrant Workers, Minorities, Peoples, Self-Determination, and Peoples, Natural Resources* (Collective Rights); and Development and Indigenous Peoples (Declaratory Rights).

*Under Peoples, Natural Resources, reference is made to the "Common Heritage of Mankind," which presents interesting issues as far as property rights are concerned.

Religion

I. The Right. (1) Everyone shall have the right to freedom of thought, conscience, and religion. This right shall include freedom to have or to adopt a religion or belief of his choice, and freedom, either individually or in community with others and in public or private, to manifest his religion or belief in worship, observance, practice, and teaching. (2) No one shall be subject to coercion which would impair his freedom to have or to adopt a religion or belief of his choice. (3) Freedom to manifest one's religion or beliefs may be subject only to such limitations as are prescribed by law and are necessary to protect public safety, order, health, or morals or the fundamental rights and freedoms of others. (4) The States Parties to the present Covenant undertake to have respect for the liberty of parents and, where applicable, legal guardians to ensure the religious and moral education of their children in conformity with their own convictions. Covenant on Civil and Political Rights, Article 18.

II. Other Sources. ECR, #9 & Prot I, #2; ACR, #13; AFR, #8; and Convention on Child, #14. Also, all conventions with provisions prohibiting discrimination on grounds of religion.

UDHR, #18; ISLAM, #18 and #25; ASEAN, #I-2-2.06

See also Declaration on the Elimination of All Forms of Intolerance and of Discrimination Based on Religion or Belief, Generally Assembly Resolution 36/35, November 25, 1981; Commission on Human Rights Resolution, 1992, entitled "Implementation of the Declaration on the Elimination of All Forms of Intolerance and of Discrimination Based on Religion or Belief"; Annual Reports, United Nations Special Rapporteur on Religious Intolerance (Angelo Vidal d'Almeida Ribeiro) established by the Commission on Human Rights, 1985. *See also Elimination of All Forms of Intolerance and of Discrimination Based on Religion or Belief,* Elizabeth Odio Benito, Special Rapporteur, Sub-Commission on Prevention of Discrimination and Protection of Minorities, 1989.

III. Expanded Definition. Religion is a right that may be exercised in "public or private" (ICPR, #18-1) while "thought and conscience" are attributes generally exercised by a person in private. The public exercise of "religion or belief of [one's] choice" is freedom to "manifest" or practice religion or belief through "worship, observance, practice, and teaching . . . individually or in community with others." This practice is to be without coercion or without mandate by a government to embrace a religion or no religion which would impair freedom of choice. A "belief" may be theological or philosophical which may or may not have a religious creed.

Freedom of religion in international human rights law is at some variance with freedom of religion in United States constitutional law and jurisprudence. Article 18-3 of ICPR places extensive restrictions on freedom of religion and belief "as prescribed by law and are necessary to protect public safety, order, health, or morals . . ." This provision gives a government extensive latitude to limit freedom of religion on many grounds. State restrictions in #18-3, ICPR, could seriously compromise the prohibition on coercion in #18-2. Article #18-3 also includes the limitation of protecting the "fundamental rights and freedoms of others," which is a limitation on most rights.

Further, ICPR #18-4 asserts the right of parents or legal guardians "to ensure the religious and moral education of their children in conformity with their own convictions." This provision may impair freedom of religion for any person below the age of eighteen. The authority granted to parents and legal guardians in #18-4 is also in ECR Protocol One, #3, and ACR #13-4. The United Nations Commission on Human Rights in a resolution of March 8, 1989, recognized the right of everyone to have conscientious objections to military service as a legitimate exercise of the right to freedom of thought, conscience, and religion.

IV. Landmarks. Religion, by whatever definition in terms of belief and theology, is basic to the person, even if one chooses not to embrace any faith or religious belief or practice. However, "the disregard and infringement . . . of the right to freedom of thought, conscience, religion or whatever belief (has) brought, directly or indirectly, wars and great suffering to mankind . . . and amount to kindering hatred between peoples and nations . . ." (Preamble, *Declaration on the Elimination of All Forms of Intolerance and of Discrimination Based on Religion or Belief.* Religious and belief system intolerance and discrimination have brought forth the worst atrocities and violations of humans' physical and mental well-being in recorded history, and their damage continues to undermine the goals and texture of human rights.

Religions and belief systems have many dimensions. Landmarks in the right to religious freedom are prominent in many historical eras, societies, and cultures but largely revolve around the person's freedom to believe and worship without dictation by government or discrimination and intolerance from any source. Over the centuries, however, governments have demanded people's conformity to state religion, accompanied or followed by discrimination, intolerance, and often severe punishment for any deviation from the identity of "church and state" or the prescribed belief system. The history of Western imperialism is remembered well in many parts of the world where Christianity was imposed as the imperial creed.

Jesus in Matthew 22:21 sought to distinguish between church and state in his pronouncement "Render therefore unto Caesar the things which are Caesar's; and unto God the things that are God's." Although what is "Caesar's" and what is "God's" continues to have ambiguity for many today, the person's right to make this decision is the essence of the freedom of religion and belief.

Over the ages, the "Caesar's" of the state identified themselves with God, and many were convinced of their "divine right" to rule. The Renaissance and Reformation in Europe led to the wars of religion which, in turn, brought about the brief Peace of Augsburg in 1555. One could worship as a Catholic or a Lutheran if the person's prince were Catholic or Lutheran; some Free Cities permitted both. Calvinists and others were ignored. The Peace opened the door to toleration which was widened with the treaties of the Peace of Westphalia of 1648, introducing the modern state system. On the Continent, in 1579 religious strife in Holland moved the Protestants in the Union of Utrecht to affirm their faith in the North Low Countries but not to prosecute Catholicism in the South. Holland then became the first home of religious toleration on the Continent.

Religious turmoil in England in the sixteenth century led to the establishment of the Anglican Church by Henry VIII in 1534 and to the religious controversies and Civil War of the seventeenth century. The English Toleration Act of May 1689 was a beginning of religious freedom for some, but it was far behind the momentum toward rights of religion and belief in the American colonies. As for other colonies of the European states, which were expanding in Africa and Asia in particular, religious toleration was usually ignored, and religious imperialism with the Christian Cross was often the symbol of intolerance and domination.

Royal and Church opposition to dissenters in England led some "Separatists" (separate from the Church of England) to find asylum in Holland as early as 1593. They were joined by other Separatists from Scrooby, England, in 1608 who decided to emigrate to America. They set out on the *Mayflower* on September 16, 1620, for Virginia but found themselves at the tip of Cape Cod in November. Their famous Mayflower Compact of November 11, 1620, provided for "just and equal laws" in their mutual contract in the "Presence of God" for a "civil Body Politik." The Puritans came in 1630 but, ironically, would not tolerate dissenters. Many others voyaged to the new English lands for some religious freedom from Royal dictation and warfare, and over some one hundred and fifty years established historic religious rights.

Religious tolerance was first proclaimed in America in Maryland in 1632, although it did not encompass all religious beliefs by any means. Roger Williams fled from the Massachusetts theocracy in 1636 to establish religious freedom from government authority. The Charter of Rhode

Island and Providence Plantations of July 8, 1663, was the first colonial document to proclaim "a full libertie in religious concernments. . ."

The march toward enhanced freedom to worship is recorded in the charters and constitutions of many colonies. Many expressed clear preference for one denomination or another, which was hardly a separation of church and state. However, documents such as the Charter of Fundamental Laws of West New Jersey of March 13, 1667 (#XVI, "Liberty of Conscience"); Pennsylvania Charter of Privileges of October 28, 1701, under William Penn ("FIRST—Liberty of Conscience"); and the constitutions of most colonies in the mid-eighteenth century gradually moved toward more full religious freedom. Thomas Jefferson's famous Virginia Statute of Religious Liberty of 1786 demanded that no one should be "enforced, restrained, molested, or burthened" for religious opinion or belief. After considerable debate, the heart of the Statute was incorporated into the First Amendment to the United States Constitution of December 15, 1791, and stated that "Congress shall make no law respecting the establishment of religion, or prohibiting the free exercise thereof. . ."

In a letter of 1802, Jefferson referred to the First Amendment provision on religion as "building a wall of separation between church and state." Jurisprudence in the United States has addressed itself ever since to defining the Amendment and the "wall," and that contention will continue. Most other states continued to ignore Matthew 22:21 and many continue to do so today. Many states moved toward enhanced religious freedom. However, the "wars and great suffering to mankind" based on religious imperialism of one brand or another reflect the words in the Preamble of the Convention on Religious Freedom cited above.

Article 10 in the French Declaration of the Rights of Man and the Citizen of August 26, 1789, declared that "nobody must be persecuted on account of his opinions, including religious ones, provided that the manifestation of those does not disturb the public order established by legislation." Article 10 formally terminated any divine right to rule in France and over time became the foundation for religious tolerance in France and countries embracing the code of civil law.

In his famous Four Freedoms address of January 6, 1941, President Franklin D. Roosevelt launched the internationalization of freedom of religion in declaring the second freedom to be that "of every person to worship God in his own way—everywhere in the world." Prohibition against religious discrimination appears in four articles of the United Nations Charter of June 26, 1945, including the Preamble's aspiration "to practice tolerance and live together in peace with one another as good neighbors." In chairing the new United Nations Commission on Human Rights in 1946, Mrs. Franklin D. Roosevelt and her colleagues incorporated the right to religious freedom in Article 18 of the Universal Declaration of Human Rights of December 10, 1948.

V. Cross References. Assembly, Association, Discrimination, Life, Political, Press, and Speech (Civil and Political Rights); Due Process (Legal Rights); and Family and Education (Economic, Social, and Cultural Rights).

Speech

I. The Right. (1) Everyone shall have the right to hold opinions without interference. (2) Everyone shall have the right to freedom of expression; this right shall include freedom to seek, receive, and impart information and ideas of all kinds, regardless of frontiers, either orally, in writing or in print, in the form of art, or through any other media of his choice. (3) The exercise of these rights provided for in paragraph 2 of this Article carries with it special duties and responsibilities. It may therefore be subject to certain restrictions, but these shall only be such as are provided by law and are necessary: (a) for respect of the rights and reputations of others, (b) for the protection of national security or public order (ordre public), or of public health of morals. Covenant on Civil and Political Rights, Article 19. (1) Any propaganda for war shall be prohibited by law. (2) Any advocacy of national, racial, or religious hatred that constitutes incitement to discrimination, hostility, or violence shall be prohibited by law. CPR, Article 20.

II. Other Sources. ECR, #10; ACR, #13, #14; AFR, #9, Convention on Racism, #4 and #5-d-(viii); also all conventions with provisions prohibiting discrimination on grounds of expression (*see* Discrimination, Civil and Political Rights).

UDHR, #19; ISLAM, #22; ASEAN, #1-2-(2.07): Dec on Non-Nationals, #5-e.

III. Expanded Definition. Freedom of speech and freedom of the press are linked throughout the evolution of human rights as they are in #19, ICPR, in the First Amendment to the United States Constitution, and in all provisions of treaties of international human rights law. However, each has its origins and distinctive nature in law. Each stems from a person's privately held opinions, which may be conveyed by that person's overt expression of opinions in speech, publication, writing, art, or any other medium including electronic media of all kinds. Paragraphs 1 and 2 of #19, ICPR, suggest an extensive right (1) to seek information and ideas of all kinds, (2) to receive information and ideas of all kinds, (3) to impart information and ideas of all kinds, and (4) to do so without limits of frontiers of any jurisdiction, especially the State Party to the ICPR. Seeking and receiving information and ideas are essential to forming opinions in addition to those otherwise held by the person.

However, Paragraph 3 of #19 places limitations on freedom of speech. Those limitations must be provided for in the law of the state in order (1) to protect the rights of others, (2) to protect the reputations of others, (3) to protect national security, (4) to protect public order (ordre public), and (5) to protect public health or morals. Each of these limitations is extensive in scope and is subject to the determination and interpretation of the States Parties to ICPR. Each applies to the seeking, receiving, and imparting of ideas and information as noted above. In addition, Article 20, ICPR, contains additional limitations on freedom of expression through speech with such words as "propaganda," "hatred," "incitement," and others. These are significant restrictions as interpreted and applied by a State Party, an international authority, or human rights court.

Further, ECR, ACR, and especially the Convention on Racism have more stringent restrictions on the right to freedom of expression, especially #4 of the Convention on Racism. Article 14, ACR, also provides for a "right of reply" for anyone who claims injury by "inaccurate or offensive statements or ideas disseminated to the public in general by legally regulated media of communication . . ." This right is also confirmed in the United Nations Convention on the International Right of Correction, August 24, 1962. In brief, the right of expression, and especially of speech, is compromised by the right of the state to limit a person's opinions through expression by speech on many grounds.

IV. Landmarks. A person's "right" to freedom to speech has always been limited by the authority of the political community or state to place limitations on what the state considers to be a threat to its security and well-being. As such, some freedom of or latitude for speech evolved only with the emergence of the parallel right of challenge to the authority of state (or political community) leadership. The 1215 Magna Carta was such a challenge. It was followed over hundreds of years in England by the demand of members of the early Parliaments for the need and thus right to debate issues without fear of restrictions or punishment by the monarch. Strode's Act in the Parliament of 1512 was the first statute to protect such early freedom of expression, although limited to members of Parliament.

Elizabeth I and James I often challenged rights of expression in Parliament, and Parliament members protested such limitations. The emerging expansion of expression by print and the press complemented the demand for freer speech. However, battles between Parliament and political leaders on the one hand, and the Crown on the other, raged throughout the seventeenth century. Finally, after the Revolution of 1688, the English Bill of Rights of December 16, 1689, formally recognized considerable freedom of speech in the Parliament in Article 9. It declared that "freedom of speech, and debate or proceedings in parliament, ought not to be impeached or questioned in any court or place out of parliament."

As was often the case, the American colonies outpaced their English superiors in proclaiming rights. The Fundamental Orders of Connecticut of January 14, 1639, led the way with Article 10: the "Courte [General Court or legislature] the Gouernour or Moderator shall haue power to order the Courts to give liberty of speech . . ." The Massachusetts Body of Liberties of December 10, 1641, affirmed that "every man . . . free or not shall have liberty to come to any [public meeting] and either by speech or writing . . . to present any . . . information . . ." Freedom of speech for one's religious beliefs was guaranteed in Rhode Island in 1663, and colonial legislatures all honored freedom of speech in their halls. Most colonies joined the freedom of speech with freedom of the press as basic to the other liberties they brought from England and enshrined in their constitutions. The Constitution of Vermont of July 8, 1777, put it this way: ". . . the free communication of thoughts and opinions is one of the invaluable rights of man; and every citizen may freely speak, write, and print on any subject, being responsible for the abuse of that liberty."

Freedom of speech in the United States Constitution of September 17, 1787, is limited in Article I, Section 6, to "members of Congress." However, the First Amendment to the Constitution of December 15, 1791, declares that "Congress shall make no law . . . abridging the freedom of speech, or the press . . ." The French Declaration of the Rights of Man and the Citizen of August 26, 1789, commented in Article 11 that "the free communication of thoughts or opinions being one of the most precious rights of man; every citizen may speak, write and publish freely, save that he answer for the abuse of such freedom according to the cases established by legislation."

The French Declaration flowed into French civil law and thus into most other nations basing their legal systems on that law. Rights in England are determined by acts of Parliament, unlike the United States constitutional system with the strong role of the courts in interpretation and judicial decisions. All states, however, have always had contention between freedom of speech and the interests of the state with respect to how free speech may be and therefore what restrictions are necessary for national security and well-being. The Constitution of Vermont and the French Declaration emphasize the obligation of the person engaged in speech not to abuse his/her liberty.

V. Cross References. *See* Discrimination, Dignity, Press, Property, and Political (Civil and Political Rights); Due Process and Privacy (Legal Rights); and Author and Culture (Economic, Social, and Cultural Rights).

Territory, Movement in

I. The Right. (1) Everybody lawfully within the territory of a State shall, within that territory, have the right to liberty of movement and freedom to choose his residence. (2) Everyone shall be free to leave any country, including his own. (3) [Restrictions include] "national security, public order (ordre public), public health or morals or the rights and freedoms of others . . ." (4) No one shall be arbitrarily deprived of the right to enter his country. Covenant on Civil and Political Rights, Article 12.

II. Other Sources. ECR, Protocol 4, #2, & #3; ACR, #22 (in considerable detail, paras 1–9); AFR, #12, 1-5; Convention on Racism #5-D (i) (ii); Convention on Women, #15-4; Convention on Apartheid, #2-c; Convention on Refugees, #31, #32, and #33 (no "Refoulement"); and Convention on Stateless, #26;

UDHR, #13; Eur. Charter, I-#18 and II-#19; ISLAM, #12; ASEAN, #1-2-(2.04); and Dec on Non-Nationals, #5-3.

III. Expanded Definition. The free mobility of people in and out of territories of states with natural law and natural rights jurisprudence is based on the inherent right of liberty. In other states, this freedom is statutory or judicial but not a natural right of liberty. Each state preserves the right under its constitution, legislation, and court decisions to place restrictions on freedom of movement in and out of territory and within the territory as well. State Parties to ICPR are bound by the limitations of #12-4 or other restrictions states may choose to apply to the freedom of movement. "National security" is a widely used restriction, especially with respect to the right of emigration. National and international laws concerning asylum, aliens, indigenous peoples, migrants, minorities, refugees, stateless persons, criminals, and others are detailed and complex on movement in and out of territory.

IV. Landmarks. Mobility of people within, in, and out of territory has always been regulated by political communities. Such movement was not viewed as a "right" until the Magna Carta of June 15, 1215. Article 42 was generous to relative freedom of movement.

> It is allowed henceforth to anyone to go out from our kingdom, and to return, safely and securely, by land and by water, saving their fidelity to us, except in time of war for some short time, for the common good of the kingdom; excepting persons imprisoned and outlawed according to the law of the realm, and people of a land at war with us, and merchants.

Article 41 of the Magna Carta further stipulated that merchants "shall be safe and secure in going out from England and coming into England and in remaining and going through England . . ." Articles 41 and 42 compare nicely with #12, ICPR, including the right and its restrictions, especially for national security.

Mobility of persons remained primarily under the law and authority of the sovereign political community or state. However, customary international law recognized reciprocities between and among states for mobility, tempered, of course, by restrictions imposed by each state. The Constitution of Vermont of July 8, 1777, brought movement into the frame of human rights with Article XVII, which stated that "all people have a natural and inherent right to emigrate from one state to another, that will receive them . . ." This right entered into the Articles of Confederation of March 1, 1781, which provided that "the people of each state shall have free ingress and regress to and from every other state . . ." Movement in and out of states of the new United States and into and out of the United States was considered a dimension of the inalienable right to liberty. By the time of the Universal Declaration of Human Rights of

December 10, 1948, and its Article 13, constitutions or laws of most members of the United Nations provided for freedom of movement. Variations in restrictions by states on freedom of movement remains a state prerogative.

V. Cross References. Asylum and Nationality (Civil and Political Rights); Due Process (Legal Rights); Family (Economic, Social, and Cultural Rights); Aliens, Apartheid, Migrant Workers, Minorities, and Refugees (Collective Rights); and Indigenous Peoples (Declaratory Rights). *See also United Nations Action,* pp. 106–108.

Women

I. The Right. The States Parties to the present Covenant undertake to ensure the equal right of men and women to the enjoyment of all civil and political rights set forth in the present Covenant. Covenant on Civil and Political Rights, Article 3. ICPR also states in #26 that "the law shall prohibit any discrimination . . . on any grounds such as race, colour, sex . . ."

II. Other Sources. The principal source on rights for women is the Convention on the Elimination of All Forms of Discrimination Against Women, December 18, 1979, with the Convention's Committee on the Elimination of Discrimination Against Women (CEDAW). *See also* the Convention on the Political Rights of Women, 1952 (the first treaty exclusively on women's rights); the Convention on the Nationality of Married Women, 1957; and the Convention on Marriage, 1962.

Also, ESCR, #3; ECR, #1 and #14; ACR, #1; AFR, #2 and #18-3. For the pace-setting and extensive International Labor Organization Conventions between 1919 and 1982, *see United Nations Action,* paragraphs 1911–1917, pp. 231, 232. *Also* all conventions with provisions prohibiting discrimination on the grounds of sex (*see* Discrimination, Civil and Political Rights). UDHR, #2; Eur. Charter, I-8, 17, and II-8, 17; ISLAM, #6; ASEAN, #5-9.

III. Expanded Definition. Women—adults and children—comprise slightly over one half of the world's population. However, throughout history and in about all societies, they have received far less than treatment equal to that accorded to men. The United Nations era has sought to redress this imbalance through international human rights law.

Women perform two-thirds of the world's work and receive one-tenth of the world's income. They own less than one-hundredth of the world's property and comprise two-thirds of the adult illiterates in the world. About 80 percent of the world's almost 20,000,000 refugees are women. Many cultures engage in dehumanizing treatment of women, such as genital mutilation and female infanticide. An expanded definition of women must thus record the historical and current patterns of discriminatory treatment of women of all ages. The Convention on Elimination of All Forms of Discrimination Against Women, with its eloquent Preamble, expands fully on the rights of women, with CEDAW monitoring State Parties' compliance with the rights they are obligated to implement in national law.

IV. Landmarks. The status of women in any society of the past must be examined within the law and culture of that society, especially those in Africa, Asia, the Americas, and their subsocieties as well. In fifth-century Athens, the adult, affluent, male Athenian citizen was the principal civic person, and women were objects rather than subjects. Plato (427–347) called for full equality for both sexes, but this prescription was in theory and not in Athenian policy. Throughout Western civilization, woman had few if any rights but in all societies was often treated well as a person. The variations were many depending on cultural relativism and, of course, the social and economic status of women in all societies. Although many women were educated and highly cultivated, they had few if any rights. Religions and their theologies had much influence on the treatment and law of women; this continues to prevail in most societies today. Jefferson's man in "all men are created equal" in the United States Declaration of Independence of July 2, 1776, was the same "man" as in ancient Athens—the adult, white, property owner who was hardly the equal of others who did not have these attributes of "man."

The movement toward more rights for women occurred with varying degrees and speeds in all societies. It was usually by initiative of women such as Mary Wollstonecraft, whose *Vindication of the Rights of Women* in 1792 was an initial contribution toward the elevation of women in society. The Industrial Revolution gradually led to legislation for some protection for working women and children, and educational rights were also included in this slow-paced agenda for women.

The convention on women's rights in Seneca Falls, New York, in July 1848 produced under the leadership of Elizabeth Cady Stanton a "Declaration of Sentiments," which pronounced that "All men and women are created equal." The drive for women's suffrage was launched, which finally led so many years later to the Nineteenth Amendment to the United States Constitution of 1919—"The right of citizens of the United States to vote shall not be denied or abridged by the United States or by any State on account on sex." England embraced women's suffrage in 1918 and 1919, as did many other states, although rights in many other areas were long denied to women. In Turkey, Kemal Ataturk (1881–1936) modernized legislation for women, beginning with his presidency in 1923, and launched their right to vote in 1932.

At the international level, several conferences were convened early in 1902 and 1906 on women's working rights that led to Article 23 (a) of the Covenant of the League of Nations and the commitment "to secure and maintain fair and human conditions of labor for men, women, and children." Section 23 (c) called for "agreements with regard to traffic in women and children. . ." Under the League Assembly, the Committee on Traffic in Women and Children was broadened to include many forms of exploitation. An extensive 1935 League study on the status of women and the International Labor Organization's early concerns and modest conventions on women in the workplace were placed on hold with the advent of World War II in 1939.

The manifold contributions of women in all nations during the war were accompanied by many states' legislation enhancing women's rights. They also led to the indelible imprint of women's rights in the United Nations Charter of June 26, 1945, in the second paragraph of the Charter's Preamble, which "reaffirms . . . the equal rights of men and women." The Charter details four times "promoting and encouraging respect for human rights and fundamental freedoms for all without discrimination as to race, sex . . ." The word "sex" was an addition by the Soviet Union. Mrs. Franklin Delano Roosevelt became chairman of the new UN Commission on Human Rights and led the Commission's affirmation of equality of gender in the provisions of the Universal Declaration of Human Rights of December 10, 1948.

IV. Cross References. Child, Discrimination, and Political (Civil and Political Rights); Due Process and Equal Protection of the Law (Legal Rights); Family (Economic, Social, and Cultural Rights); and Refugees (Collective Rights).

See "Advancement of Women," *United Nations Action,* pp. 196–232, for a partial record of the extensive activity of the United Nations in women's rights, especially in the areas of equality and development. See in particular para 1877, p. 225, "Categories of Women." The Commission on the Status of Women was established by the Economic and Social Council in 1946. Located in Vienna, the thirty-two-member Commission has exercised strong leadership in women's rights and policy, including the sponsorship of the UN Decade for Women, 1975–1986, and major conferences in Mexico City (1975), Copenhagen (1980), and Nairobi (1985). The Nairobi conference led to the extensive Nairobi Forward-looking Strategies for the Advancement of Women with an expansive program and logistics for implementation. The fourth world conference on women, "Womens' Action for Equality, Development and Peace," was held in the Peoples Republic of China from September 4 to 15, 1995.

The eleven-member International Research and Training Institute for the Advancement of Women, established in 1976, is located in Santo Domingo, Dominican Republic. Initiatives and resolutions on women's rights were at the top of the agenda of the 1993 Vienna World Conference on Human Rights. The forty-eighth General Assembly in 1993 adopted the Declaration on the Elimination of Violence Against Women, which was followed by the Commission on Human Rights' creation of a Special Rapporteur on Violence Against Women in March 1994. Sri Lankan jurist Radhika Coomaraswamy was appointed by the Commission to this post.

II

Legal Rights

Introduction

International human rights law, with respect to legal rights, seeks to protect the legitimate interests of the person within the context of the public order of the state or other political community. The person has a series of rights and an obligation to recognize the rights of others. The state has the obligation to protect those rights as well as the security and well-being of the state as a community of many persons. Articles 4 and 5 of the 1789 French Declaration of the Rights of Man and the Citizen and Article 29 of the 1948 Universal Declaration of Human Rights both state the equation of individual rights within the context of rights of others and the public order of the state.

Each right is distinctive, but all legal rights are related to each other in the context of the due process of the law. Legal rights are substantative (right to legal assistance), procedural (right of counsel to examine witnesses), and occasionally both (right of equal protection of the law). The entries for legal rights are listed in alphabetical order. The entry on Due Process provides a sequential overview of most of the legal rights in international human rights law.

Foundations for the enjoyment of legal rights include specific rights in ICPR that are fundamental to the protection by and enhancement of all legal rights. They are the right of life, the right to a remedy, and dimensions of equality and nondiscrimination.

A. Life

Every human being has the inherent right to life. Article 6, paragraph 1, ICPR, and in all international human rights treaties (*see* Life, Civil and Political Rights).

B. Remedy

"Each State Party to the present Covenant undertakes . . . to ensure that any person whose rights or freedoms as herein recognized are violated shall have an effective remedy, notwithstanding that the violation has been committed by persons acting in an official capacity." ICPR, #2-3;

ECR, #13; ACR, #25; AFR, #7-1; Convention Against Racism, #6; UDHR, #8; and ISLAM, #19-b.

A remedy in law is a legal recourse for a person denied his human rights and an attribute of protection beyond having the right itself. A statement of remedy over 200 years ago is as follows: ". . . every freeman for every injury done him . . . ought to have a remedy in the course of the law of the land," Section 12, Delaware Declaration of Rights, September 11, 1776, and in other state constitutions and declarations as well. "The law of the land" is from the June 15, 1215, Magna Carta, which included many remedies sought by the English Barons from King John. The right to remedy is the right to fulfillment of all rights. The last sentence in #2, ICPR, is particularly important: Each State Party undertakes "to ensure that competent authorities shall enforce such remedies when granted" (*see* Issues and Contexts, G., Implementation of Rights).

C. Equality before the Law and Protection against Discrimination

All persons are equal before the law and are entitled without discrimination to the equal protection of the law. In this respect, the law shall prohibit any discrimination and guarantee to all persons equal and effective protection against discrimination on any ground, such as race, color, sex, language, religion, political or other opinion, national or social origin, property, birth, or other status: #26, ICPR. Also ECR, #14; IACR, #24 & #1; AFR, #3-1 & #2; and the Convention Against Racism, #5.

Equality before the law was first enshrined in Article 1 of the French Declaration of the Rights of Man of August 26, 1789: In respect to their rights men are born and remain free and equal. Equal Protection of the Law is an entry under Legal Rights with Landmarks and Cross References. Equality and the prohibition against discrimination of all kinds are almost inseparable.

The United Nations Charter of June 26, 1945, in Article 1, paragraph 3, "The Purposes of the United Nations," calls for "promoting and encouraging respect for human rights and for fundamental freedoms for all without distinction as to race, sex, language, or religion. . ." This goal was universalized and woven in with equality in the 1948 UN Universal Declaration of Human Rights in Article 7: "All are equal before the law and are entitled without any discrimination to equal protection of the law. All are entitled to equal protection against any discrimination in violation of this Declaration and against any incitement to such discrimination."

Equality of persons before courts and tribunals is guaranteed in ICPR in #14-1 and in the Convention on Race, #5-a. Minimum guarantees of full equality for due process of law are included in ICPR, #14-3. Equality is a constant theme and requirement in international legal rights, as are prohibitions against discrimination on many grounds, as cited above in references to articles in many human rights conventions.

These foundation rights and duties for international human rights law are fundamental to the legal rights in this part of the dictionary. The ICPR is the basic treaty for international legal rights. The Human Rights Committee under Part IV of the ICPR is responsible for monitoring State Parties' compliance and implementation of the legal rights as appraised in the Introduction to Civil and Political Rights in part 1 of the dictionary.

Appeal

I. The Right. Everyone convicted of a crime shall have the right to his or her conviction and sentence being reviewed by a higher tribunal according to law. Covenant on Civil and Political Rights, Article 14, para 5. Anyone sentenced to death shall have the right to seek pardon or commutation of the sentence. Amnesty, pardon, or commutation of the sentence of death may be granted in all cases. ICPR, #6-4.

II. Other Sources. ECR, Protocol Seven, #2; ACR, #8-2-h & #4-6; AFR, #7-1-a.

III. Expanded Definition. Resort to a superior (i.e., appellate) court to review the decision of an inferior (i.e., trial) court or administrative agency (Black, 88). Nearly all legal systems have a hierarchy of courts from the lower level to the highest court of the jurisdiction, such as the United States Supreme Court. Most recognize the right of appeal by the party found guilty to a dispute to a higher court for review and possible retrial. Where one enjoys the right not to be tried twice for the same crime, the prosecution cannot appeal an acquittal. The right to appeal has many technicalities and in general is governed by constitutions and legislative statutes which define those technicalities under the authority of the appellate courts, tribunals, and judges.

IV. Landmarks. The right to appeal a decision to a higher authority is rooted in customary law and later in both civil and common law. In England, "appeal" originally meant a formal accusation made by one private person against another of having committed some heinous crime (Black, 123). This private suit was gradually replaced when public or state prosecution appeared at the end of the twelfth century. The right to appeal a prosecution evolved with the emergence of juries. In common law, one could appeal on a question of law but not of fact, on which the jury had the last word. In civil law in Europe, appeal could be on both fact and law.

In England Henry II (1133–1189) and Edward I (1239–1307) furthered the centralization of government as well as the law and its administration. Three courts grew out of the original King's Council or Curia Regis. The Court of the Exchequer, the Court of Common Pleas, and the King's Bench at first handled original jurisdiction but evolved into courts of appeal from the local courts in England. Statutes of Parliament defined the process of appeals and much else in the legal system. "Appeal" in this sense is not a right but a procedure granted and defined by Parliament. On the Continent, appeal varied given the extensive decentralization of authority including legal systems for the Church, merchants, and others.

Appeal and reference to a higher court was recognized in the American colonial courts but varied in colonial legal and constitutional documents. In Article 31 of the Massachusetts Body of Liberties of December 10, 1641, for instance, if there is a difference in the lower courts between Bench and Jurors "the case shall be referred to the General Court, who shall take the question from both and determine it." In the United States Constitution, the Supreme Court in Article III is established along with "such inferior courts" as the Congress may establish. The Supreme Court has specific original jurisdiction in Article III and "appellate jurisdiction, both as to law and fact, with such exceptions, and under such regulations, as the Congress shall make." Appeal is thus a right only as determined and defined by federal and/or state statutes. It has become, however, a right in international human rights law and especially in the Inter-American Convention and Protocol Seven, ECR.

V. Cross References. Courts/Tribunals, Double Jeopardy, Due Process, Judgment and Sentencing, Trial, and Trial Procedure (Legal Rights).

Arrest

I. The Right. (1) Everyone has the right to liberty and security of person. No one shall be subjected to arbitrary arrest or detention. No one shall be deprived of his or her liberty except upon such grounds and in accordance with such procedures as are established by law. (2) Anyone who is arrested shall be informed, at the time of arrest, of the reasons for his or her arrest and shall be promptly informed of any charges against him or her. (3) Anyone arrested or detained on a criminal charge shall be brought promptly before a judge or other officer authorized in law to exercise judicial power and shall be entitled to trial within a reasonable time or to release. Covenant on Civil and Political Rights, Article 9, paras 1, 2, and 3.

All persons deprived of their liberty shall be treated with humanity and with respect for the inherent dignity of the human person. ICPR, Article 10, para 1.

II. Other Sources. ECR, #5; ACR, #7-1-5; AFR, #6; Convention on Child, #37; Convention on Apartheid, #II-a (iii);

UDHR, #9; ISLAM, #25; ASEAN, #I-2 (2.04); Dec on Non-Nationals, #5-1 (a); Declaration of Basic Principles of Justice for Victims of Crime and Abuse of Power, General Assembly Res. 40/34 (1985), and Declaration on the Protection of All Persons from Enforced Disappearances, General Assembly Res. 47/33 (1992).

III. Expanded Definition. Arrest is the deprivation of a person's liberty by legal authority. It is taking, under real or assumed authority, custody of another for the purpose of holding or detaining him or her to answer a criminal charge or civil demand (Black, 141). In its broader meaning and within the context of human rights law, arrest also includes (1) prohibition against arbitrary arrest or arrest without the components of due process of the law; (2) arrest on the basis of existing law specifying grounds for arrest; (3) informing the person of those reasons or grounds for arrest; (4) informing the person of the specific charges against the person; and (5) assuring the person of his or her right to be brought before judicial authority for determination of either a trial or for release. Due process of arrest also includes presumption of innocence of the person, the right to bail, and the rights associated with detention and detention conditions. Arrest is thus broader than the actual deprivation of liberty as set forth in ICPR and other conventions and declarations. This reflects the expansion of due process of the law of arrest in the twentieth century.

It should be noted that Article 9, paragraph 3, ICPR, specifies "criminal charge." Requirements in this paragraph for judicial decision and entitlement to trial may not apply in a civil charge. However, the requirement in paragraph 4 for judicial determination of lawfulness of detention still applies.

IV. Landmarks. Arrest has been a feature of political communities for over 5,000 years. The actual apprehension of a person and deprivation of liberty requires little historical analysis other than the advent of essential rights of the arrested person. These rights evolved in many different political communities and, in a more concrete manner, with the growth in English law of individual rights against arbitrary governance. Article 39 of the Magna Carta of June 15, 1215, is the central landmark of the triumph of human rights against arbitrary arrest. "No free man shall be taken or imprisoned . . . except . . . by the law of the land." Article 39 does not speak of "arbitrary arrest." However, its intention was to modify the practice of arrest without cause.

Arbitrary arrest, of course, did not end in 1215 or, indeed, in 1996. However, the growth and development of other branches of the due process of the law over the centuries moderated the indiscriminate taking of a person into custody. Anyone subjected to such a procedure at the very least has the law on his or her side, especially the IHRL condemning arbitrary arrest.

V. Cross References. Bail, Compensation, Detention, Due Process, Equal Protection of the Law, Habeus Corpus, Innocence Presumption, Legal Assistance, Person before the Law, Security of Person, and Self-Incrimination (Legal Rights).

*See also (*1) Annual reports of the United Nations Commission on Human Rights Working Group on Arbitrary Detention. Established by the Commission in 1991 as a thematic mechanism for the implementation of the right to be protected against arbitrary detention, the Working Group is putting into practice the "Body of Principles for the Protection of All Persons under Any Form of Detention or Imprisonment," General Assembly Resolution 43/173, December 9, 1988. (2) Annual reports of the United Nations Commission on Human Rights Working Group on Enforced and Involuntary Disappearances. Established in 1980 as the Commission's first thematic mechanism for implementation of human rights law, this Working Group of Five was created to respond to the widespread phenomenon of missing persons who were allegedly involved with opposing policies, especially in Argentina. "Disappearances are cases in which an individual has been seized, often by persons in plainclothes and either in government service or protected by government agencies, and not seen or heard from again. The government denies any knowledge of these individuals or any responsibility for their whereabouts, and the practice has a chilling effect: eliminating citizens, terrorizing the population, and rendering the government unaccountable" (*A Global Agenda,* 1991–92, p. 174). (3) *United Nations Action,* "Protection Against Arbitrary Arrest and Detention," pp. 92–100.

Bail

I. The Right. It shall not be the general rule that persons awaiting trial shall be detained in custody, but release may be subject to guarantees to appear for trial, at any other stage of the judicial proceedings, and, should occasion arise, for execution of the judgment. Covenant on Civil and Political Rights, Article 9, paragraph 3.

II. Other Sources. ECR, #5-3; ACR, #7-5.

III. Expanded Definition. To procure the release of one charged with an offense by insuring his future attendance in court and compelling him to remain within the jurisdiction of the court (Black, 127). "Guarantees" in ICPR is usually a sum of money, also called "bail." Black also defines bail as a noun meaning "the surety or sureties who procure the release of a person under arrest by becoming responsible for his [or her] appearance at the time and place designated." The right to post bail and gain freedom from detention until judicial procedure takes place and judgment is rendered is essential to the basic right to liberty of the person, the presumption of innocence until or unless guilt is proven by the state and thus the right to due process of the law.

IV. Landmarks. Black notes that "in its more ancient signification, [bail] includes the delivery of property, real or personal, by one person to another." Such a delivery of something of value became, in time, a guarantee by a person in detention or his or her agent to an official that he or she shall gain freedom until his case is heard by a judicial official. Refusal of bail to detained high officials in the "Five Knights Case" in 1628, along with other major grievances filed against King Charles I, led to the famous Petition of Right in the English Parliament of June 7, 1628. The Knights' attorneys held that the grievances were a denial of the due process of the law and, in turn, of the "law of the land" in Article 39 of the Magna Carta of June 15, 1215. King Charles II assented to the Petition for redress of grievances with the words "let right be done as is desired."

In order to circumvent the Writ of Habeas Corpus and the Habeas Corpus Act of 1679, King James II charged excessive bail for adversaries in detention. The English Bill of Rights of 1689 complained of this procedure and declared in Article 10 of the "Rights of the People" that "excessive bail ought not to be required, nor excessive fines imposed . . ."

The right of bail was transposed to the American colonies in the company of many other English rights. It was first engraved in American colonial law in the Frame of Government of Pennsylvania of April 25, 1682, in Article XI. It is declared in the Frame "that all prisoners shall be bailable for sufficient sureties, unless for capital offences, where the proof is evident, or the presumption great." Another example is in the Constitution of Virginia of December 15, 1776, in Section 9. "That excessive bail ought not to be required, nor excessive fines imposed. . ." Finally, this right is incorporated in the Eighth Amendment to the United States Constitution of December 15, 1791, with the familiar wording "Excessive bail shall not be required, nor excessive fines imposed . . ."

V. Cross References. Arrest, Courts/Tribunals, Detention, Due Process, Punishment, Security of Person, Trial, and Trial Procedure (Legal Rights).

Compensation

I. The Right. Anyone who has been a victim of unlawful arrest or detention shall have an enforceable right to compensation. Covenant on Civil and Political Rights, Article 9, para 5.

When a person has by a final decision been convicted of a criminal offence and when subsequently his or her conviction has been reversed or he or she has been pardoned on the ground that a new or newly discovered fact shows conclusively that there has been a miscarriage of justice, the person who has suffered punishment as a result of such conviction shall be compensated according to law, unless it is proved that the non-disclosure of the unknown fact in time is wholly or partly attributable to him or her. ICPR, Article 14, para 6.

II. Other Sources. ECR, #5-5 & Protocol 7, #3; ACR, #10; Convention on Torture, #14;

ASEAN, #10-3, #11-4 (e); Declaration of Basic Principles on Justice for Victims of Crimes and Abuse of Power (1985), #8-11 and #12 and #13.

III. Expanded Definition. A person has a right to compensation for a miscarriage of justice. Under ICPR, compensation may be sought for a miscarriage (1) at the detention and/or arrest level (#9-5) and (2) at the punishment or post-punishment level (14-6).

Compensation is a principle of justice that is incorporated in many declarations. The Declaration of Basic Principles of Justice for Victims of Crime and Abuse of Power [General Assembly Resolution 40/34 (1985)] calls for restitution to victims by offenders for a miscarriage (Articles 8–11). "When compensation is not fully available from the offender or other sources, States should endeavor to provide financial compensation to: a) victims who have sustained significant bodily injury or impairment of physical or mental health as a result of serious crimes; b) the family, in particular dependants of persons who died or become physically or mentally incapacitated as a result of such victimization. The establishment, strengthening, and expansion of national funds for compensation to victims should be encouraged. Where appropriate, other funds may also be established for this purpose, including those cases where the State of which the victim is a national is not in a position to compensate the victim for the harm" (Articles 12 and 13).

Compensation for expropriation by a state of property belonging to another state or belonging to a national of another state (e.g., a corporation) is a firm rule of international law. The compensation is required to be prompt, adequate, and effective. This norm has been challenged by many new states in the past thirty years with claims of a "New International Economic Order." *See* Peoples, Natural Resources (Collective Rights).

IV. Landmarks. Compensation for victims of a miscarriage or corrosion of justice is a fairly new right per se. However, compensation for violation of due process of law is ingrained in ancient and medieval customary law and in the emerging common law of England. The Magna Carta of June 15, 1215, was basically a claim by the Barons for a redress of grievances for violations of customary law and ancient rights and privileges by King John. The power of the state to take private property for public use (eminent domain, Black, 470) was long recognized, but in time the state recognized the necessity to provide compensation for this exercise of "the highest and most exact idea of property remaining in the government" (Black, 470). Thus the Fifth Amendment to the United States Constitution states "nor shall private property be taken for public use, without just compensation."

Demands on governments for redress of grievances in miscarriages of justice were formalized in #8 of the 1948 Universal Declaration of Human Rights: "everyone has the right to an effective remedy by the competent national tribunals for acts violating the fundamental rights granted him by the constitution or by law." Article 8 flowed into #2-3 of the ICPR with respect to the right of an effective remedy and thus into the right for compensation in #9-5 and #14-6, ICPR.

V. Cross References. Property (Civil and Political Rights); Appeal, Arrest, Courts/Tribunals, Detention, Due Process, Judgment and Sentencing,

Punishment, Security of Person, Trial, and Trial Procedure (Legal Rights); and Peoples, Natural Resources (Collective Rights). *See also* Subcommission of UN Commission on Human Rights Task Force study on restitution and a fair and just compensation, established in 1989 and in continuation.

Contract Inability

I. The Right. No one shall be imprisoned merely on the ground of inability to fulfil a contractual obligation. Covenant on Civil and Political Rights, Article 11. [There shall be no] derogation from Article 11 . . . ICPR, #4-1.

II. Other Sources. ECR Fourth Protocol, #1.

III. Expanded Definition. A contract is a promissory agreement between two or more persons that creates, modifies, or destroys a legal relation (Black, 421). ICPR prohibits imprisonment for inability to fulfil a contractual obligation which, in nearly every jurisdiction, would not be a punishment in any event. However, the article was considered important to some states which had experienced such an extreme penalty. ECR Fourth Protocol, #1, states "no one shall be deprived of his [or her] liberty . . . on inability to fulfill a contractual obligation."

IV. Landmarks. The contract is a historical and formidable instrument binding two or more actors for some specified obligation with mutual benefits. There is extensive law of contracts which are considered very fundamental for the security and well-being of and within any political community. The American Northwest Ordinance of 1787 states in #II that "no law . . . shall . . . interfere with or affect private contracts . . ." A proposal to place such a statement in the United States Constitution with respect to the federal government did not succeed. However, Article I, paragraph 10, of the Constitution declares that "no State shall. . . . pass any . . . law impairing the obligation of contracts . . ." Any penalty for "inability to fulfil a contractual obligation" (ICPR, #11) is usually a judicial decision which would not today involve any imprisonment.

V. Cross Reference. Political and Property (Civil and Political Rights) and Due Process and Punishment (Legal Rights).

Courts/Tribunals

I. The Right. In the determination of any charge against him or her, or of his or her rights and obligations in a suit of law, everyone shall be entitled to a fair and public hearing by a competent, independent, and impartial tribunal established by law. Covenant on Civil and Political Rights, Article 14, paragraph 1.

II. Other Sources. ECR, #6-1; ACR, 8-1; AFR, 7-1-d; UDHR, #10; ASEAN, #1-2 (2.03).

III. Expanded Definition. An organ of government, belonging to the judicial department, whose function is the application of the laws to controversies brought before it and the public administration of justice (Black, 457). An international court or tribunal is a judicial organ established by treaty for the application of the laws specified in the treaty. Judges sitting as courts and tribunals may make determinations with respect to the arrest and detention of a person (ICPR, #9-3) as well as courts and tribunals engaged in a "suit in law" (ICPR, #14-1).

Indispensable to any court or tribunal are judges or other judicial authorities whose election or appointment, qualifications, and jurisdiction are based on provisions in constitutions or treaties. A "competent, independent, and impartial tribunal" in ICPR, #14-1, implies judicial authorities who possess these qualities. Qualifications for judges are included in treaties dealing with tribunals and courts. One set of qualifications is in ECR, #39-3, for the members of the European Court of Human Rights. These qualifications call for "persons of high moral character [who] must either possess the qualifications required for appointment to high judicial office or be jurisconsults of recognized competence." *See also* Articles 2, 6, and 9, Statute, International Court of Justice, for judges' qualifications for the International Court. Judges on international tribunals are also required to "serve in their personal capacity" (e.g., ICPR, #28-3), rather than in the service of the state of their nationality or in the interests of another state.

IV. Landmarks. Courts and tribunals, however primitive or sophisticated, have served as instruments of political leaders and communities for authoritative decision making on contentious issues since the beginnings of organized civilization. Tribunals in all areas of the world served and continue to serve the jurisprudence of their sovereign jurisdictions.

The court system in England paved the way for the courts and tribunals that serve international human rights law today. The medieval Curia Regis, or King's Council, was a many-faceted organ of administration and judicial authority under the Norman kings after William I's conquest in 1066. The Curia served as a mechanism of consolidation of monarchial power and authority and especially, over the years, of centralized judicial control over local courts. It was comprised of men closest to the King in serving his interests and legal authority. The Curia became decentralized with the advancing complexities of society in the thirteenth and fourteenth centuries as other courts including the Exchequer, the King's Bench, and the Common Pleas assumed specialized roles and functions. The June 15, 1215, Magna Carta, especially Article 39, confirmed an essential due process of the law which over the ages gradually defined the procedure for the courts in civil and criminal suits in law.

On the other hand, the infamous judicial body the "Court of the Star Chamber" emerged in the fifteenth century to serve the King's business outside the frame of the common law. By the early seventeenth century, the Star Chamber had assumed vast powers and challenged other courts and the common law in its authoritarian bent under James I. The challenges by Parliament and Sir Edward Coke to monarchial power led to the 1641 abolishment of the Star Chamber.

The famous Bushell's Case, decided in England by Chief Justice Vaughan in 1671, is a landmark in the major curtailment of judges and courts exercising extraordinary biased and arbitrary authority. The enhanced role of judges and courts in the administration of justice under the common law led to the gradual consolidation of "competent, independent, and impartial tribunals" in England and the American colonies. Article V of the Frame of Government of Pennsylvania of April 25, 1682, stated that "all courts shall be open . . ." Section 22 of the Delaware Declaration of Rights of September 11, 1776, and Article XXX of the Constitution of Maryland of November 3, 1776, declared that "independency and uprightness of judges are essential to the impartial administration of justice . . ." Article XXIX of the Constitution of Massachusetts of October 25, 1780, provides for qualifications of judges ("free, impartial, and independent as the lot of humanity will admit . . .") along with other colonial constitutions and documents.

In France, the "parlements" were courts serving the monarchial regimes. However, decentralization and fragmentation of justice continued there and elsewhere in Europe. The emergence of the Napoleonic

Code, based on the Roman law, in the early nineteenth century stressed the letter of the law rather than the independence and authority of courts and tribunals under the common law. Clearly the treaties in international law and especially in international human rights law seek to unite the authority of courts and tribunals as representative of the "main forms of civilization and of the principal legal systems of the world . . ." (#9, Statute of the International Court of Justice).

V. Cross References. Arrest, Detention, Due Process, Trial, and Trial Procedure (Legal Rights).

See also (1) Basic Principles on the Independence of the Judiciary ("The Milan Principles"), adopted by the Seventh UN Congress on the Treatment of Offenders, Milan, Italy, 1985. *The Review,* International Commission of Jurists, December 1986. Procedures for Implementation of Milan Principles, Economic and Social Council Resolution 1989/60. (2) Appointment of Special Rapporteur on Independence of Judiciary, UN Commission on Human Rights, 1994. (3) Center for the Independence of Judges and Lawyers, International Commission of Jurists, Geneva.

Death Penalty

I. The Right. In countries which have not abolished the death penalty, sentence of death may be imposed only for the most serious crimes in accordance with the law in force at the time of the commission of the crime and not contrary to the provisions of the present Covenant and to the Convention on the Prevention and Punishment of Genocide. This penalty can only be carried out pursuant to a final judgment rendered by a competent court. Covenant on Civil and Political Rights, Article 6, paragraph 2. Paragraphs 3, 4, 5, and 6 of Article 6 deal with the death penalty. Paragraph 5 is of particular interest. It states that "sentence of death shall not be imposed for crimes by persons below eighteen years of age and shall not be carried out on pregnant women."

Article 6 of ICPR is substantially broadened in the ICPR's Second Optional Protocol on Capital Punishment, December 15, 1989. Article 1, paragraph 1: "no one within the jurisdiction of a State Party to the present Protocol shall be executed"; and paragraph 2: "each State Party shall take all necessary measures to abolish the death penalty within its jurisdiction."

II. Other Sources. ECR, Protocol 6, #1; ACR, #4-1 to 6; Convention on Child, #37 (a); Convention on the Prevention and Punishment of Genocide, #II-a; ISLAM, #2-a).

III. Expanded Definition. The death penalty is the deprivation of a person's life as the result of a judgment and sentence by a judicial authority for the commission of a specific crime. Death by official execution is also termed a capital punishment. Each jurisdiction may determine (1) whether to inflict the punishment of death for the commission of a crime; (2) what crimes may be included as demanding the penalty of death; and (3) the means of inflicting the death penalty. Among the purposes of the death penalty are punishment for commission of extreme crimes, deterrent to others not to commit such crimes, removing the accused person entirely from society of any kind, and inflicting a punishment in reciprocity if the condemned person has committed an act of homicide.

The covenants and conventions cited above have a number of waivers to the death penalty, unlike the Convention on Torture, which provides no waiver to the crime of torture. The United States does not recognize the prohibition of the death penalty to persons under the age of eighteen as do most other nations.

IV. Landmarks. Thou shalt not kill, Exodus 20:13. However, the penalty of death for many and varied crimes has been inflicted throughout the ages as the principal exception, save in war, to the mandate in the Old Testament of the Bible and of many other doctrines of the world's religions. The punishment of death has been historical and universal, as have been the means of execution, some so hideous that death was a blessing. Article 39 of the 1215 Magna Carta states that "no free man shall be . . . in any way destroyed . . . except . . . by the law of the land." But Article 39 and subsequent amplifications of the Magna Carta and Statutes of Parliament were not modest in defining "destroyed" or the number of crimes requiring capital punishment.

The number of crimes specifying the death penalty reached an all-time high in England around 1800, but change was in the air. The advent of natural rights, the creed of "life and liberty" in the American and French Declarations of Rights, the revulsion of the guillotine in the "French Reign of Terror," and the gradual emergence of democracy in the nineteenth century led to substantial reductions in crimes calling for capital punishment and an increase in humanity in the means of execution. The writings of Montesquieu and Voltaire in the eighteenth century and Bentham and Romilly in the nineteenth led to progressive legislation in the emerging democracies to reduce the harshness of the death penalty. Pennsylvania limited the death penalty to first degree murder in 1794, and many other jurisdictions followed suit. Capital punishment was retired in Luxembourg in 1822 and eliminated in the Netherlands in 1870, Norway in 1905, and Sweden in 1921. On the other hand, the 1994 United States federal crime legislation specified approximately seventy crimes that will carry the death penalty for federal offenses in addition to capital crimes in the individual states.

V. Cross References. Life (Civil and Political Rights); Appeal, Detention, Due Process, Judgment and Sentencing, Punishment, Security of Person, and Torture (Legal Rights); and Apartheid and Genocide (Collective Rights).

See also (1) "Capital Punishment," *United Nations Action,* pp. 69–73. (2) Annual Reports of the United Nations Special Rapporteur on Summary and Arbitrary Executions. This position was established by the Economic and Social Council on May 25, 1984 (Res. 1984/50) after General Assembly resolutions deploring summary and extrajudicial executions (December 15, 1980, and November 9, 1981). It is one of the Commission on Human Rights most important thematic mechanisms for implementation of human rights law. The Special Rapporteur has constantly cited military and national security issues and indiscriminate violence (especially terrorism and hostage taking) as prime causes of summary and arbitrary executions. Special Rapporteur annual reports include specific legal bases for his investigations and reports to the General Assembly. (3) Annual reports of UN Commission on Human Rights Working Group on Enforced or Involuntary Disappearances and UN Declaration on the Protection of All Persons from Enforced Disappearance, General Assembly Resolution 133, 1992. Such "disappearances" often lead to summary execution. (4) Reports of the United Nations Congresses on Prevention of Crime and Treatment of Offenders which have stimulated extensive United Nations activity in the area of capital punishment, especially Congress recommendations for safeguards for those facing capital punishment of any kind. *See* index, *United Nations Action.* (5) *Manual on the Effective Prevention and Investigation of Extra-legal, Arbitrary and Summary Executions,* UN Secretariat, 1991, and based on Economic and Social Council Resolution, May 24, 1989; and Safeguards Guaranteeing Protection of the Rights of Those Facing the Death Penalty, Economic and Social Council Resolution, May 25, 1984.

Detention

I. The Right. (1) Everyone has the right to liberty and security of person. No one shall be subjected to arbitrary arrest or detention. No one shall be deprived of liberty except on such grounds and in accordance with such procedures as are established by law. (2) Anyone arrested or detained on a criminal charge shall be brought promptly before a judge or other officer authorized by law to exercise judicial power and shall be entitled to trial within a reasonable time or to release. It shall not be the general rule that persons awaiting trial shall be detained in custody. (3) Anyone who is deprived of his or her liberty by arrest or detention shall be entitled to take proceedings before a court, in order that the court may decide without delay on the lawfulness of his or her detention and order his release if the detention is not lawful. Covenant on Civil and Political Rights, Article 9. (1) All persons deprived of their liberty shall be treated with humanity and with respect for the inherent dignity of their human person. (2) (a) Accused persons shall, save in exceptional circumstances, be segregated from convicted persons and shall be subject to separate treatment appropriate to their status as unconvicted persons; (b) Accused juvenile persons shall be separated from adults and brought as speedily as possible for adjudication. ICPR, Article 10.

II. Other Sources. ECR, #5; ACR, #7; AFR, #6; Convention on the Crime of Apartheid, #II, (a), (iii);

UDHR, #9; ASEAN, #1-2 (2.04); Human Rights of Persons Detained or Imprisoned, Subcommission, Commission on Human Rights, 1974; Standard Minimum Rules for Prisoners; Code of Conduct for Law Enforcement Officials (1979); Dec on Non-Nationals, #5-1-a.

III. Expanded Definition. Detention is the arrest and placing in custody by a government of a person alleged to have violated a law. The detained person is not accused of violation of the law and is presumed innocent. Detention is prior to any subsequent judicial determination of innocence or guilt.

The period of detention is often one of violation of rights of the detained person by governments which may seek to apply cruel or unusual punishment, including torture, to the person in order to physically and/or mentally damage the person and/or to gain a confession of any alleged crime. Detention is the period and condition when an arrested person is most vulnerable to severe bodily harm by a government which may apply extrajudicial punishment for many and varied reasons. This is particularly the case with persons accused of "political crimes," however defined, against the detaining government. Administrative detention is unusually harsh confinement whereby individuals may be detained or interned by the administrative authorities, without charge or trial by an independent judicial body and without any protection for their human rights (*Encyclopedia of Human Rights*, 390). ECR #5-l-e is innovative in human rights law in stating that there may be "the lawful detention of persons for the prevention of the spreading of infectious diseases, of persons of unsound mind, alcoholics or drug addicts, or vagrants."

IV. Landmarks. Detention of a person or persons considered guilty of a violation of any law or of any offense against an authoritative official of any institution—government, religious, or other—is rooted in human history. Early societies some 5,000 years ago developed procedures of arrest, trial, and formal sentencing which evolved over the ages to more stable processes in many societies and areas of the world. The Magna Carta of June 15, 1215, places detention in this context of legal procedure. More humane treatment of the detained person with more humane legal processes of presumption of innocence, right of habeus corpus, and the dignity of the person before the law were gradually incorporated into the common and the civil law.

V. Cross References. Arrest, Bail, Due Process, Equal Protection of the Law, Habeus Corpus, Innocence Presumption, Punishment, Security of Person, and Torture (Legal Rights).

See also (1) Body of Principles for the Protection of All Persons under Any Form of Detention or Imprisonment, General Assembly Resolution 43/173, December 9, 1988. (2) Annual Reports of United Nations Commission on Human Rights Working Group on Arbitrary Detention. Established in 1991, this Working Group of Five is one of the Commission's thematic mechanisms for implementation of human rights law. It is particularly concerned with political prisoners ("prisoners of conscience"), engages in global fact-finding and investigation of detention, and reports annually to the Commission on Human Rights. (3) Annual Reports of the United Nations Commission on Human Rights Working Group on Enforced and Involuntary Disappearances. Established in 1980 as the Commission's first thematic mechanism for implementation of human rights law, the Working Group of Five was created to respond to the widespread phenomenon of missing people who were alleged to have been in assertive and overt opposition to government policy, especially in Argentina. In 1992, the UN Commission on Human Rights adopted the Declaration on the Protection of All Persons from Enforced or Involuntary Disappearances. Number 4 of the Declaration deals with the contentious issue of impunity with respect to violators of human rights. "Disappearances are cases in which an individual has been seized, often by persons in plainclothes and either in government service or protected by government agencies, and not seen or heard from again. The government denies any knowledge of these individuals or any responsibility for their whereabouts, and the practice has a chilling effect: eliminating citizens, terrorizing the population, and rendering the government unaccountable" (*A Global Agenda,* 1991–92, p. 174). (4) *United Nations Action,* "Protection Against Arbitrary Arrest and Detention," pp. 94–100, including review of UN measures with respect to detention, including annual review of detention by the Commission's Subcommittee on Prevention of Discrimination and Protection of Minorities, concerns about detention of United Nations staff members, and detention of special categories of people, including those struggling against violations of human rights, detention due to trade union activities, detention of people with mental illnesses, and detention of people in national emergencies.

Double Jeopardy

I. The Right. No one shall be liable to be tried or punished again for an offense for which he or she has already been finally convicted or acquitted in accordance with the law and penal procedure of each country. Covenant on Civil and Political Rights, Article 14, paragraph 7.

II. Other Sources. ECR, Protocol Seven, #4; ACR, 8-4.

III. Expanded Definition. Double jeopardy is the placing of a person twice in jeopardy—danger of a conviction and punishment which a defendant in a criminal action incurs (Black, 749). It is a prohibition on the authority of the state over the legitimate interests of the person. Once a judicial determination has been made of innocence or guilt of a defendant, the state may not again prosecute the person for the same offense. The person, however, has the right of appeal if found guilty, to be tried again by a court superior to the lower court making the first judgment. The prohibition of double jeopardy, however, does not always protect the defendant if he or she is tried in another jurisdiction (state or federal in the United States), depending on legislation and constitutional (state) provisions and court decisions. *See* ECR, Protocol Seven, #4-2, for exception to above.

IV. Landmarks. "Freedom from double jeopardy had long been considered one of the rights of Englishmen embodied in the common law. 'It is contrary to the genius and spirit of the law of England to suffer any man to be tried twice for the same offense in a criminal way, especially if acquitted upon the first trial"' (Perry, 381).

In the American colonies, the Massachusetts Body of Liberties of December 10, 1641, stated in Article 42 that "no man shall be twise sentenced to Civil Justice for one and the same Crime, offence or Trespasse."

The Constitution of New Hampshire of June 2, 1784, included the first constitutional provision on double jeopardy in Article XVI: "no subject shall be liable to be tried, after an acquittal, for the same crime or offence." The new and revised Constitution of Pennsylvania of 1790 was accompanied by a Declaration of Rights providing that "no person shall, for the same offence, be twice put in jeopardy of life and limb." The Fifth Amendment to the United States Constitution of December 15, 1791, declares "nor shall any person be subject for the same offence to be twice put in jeopardy of life or limb . . ."

V. Cross References. Appeal, Arrest, Courts/Tribunals, Due Process, Punishment, Judgment and Sentencing, Trial, and Trial Procedure (Legal Rights).

Due Process

I. The Right. Due process of the law is the exercise of the powers of government to provide protection to one accused of violation of the law and to afford the accused of his or her rights of protection if or until a determination of the accusation is made by judicial authority.

II. Other Sources. As a single right, due process of the law is not mentioned in the covenants or conventions on international human rights law. In treaty law, a series of legal rights collectively provides due process of the law as set forth below. The sources of these rights are in the Landmark sections for Legal Rights in the dictionary.

III. Expanded Definition. "The history of liberty has largely been the history of the observance of procedural safeguards" (United States Supreme Court Justice Felix Frankfurter). Collectively, the due process rights are much more specific and extensive than those in the United States Constitution, Amendments to the Constitution, or any state document on legal rights.

In the Introduction to Legal Rights, a series of foundation rights in the ICPR includes right to life (#6), prohibition against discrimination (#27), equality before the law (#26), equal protection of the law (#26), liberty and security of person (#6-1 and #9-1), and effective remedy for violation of rights (#2-3). These foundation rights are basic to the enjoyment of due process of the law.

The five categories of due process rights are arrest, detention, trial, post-trial, and punishment. In the detention category, a grand jury in the common law usually makes a determination if there is sufficient evidence to bring the accused to trial. There is no provision for the grand jury in IHRL. In the trial category, a jury is impanelled to determine the facts or evidence of the case while the judge determines the law. There is no provision for the jury in IHRL. The source and citation of these rights is the ICPR, although ECR and AFR are cited three times. Each of these rights in the dictionary includes other sources as well. *See also* V, Cross References.

A. Arrest Due Process
   1. No arbitrary arrest or detention, #9
   2. Treatment with humanity and respect, #10

B. Detention for Alleged Cause Due Process
   1. Basic causes for arrest, ECR, #5-1
   2. Information of reasons for arrest and charges, #9-2
   3. Right of habeus corpus, #9-4
   4. Hearing before judicial authority, #9-3
   5. Hearing without delay, #9-3
   6. No coercion, #7
   7. Bail, #9-3
   8. To a court for judicial determination, #9-3, 4
   9. Compensation for error, #9-5
   10. Detention conditions, #10-5

C. Trial Due Process
   1. Basic Rights
      a. Presumption of innocence, #14-2
      b. Equality before tribunals, #14-1

c. Fair and public hearings, #14-1 (Derogation for public trial [national security, public order, morals, other])
d. Competent, independent, and impartial tribunal, #14-3

2. Information of any criminal charge, #14-3
3. Information on nature and cause of charge, #14-3
4. Information in language defendant understands, #14-3 (a)
5. Time to prepare defense, #14-3 (b)
6. Facilities to prepare defense, #14-3 (c)
7. Trial without delay, #14-3 (c)
8. To be tried in (defendant's) presence, #14-3 (d)
9. Legal assistance, #14-3 (d)
10. Information of right to legal assistance, #14-3 (d)
11. Legal assistance without payment if defendant lacks sufficient means, #14-3 (d)
12. Right (of defendant) to defend himself, #14-3 (d)
13. Examination of witnesses against defendant, #14-3 (e)
14. Obtain attendance and examination of witnesses on defendant's behalf on same basis as witnesses against defendant, #14-3 (e)
15. Free assistance of interpreter (if needed), #14-3 (f)
16. Defendant not compelled to testify against himself or herself (no self-incrimination), #14-3 (g)
17. Defendant not compelled to confess guilt, #14-3 (g)
18. Public judgment, #14-1
19. Penalty must be in law, #15-1
20. Penalty must be personal, AFR, #7-2
21. Procedure for juveniles, #14-4

D. Post-Trial Due Process
1. Compensation for error, #14-6
2. Protection against double jeopardy, #14-7
3. Right of appeal, #14-5

E. Punishment Due Process
1. Detention punishment to be humane, with respect for inherent dignity of the human person, #10-1
2. No cruel or unusual punishment, #7
3. No death penalty except for specific reasons or crimes, #6 and Second Optional Protocol, ICPR
4. Punishment only of the offender, AFR, #7-2
5. Detention punishment provisions for juveniles, #10-2 (b) and #10-3
6. Aim of penitentiary system is reformation and social rehabilitation, #10-3

IV. Landmarks. No free man shall be taken or imprisoned or dispossessed, or outlawed, or banished, or in any way destroyed, nor will we go upon him, nor send upon him, except by the legal judgment of his peers or by the law of the land. Article 39, Magna Carta, June 15, 1215. "The law of the land" became "due process of the law" under King Edward III in 1355. In the Fifth and Fourteenth Amendments to the United States Constitution, no one shall "be deprived of life, liberty, or property, without due process of law . . ."

"The law of the land" of 1215, later "due process of the law," was evolving common law in England, which had its roots in part in the use of law by William the Conqueror (William I, 1027–1087) to unify his new kingdom after 1066. Gradual centralization of the law under the monarch (over local courts) had as its objective a common law for all. In part, the common law was also derived from strands of law in Europe, including trial by a jury of one's peers. Henry I (1068–1135) in 1100 cited in his own "Charter of Liberties" the tradition of law under Edward the Confessor (1045–1066). The Magna Carta was thus rooted in ancient law and custom, which no monarch may arbitrarily replace by fiat or arbitrary rule. This obligation, of course, was breached many times, but the enduring plea of guardians against arbitrary rule was "the law of the land must prevail."

Due process of the law, along with the body of English law and jurisprudence, was transported to the American colonies and their legal systems. Article 1 of the Massachusetts Body of Liberties of December 10, 1641, is an expanded statement of #39 of the Magna Carta. Due process of the law was central to the evolving American constitutional law. James Madison was largely responsible for incorporating due process into the Fifth Amendment to the Constitution of December 15, 1791. It later became the centerpiece of the Fourteenth Amendment of 1868.

V. Cross References. All legal rights are embraced by due process of the law. *See also* Human Rights of Persons Detained or Imprisoned, Subcommittee, Committee on Human Rights, 1974. This declaration has an extensive statement on due process, as does #40, Covenant on Child.

See also #10, 1983 ASEAN Declaration, for extensive due process procedures for persons arrested "to question the legality of the arrest and detention." *See also* Stanislav Chernichenko and William Treat, The Right to a Fair Trial: Current Recognition and Measures Necessary for

Its strengthening, June 3, 1994. This is the final report by the two Special Rapporteurs to the Subcommittee on the Prevention of Discrimination and the Protection of Minorities, UN Commission on Human Rights, dealing with an array of due process procedures necessary for a fair trial. Previous reports by the Special Rapporteurs contain extensive material on due process and the administration of justice.

Equal Protection of the Law

I. The Right. All persons are equal before the law and are entitled without any discrimination to the equal protection of the law. In this respect, the law shall prohibit any discrimination and guarantee to all persons equal and effective protection against discrimination on any ground such as race, color, sex, language, religion, political or other opinion, national or social origin, property, birth, or other status. Covenant on Civil and Political Rights, #26.

II. Other Sources. ECR, #14; ACR, #24; AFR, #3-1, 2; UDHR, #7; ASEAN, #1-2-(2.03).

III. Expanded Definition. "The equal protection of the laws of a state is extended to persons within its jurisdiction, within the meaning of the constitutional requirement, when its courts are open to them on the same conditions as to others, with like rules of evidence and modes of procedure, for security of their persons and property, the prevention and redress of wrongs, and the enforcement of contracts; when they are subjected to no restrictions in the acquisition of property, the enjoyment of personal liberty, and the pursuit of happiness, which do not generally affect others; when they are liable to no other or greater burdens and charges than such are laid upon others; and when no different or greater punishment is enforced against them for a violation of the laws" (Black, 671). "The guarantee of equal protection of the laws means the protection of equal laws" (*Yick Ho v. Hopkins,* 118 US 356).

IV. Landmarks. The Massachusetts Body of Liberties of December 10, 1641, pioneered equal protection with its Article Three: "every person . . . shall enjoy the same justice and law, that is general for the plantation . . ." This right was not included in other colonial constitutions nor, indeed, in the United States Constitution.

The concept of equality in the law, however, was advanced in the French Declaration of the Rights of Man and the Citizen of August 26, 1789: #1, "in respect to their rights men are born and remain free and equal"; #4, ". . . individuals (enjoy the) same rights (as) all other individuals . . ."; #6, ". . . all citizens are equal in its (legislation) eyes . . ."; #7, "no individual may be accused, arrested, or detained except in cases prescribed by legislation . . ."

Equal protection of the law did not enter United States constitutional law until the Fourteenth Amendment to the Constitution of July 9, 1868, "no state shall . . . deny to any person within its jurisdiction the equal protection of the laws." It has taken well over a hundred years for this right to provide equal protection of the law for the pluralistic United States society in civil rights, education, and public accommodations. It is important to note that the Fourteenth Amendment is clearly restricted to the states. There is no provision in the Constitution or any amendment requiring the federal government to guarantee "equal protection of the law."

V. Cross References. Equal Protection of the Law applies to all human rights.

Ex Post Facto Law

I. The Right. (1) No one shall be held guilty of any criminal offence on account of any act or omission which did not constitute a criminal offence under national or international law at the time when it was committed. Nor shall a heavier penalty be imposed than the one that was applicable at the time when the criminal offence was committed. If, subsequent to the commission of the offence, provision is made by law for the imposition of a lighter penalty, the offender shall benefit thereby. (2) Nothing in this article shall prejudice the trial and punishment of any person for any act or omission which, at the time when it was committed, was criminal according to the general principles of law recognized by the community of nations. Covenant on Civil and Political Rights, Article 15.

II. Other Sources. ECR, #7-1, 2; ACR, #9; AFR, #7-2;
UDHR, #11-2.

III. Expanded Definition. An ex post facto law is a law passed after the occurrence of a fact or commission of an act which retrospectively changes the legal consequences or relations of such a fact or deed (Black, 520). This law includes not only retroactive legislative enactments with respect to offenses but also enhanced punishments after the fact. "Such laws are unfair because they attach illegality to activities of persons who, when they acted, had no notice of the illegality" (Perry, 333). Paragraph two of Article 15 (Article 11, paragraph two, UDHR) was included to recognize the legality of the Nuremberg indictment and trial of the German war criminals in 1945 and 1946. Counsel for the accused and a number of others criticized much of the "Nuremberg Law" as ex post facto and not substantative or procedural law prior to the arrest and trial of the accused. Paragraph two, therefore, affirms the Nuremberg indictment and judgment, which were subsequently approved by the General Assembly of the United Nations in its resolution of December 11, 1946, "Affirmation of the Principles of International Law Recognized by the Charter of the Nuremberg Tribunal."

IV. Landmarks. The ex post facto law is a denial of basic fairness and justice, which are rooted in natural law and human dignity. Article 39 of the June 15, 1215, Magna Carta implies the prohibition of such a law in denying imprisonment or any penalty upon a person "except by the legal judgment of his peers or by the law of the land." Hundreds of years passed before ex post facto laws were banished. In seventeenth-century England, the Levellers, led by John Lilburne, proclaimed and wrote with intense protest against such laws. The English Parliament, however, is supreme. It has historically rejected any restriction on its passage of any law. On the other hand, the United Kingdom is now bound by international human rights treaties which proscribe ex post facto laws.

The French Declaration of the Rights of Man and the Citizen of August 26, 1789, affirms in Article 7 that "no individual may be accused, arrested or detained except in cases prescribed by legislation and according to the procedures it has laid down." In Article 8 "the only punishments established by legislation must be ones that are strictly and obviously necessary, and no individual may be punished except by virtue of a law passed and promulgated prior to the crime and applied in due legal form."

In the American colonies, the Massachusetts Body of Liberties of December 10, 1641, forbade any punishment except by law "established by the general Court and sufficiently published . . ." Section II of the Delaware Declaration of Rights of September 1, 1776, states "that retrospective laws, punishing offences committed before the existence of such laws, are oppressive and unjust, and ought not to be made." Article I, Section 9, paragraph 3, and Article I, Section 10, paragraph 1, of the United States Constitution preclude the Congress and the states respectively from passing ex post facto laws, as do the constitutional systems of most nations.

V. Cross References. Appeal, Arrest, Courts/Tribunals, Detention, Due Process, Punishment, Self-Incrimination, Judgment and Sentencing, Trial, and Trial Procedure (Legal Rights).

Habeas Corpus

I. The Right. Anyone who is deprived of his or her liberty by arrest or detention shall be entitled to take proceedings before a court, in order that the court may decide without delay the lawfulness of his or her detention and order his or her release if the detention is not lawful. Covenant on Civil and Political Rights, Article 9, paragraph 4.

II. Other Sources. ECR, #5-4; ACR, #7-6.

III. Expanded Definition. Habeas corpus in English means "you have the body." In law, it means bringing a party before a court or judge (Black, 638). A writ of habeas corpus is a court order directing a sheriff, warden, or other public officer or a private person, who is detaining another person, to "produce the body" of the one being held in order that the legality of the detention may be determined by the court. The right to have a judicial determination of one's detention or arrest is integral to the due process of the law. It is a mechanism for the protection of the basic right of personal liberty (Perry, 189).

IV. Landmarks. Official determination of the legality of detention or arrest has ancient origins on the grounds of fairness and justice, irrespective of past and present violations. The right was affirmed in the June 15, 1215, Magna Carta guarantee to privileged English subjects in Article 39 in that "no freeman shall be taken or imprisoned or dispossessed, or outlawed . . . except by the legal judgment of his peers or by the law of the land." While habeas corpus is not specifically mentioned in the Magna Carta, the concept is clear, and it became a well-used remedy by the end of the sixteenth century.

In England, however, the Stuart monarchy transgressed on this and many other rights, leading the Parliament into a reconfirmation of many traditional rights. Article V of the Parliament's Petition of Right of June 7, 1628, denounced the violations of the "writs of habeas corpus" by the King's authorities and demanded in Article X that "no freeman, in any such manner as before-mentioned, be imprisoned or detained . . ." The abolition of the Star Chamber in an enactment of July 5, 1641, ended the principal court of prerogative judgment. Article VIII of the Act of Abolition made clear the guarantee to a "writ of habeas corpus" to any person who "shall hereafter be committed, restrained of his liberty or suffer imprisonment, by any order or decree of such court of start-chamber, or any other court . . ."

The Habeas Corpus Act of May 27, 1679, firmly established the right of the writ of habeas corpus. The twenty-one articles of the Act conveyed in detail both the substantive and procedural dimensions of the right, including penalties for judges failing to issue writs and exceptions for its application. King James II sought to derail the writ by imposing excessive if not impossible bail on targeted victims. James was overthrown in 1688, and the English Bill of Rights of December 16, 1689, declared in Article 10 of "Rights of the People" that "excessive bail ought not to be required, nor excessive fines imposed . . ."

In the American colonies, the right of habeas corpus was incorporated in a 1692 Massachusetts statute much broader in scope than the one in England. South Carolina followed, also in 1692, Virginia in 1710, and most other colonies as well. "The Inhabitants (of the Northwest territory) shall always be entitled to the benefits of the writs of Habeas Corpus . . ." in the Congressional Northwest Ordinance of July 13, 1787. Article I, Section 9, paragraph 2, of the United States Constitution states that "the privilege of the Writ of Habeas Corpus shall not be suspended, unless when, in cases of rebellion or invasion, the public safety may require it."

V. Cross References. Arrest, Bail, Courts/Tribunals, Detention, Due Process, Ex Post Facto Law, Innocence Presumption, Person before the Law, Punishment, Security of Person, Judgment and Sentencing, Trial, and Trial Procedure (Legal Rights).

See also the reports of the United Nations Commission on Human Rights Working Group on Arbitrary Detention. This group of five experts was established in 1991 to deal with issues of detention, including the need of governments to strengthen basic detention human rights and especially the right of habeas corpus.

Innocence Presumption

I. The Right. Everyone charged with a criminal offence shall have the right to be presumed innocent until proved guilty according to law. Covenant on Civil and Political Rights, Article 14, paragraph 2.

II. Other Sources. ECR, #6-2; ACR, #8-2; and AFR, #7-1-b;

UDHR, #11-1; Standard Minimum Rules for the Treatment of Prisoners (1977), #84-2; Human Rights of Persons Detained or Imprisoned, Subcommission of UN Commission on Human Rights (1974).

III. Expanded Definition. The presumption of a person as innocent before, if, or until the state proves otherwise, is central to the right of a person to due process of the law, as UDHR, #11-1, makes clear. It is the prime procedural safeguard for the accused person, who must be presumed to be a member of the community in good standing unless or until proven otherwise by the judicial process. It is the obligation of the state to demonstrate a proof of guilt before the presumption of innocence is in any way altered.

Express or implied expressed opinion or judgment about the guilt of an accused person certainly may be challenged by the accused on the grounds of libel or slander if and when judged truly innocent.

IV. Landmarks. The presumption of innocence of an accused person until or unless proven otherwise by judicial process is implicit in Article 39 of the 1215 Magna Carta, which requires "legal judgment of his peers or by the law of the land" before any punishment. The principle is rooted in old Anglo-Saxon law and became part of the customary law of England that was upheld in the Magna Carta. The presumption of innocence is also implicit in the English Petition of Right of June 7, 1628, and permeated many other legal systems in due couse.

The right was specifically included in the French Declaration of the Rights of Man and the Citizen of August 26, 1789. Article 9 of the Declaration states that "since every individual is presumed innocent until found guilty, legislation must severely repress all use of force beyond that which is necessary to secure his person in those cases where it is deemed indispensable to arrest him."

The presumption of innocence is not in the United States Constitution or Amendments, as it was considered implicit in all aspects of the due process of the law, especially in the Fifth and Fourteenth Amendments.

It was also taken for granted in the negotiating history of the 1948 Universal Declaration. It was nevertheless incorporated in the April 1948 draft of the Declaration and became #11-1 of the December 10, 1948, Declaration. The universalizing of this principle was particularly important with respect to the jurisprudence of any state which had placed the command and authority of the state before the rights of the person.

IV. Cross Reference. Arrest, Courts/Tribunals, Detention, Due Process, Habeus Corpus, Person before the Law, Punishment, Security of Person, Self-Incrimination, Judgment and Sentencing, Trial, and Trial Procedure (Legal Rights).

See also annual reports of United Nations Commission on Human Rights Working Group on Arbitrary Detention, established in 1991, with legal concerns about presumption of innocence.

Judgment and Sentencing

I. The Right. Any judgment rendered in a criminal case shall be made public except where the interest of juvenile persons otherwise requires or the proceedings concern matrimonial disputes or the guardianship of children. Covenant on Civil and Political Rights, Article 14, paragraph 1. Nor shall a heavier penalty be imposed than one that was applicable at the time when the criminal offence was committed. If, subsequent to the commission of the offence, provision is made by law for the imposition of the lighter penalty, the offender shall benefit thereby. ICPR, #15-1.

II. Other Sources. ECR, #6-1, 7-1; ACR, #8-5; AFR, 7-2;
UDHR, #11-2.

III. Expanded Definition. Judgment is by "a competent, independent, and impartial tribunal" (ICPR, #14-1) following due process for the accused and includes a sentence that may or may not involve a specific penalty or a specific punishment. The judgment must be public to protect the interests of the State Party as well as the accused person. However, the exceptions to public sentencing are included to protect the interests of juveniles and persons involved in matrimonial adversity. With the exception of the provisions in the covenants and conventions on the death penalty, the actual sentence and possible penalty are dictated by the law of the State Party to the covenants and conventions. Article 7, paragraph 2, of the African Charter asserts that "punishment is personal and can be imposed only on the offender." This is a specific statement that the judgment and sentence must be on the person and not on any group to which the person might belong. Personal punishment as a sentence is implied in other covenants and conventions.

IV. Landmarks. Judgment and sentencing are basic final steps in due process but require the conditions stated in the above articles of covenants and conditions. "Public" judgment and sentencing emerged out of seventeenth-century England's statutes concerning evolving due process, especially habeas corpus.

V. Cross References. Appeal, Contract, Compensation, Due Process, Double Jeopardy, Ex Post Facto Law, Punishment, Trial, and Trial Procedure (Legal Rights).

Juvenile Due Process

I. The Right. In the case of juvenile persons, the procedure shall be such as will take account of their age and the desirability of promoting their rehabilitation. Covenant on Civil and Political Rights, Article 14, paragraph 4. Any judgment [resulting from a trial] rendered in a criminal case or in a suit at law shall be made public except where the interest of juvenile persons otherwise requires. ICPR, Article 14, paragraph 1. Accused juvenile persons [in detention] shall be separated from adults and brought as speedily as possible for adjudication. Juvenile offenders shall be segregated from adults [in the penitentiary] and be accorded treatment appropriate to their age and legal status. ICPR, Article 10, paragraphs 2-b and 3. Sentence of death shall not be imposed for crimes committed by persons below the age of eighteen. ICPR, Article 6, paragraph 5.

II. Other Sources. Covenant on the Rights of the Child (November 20, 1989), with extensive provisions for protection and due process for the child in #40, is the principal source of law for juvenile due process.

ECR, #5-1-d and #6-1; ACR, #4-5 and #5-5;

UDHR, #25-2; ISLAM, #3; Standard Minimum Rules for the Administration of Juvenile Justice (the "Beijing Rules"), Resolution of General Assembly, November 29, 1985, and Standard Minimum Rules for the Treatment of Prisoners, #8 (d) and #85 (1) and (2). *See also* International

Labor Organization conventions on the child and child labor. Article 11 in the 1930 Convention on Forced or Compulsory Labor, for instance, prohibits "able-bodied males . . . not less than eighteen" from being "called upon for forced or compulsory labor."

III. Expanded Definition. Juvenile due process in international human rights law expands on many state laws in seeking the protection and rehabilitation of a juvenile who is accused of violation of law. The child is "every human being below the age of eighteen unless, under the law applicable to the to the child, majority is attained earlier." Covenant on the Rights of the Child, Article 1. See also #10, ICPR, in citing "below the age of eighteen years of age" and Child (Civil and Political Rights) with respect to age levels. The child as a person is protected by due process in international human rights law under the provisions of all relevant covenants and conventions. However, it was not until the 1950 European Convention on Human Rights that international human rights law specifically referred to a child's right in due process (#6-1). The ICPR reinforced in greater detail protection and due process for the child, and the Covenant on the Rights of the Child of 1989 added substantially to significant procedural safeguards for the child.

IV. Landmarks. For most of history but with few exceptions, child protection and punishment were under full authority and control of parents, the broader family, and/or guardians or public overseers. Children were often treated cruelly, especially those who were deserted, orphaned, or born to neglectful parents and prisoners. Child protective measures began in the seventeenth century (*see* Child, Civil and Political Rights), but it was only in the eighteenth that modest due process measures were introduced.

With respect to separate courts for juveniles, Switzerland established the first juvenile tribunal in 1862, followed by Massachusetts in 1869, and soon by many other American states and other nations as well. Probation for juveniles was introduced in Massachusetts around 1870. England's Criminal Courts Act of 1908 and similar legislation in 1912 furthered juvenile due process.

England initiated early but limited measures for separate confinement of juveniles in the eighteenth century. The Farm Colony in Warwickshire was established in 1817 as the first significant "reformatory," followed by the New York City House of Refuge in 1825. Pennsylvania followed in 1828 and Massachusetts in 1847. France created an agricultural colony for juvenile offenders in 1839. The English Youthful Offenders Act of 1854 advanced the "reformatory movement," as did the Elmira, New York Reformatory in 1876.

Protective measures and legislation for children (*see* Child, Civil and Political Rights) were accompanied by improved due process procedures including juvenile courts and separate confinement. International Labor Conventions relating to children after 1919 introduced modest obligations by States Parties to improve juvenile treatment, protection, and due process. Family and education legislation in many nations also tempered harsh treatment for children, leading to enhanced protective and due process procedures in the twentieth century.

V. Cross References. Due Process (Legal Rights); Child (Civil and Political Rights); and Education and Family (Economic, Social, and Cultural Rights).

Legal Assistance

I. The Right. In the determination of any criminal charge, everyone shall be entitled to defend himself or herself in person or through legal assistance of his or her own choosing. Covenant on Civil and Political Rights, Article 14, paragraph 3-d. He or she "shall be informed, if he [or she] does not have legal assistance, of this right; and to have legal assistance assigned to him [or her], in any case where the interests of justice so require, and without payment by him [or her] in any such case if he [or she] does not have sufficient means to pay for it." ICPR, Article 14, paragraph 3-d.

II. Other Sources. ECR, #6-3-c; ACR, #8-2-d; AFR, #7-1-c.

III. Expanded Definition. Legal assistance to the accused is essential, given the ever expanding complexities of the law and the judicial process. The state always has counsel to prosecute, and a plaintiff, in making a case against an accused defendant, usually has legal assistance. The right to a fair hearing or trial, the presumption of innocence, and other procedural safeguards for due process of the law may be of dubious value if the accused is unable adequately to present his or her case without legal assistance. On the other hand, an accused person also has the right to refuse counsel and, under most circumstances, to defend himself or herself. The provision for payment of counsel if the accused "does not have sufficient means" to provide such assistance is another facet of the right of equal protection of the law and the broader guarantees of equality before the law and protection against discrimination.

IV. Landmarks. Until late in the seventeenth century, a person accused of a felony could not engage legal assistance, although one accused of a misdemeanor could do so. After the English Revolution of 1688–89, the Trial of Treason Act of 1696 provided for the right of defense assistance but limited it to an accusation of treason. By an act of Parliament in 1836, defense counsel began to appear in English courts in felony cases if the accused were able to provide remuneration, but only with permission of the judge. It still was not a right.

The American colonies were far more advanced than their parent England as far as right to legal assistance was concerned. The right first appeared in the Massachusetts Body of Liberties of December 10, 1641, and the right applied in "any Court." It was thus a right and privilege for decades in America, but with varying restrictions and conditions. The right became more firm in the Pennsylvania Charter of Liberties of October 28, 1701, with the provision in Article V that "all Criminals shall have the same Privileges of Witnesses and Council as their Prosecutors."

It was later incorporated into many colonial and state documents, including the New Jersey and Pennsylvania Constitutions of 1776, the Delaware Declaration of Rights of September 11, 1776, and the Constitutions of Vermont (1777), Massachusetts (1780), and New Hampshire (1784). Finally, the right was confirmed in the United States Constitution in Article VI: "in all criminal prosecutions, the accused shall enjoy the right . . . to have the assistance of counsel for his defense." In due course, the right was one to be enjoyed in "any Court."

V. Cross References. Appeal, Arrest, Courts/Tribunals, Detention, Due Process, Judgment and Sentencing, Trial, and Trial Procedure (Legal Rights).

Person before the Law

I. The Right. Everyone shall have the right to recognition everywhere as a person before the law. Covenant on Civil and Political Rights, Article 16.

II. Other Sources. ACR, #3; AFR, #5; ISLAM, #8; UDHR, #6.

III. Expanded Definition. A person before the law has legal status to engage and to be engaged fully in the broad domains of due process of the law and in the system of justice in any jurisdiction where he might be located. A person before the law "has the right to be recognized everywhere as [one] having rights and obligations and to enjoy basic civil rights" (ICDR, #17). Legal personality likewise protects the person from any deprivation of liberty and security and from bodily harm in any manner without due process of the law.

IV. Landmarks. The right to recognition everywhere as a person before the law is an ancient right but one constantly violated throughout history by governments which arrest, detain, and punish individuals without their enjoyment of any procedural safeguard against such arbitrary and inhumane treatment. This has been particularly true with respect "to all forms of exploitation and degradation of man, particularly slavery, slave trade, [apartheid], torture, cruel, inhuman, or degrading punishment . . ." (AFR, #5). The racial policy of Nazi Germany, especially its treatment of Jews and other minorities, was vivid evidence of the denial of the right of legal personality.

In his draft of the United Nations Universal Declaration of Human Rights in the spring of 1947, UN Director of the Division of Human Rights Professor John Humphrey composed an article on the right to legal personality. He reflected on deprivation of rights of slaves, minorities, and millions of humans denied legal personality and rights under the Nazi regime. It took some time and effort for Professor Humphrey to explain the importance of this right, but the Commission on Human Rights finally recognized its wisdom. He records that this right "had not been included in any of the drafts [of the declaration on human rights] on which I had worked" and thus he was the sole author of this very basic right (Humphrey, *The Great Adventure,* 40). The tragedy is that massive violations of peoples' right to legal personality continue to plague humanity and include abuses such as summary and arbitrary executions, enforced or involuntary disappearances, and many other transgressions.

V. Cross References. Arrest, Death Penalty, Courts/Tribunals, Detention, Due Process, Habeus Corpus, Punishment, Security of Person, Torture, Trial, and Trial Procedure (Legal Rights).

Privacy

I. The Right. (1) No one shall be subjected to arbitrary or unlawful interference with his privacy, family, home, or correspondence, nor to unlawful attacks on his honour or reputation. (2) Everyone has the right to the protection of the law against such interferènce or attacks. Covenant on Civil and Political Rights, Article 17.

II. Other Sources. ECR, #8; ACR, #11;

UDHR, #12; ISLAM, #18-b; ASEAN, #1-2-(2.04); Declaration on the Use of Scientific and Technological Progress, General Assembly Resolution 3384, 1975, #6; Declaration of Basic Principles of Justice for Victims of Crime and Abuse of Power, Annex 6-b, General Assembly Resolution 40/34, 1985.

III. Expanded Definition. The value, integrity, and dignity of the individual command no interference into the basic privacy of the person unless there is a compelling reason by the state to intrude on individual privacy. This extends to one's family and home, possessions and communications, reputation and honor. The right to privacy, of course, is increasingly compromised with technological advances and electronic capabilities to penetrate even the most personal human recesses and resources. The right to privacy is integral to human rights but one on which the state and others lay claims which necessitate profound vigilence.

IV. Landmarks. Individual privacy and immunity from state intrusion, except for a valid public cause, is rooted in English customary and common law. Special "writs of assistance" or search warrants issued by magistrates or other judicial officials in England were valid for search and seizure of private property for a specific purpose, such as the Licensing Act of 1662. However, general writs or warrants were blanket authorizations to search and seize and were condemned as a violation of the presumed innocence of the accused. They were finally ruled illegal by 1765.

In Massachusetts in 1761, James Otis strongly condemned general writs of assistance issued by the English Superior Court of Massachusetts as a violation of privacy and individual possessions. "Each man's house is his castle," he declared, and "this writ [English writ of assistance], if it be declared legal, would totally annihilate this privilege." The English Townshend Revenue Act of 1767 provided sweeping authority to search and seize and was one more English law that led to colonial revolutionary sentiment. The Declaration and Resolves of the First Continental Congress of October 14, 1774, condemned the revenue acts and others as "subversive of American rights."

Condemnations of invasion of privacy rights and general warrants were incorporated in the Constitution of Virginia of June 12, 1776, in Section 10 as "grievous and oppressive." Article 10 of the Constitution of Pennsylvania of August 16, 1776, targeted the general warrants as a violation of the right of the people "to hold themselves, their houses, papers and possessions free from search and seizure . . ." Other states followed suit, including Delaware in its Declaration of Rights of September 11, 1776; Maryland and North Carolina in their Constitutions, 1776; Vermont, 1777; Massachusetts, 1780; and New Hampshire, 1784. The Fourth Amendment to the United States Constitution of December 15, 1791, provides for the right of privacy: "the right of the people to be secure in their persons, houses, papers, and effects, against unreasonable searches and seizures, shall not be violated; and no warrants shall issue, but upon probable cause, supported by oath or affirmation, and particularly describing the place to be searched, and the persons or things to be seized."

V. Cross References. Dignity, Name, Property (Civil and Political Rights) and Arrest, Courts/Tribunals, Detention, Due Process, Innocence Presumption, Person before the Law, Security of Person, Self-Incrimination, Judgment and Sentencing, Trial, and Trial Procedure (Civil Rights).

Punishment

I. The Right. No one shall be subjected to torture or to cruel, inhuman, or degrading treatment or punishment. In particular, no one shall be subjected without his or her free consent to medical or scientific experimentation. Covenant on Civil and Political Rights, Article 7. The penitentiary system shall comprise treatment of prisoners, the essential aim of which shall be their reformation and social rehabilitation. ICPR, #10-3.

II. Other Sources. ECR, #3; ACR, #5-2, 3 and 6; AFR, #5 and 7-2; Convention on Women, #2-b; Convention Against Torture; Convention on the Prevention and Punishment of Genocide; UDHR, #5; ISLAM, #19-d; ASEAN, #1-2 (2.02); Principles of Medical Ethics, General Assembly Resolution 37/194, 1983.

III. Expanded Definition. Punishment is any pain, penalty, suffering, or confinement inflicted upon a person by the authority of the law and the judgment and sentence of a court, for some crime or offense committed by him or her, or for his or her omission of a duty enjoined by law (Black, 1110). "Cruel, inhuman, or degrading treatment or punishment" and especially torture are violations of the value and dignity of the individual. Debate is historical and universal on the definition of these terms, although international human rights law seeks to advance recognition and prohibition of gross violations in punishment of the individual and his or her dignity and integrity. "[R]eformation and social rehabilitation" in ICPR, #10-3, are enlightened goals for any punishment and confinement in prison. Article 5-6, ACR, declares that "punishments consisting of deprivation of liberty shall have as an essential aim the reform and social readaptation of the prisoners."

The provision in ICPR with respect to medical or scientific experimentation reflects the repulsion of the international community to such activity on thousands of prisoners and other detainees under the authority of Nazi Germany and the determination to prohibit such experimentation unless authorized by consent of the persons involved.

IV. Landmarks. Punishment of humans for alleged and actual violations of laws of political communities has an infamous history from the very beginnings of ordered political life. Religious authorities and institutions sought to place restraints on excessive punishment, especially the death penalty, but they too often violated the right of humans for many transgressions of creed and doctrine. The Magna Carta of June 15, 1215, in Article 20 placed punishment for both small and great offences "in proportion to the magnitude of the offence." This provision established an important restraint on unmitigated punishment, irrespective of the many subsequent departures from proportionality between crime and punishment. Article 39 of the Magna Carta placed punishment under the authority of the accused being judged by his or her peers or by the "law of the land."

Irrespective of parliamentary statutes calling for proportionality in punishment, penalties for treason and other major crimes, especially against the monarch, continued to be cruel and harsh. Grievances listed in the 1689 English Bill of Rights listed cruel and unusual punishment, which led to Article 10 in the Bill and its prohibition. However, severity of punishment proportionate to the offence usually continued for crimes against the throne.

In the American colonies, the experiences of severe punishment produced Article 46 in the Massachusetts Body of Liberties of December 10, 1641, which declared that "for bodilie punishments we allow amongst us none that are inhumane Barbarous or cruel." On the other hand, the same Body of Liberties in Article 94 provided for twelve crimes demanding the death penalty, eleven of which were based on sources cited from the Old Testament of the Bible.

The 1776 Constitutions of Virginia, Maryland, North Carolina, and South Carolina proscribed "cruel and unusual punishment," as did many other constitutions and declarations of rights. Article XVIII of the Constitution of New Hampshire of June 6, 1784, is eloquent on punishment:

> All penalties ought to be proportioned to the nature of the offence. No wise legislature will affix the same punishment to the crimes of theft, forgery and the like, which they do to those of murder and treason . . . a multitude of sanguinary laws is both impolitic and unjust. The true design of all punishments being reform, not to exterminate, mankind.

The Eighth Amendment to the Constitution of December 15, 1791, continues the familiar words "Excessive bail shall not be required, nor excessive fines imposed, nor cruel and unusual punishment inflicted."

V. Cross References. Life (Civil and Political Rights), Arrest, Courts/Tribunals, Death Penalty, Detention, Person before the Law, Security of Person, Judgment and Sentencing, Trial, and Trial Procedure (Legal Rights); and Apartheid and Genocide (Collective Rights).

See also Standard Minimum Rules for the Treatment of Prisoners and Human Rights of Persons Detained or Imprisoned.

Security of Person

I. The Right. Everyone has the right to liberty and security of person. Covenant on Civil and Political Rights, Article 9, paragraph 1.

II. Other Sources. ECR, #5-1; ACR, #7-1; AFR, #4;
Dec on Non-Nationals, #5-1-a.

III. Expanded Definition. Liberty of the person is enjoyment of human rights and freedom from constraint by any authority, limited only by respect for the liberty of others and the requirements of security and well-being of the political community of the person (Articles 4 and 5 of the French Declaration of the Rights of Man and the Citizen of August 26, 1789, and Article 29, UDHR). Security of the person is the enjoyment of the inherent dignity of the human and freedom from any arbitrary or extralegal impairment of the person's physical well-being. Both liberty and security of the person may only be restricted by due process of the law. This right is an affirmation of Article 6, paragraph 1, of ICPR, which states, "every human being has the inherent right to life. This right shall be protected by law. No one shall be arbitrarily deprived of his life." In human rights law, such deprivations as apartheid, arbitrary arrest and detention, coercion in detention, enforced or involuntary disappearances, genocide, slavery, summary executions, and torture, among other illegal and extrajudicial measures, are prominent violations of the liberty and security of the person.

IV. Landmarks. Liberty and security of some persons have always been recognized in all political communities but throughout history, and too often in many societies, only for elites and others in descending order from elites. The June 15, 1215, Magna Carta is basic. "No free man shall be taken or imprisoned or dispossessed, or outlawed, or banished, or in any way destroyed, nor will we go upon him, nor send upon him, except by the legal judgment of his peers or by the law of the land." "Free man," of course, was a minority of Englishmen at that time and certainly did not include women, children, aliens, and many others. Over the centuries, however, the category "free man" was greatly broadened from the elite of 1215 as liberty and security of person became more widely guaranteed.

"Liberties" or rights and freedoms in many areas were guaranteed in English statutes and other documents, especially in legal rights such as due process of the law, the right of habeus corpus, and equality before the law. Civil rights of speech and the press became gradually confirmed in seventeenth-century England. The dramatic victories of peoples' rights and liberties over arbitrary rule in that century led to the first words in the English Bill of Rights of December 16, 1689—"an act for declaring the rights and liberties of the subject . . ."

Liberty and liberties flourished in American colonial documents and constitutions, again leading to the first sentence of the United States Declaration of Independence of July 4, 1776, and the affirmation of the "self-evident" truth of the "unalienable rights . . . of life, liberty, and the pursuit of happiness." We find as the fifth of the five objectives for forming " a more perfect union" in the Preamble to the United States Constitution of September 17, 1787, to "secure the blessings of liberty . . ." The rights of "life, liberty, and property" are confirmed in the Fifth and Fourteenth Amendments to the Constitution (1791 and 1868). In Article 2 of the French Declaration of the Rights of Man and the Citizen of August 26, 1789, "the final end of every political institution is the preservation of the natural and imprescriptible rights of man. These rights are those of liberty, property, security, and resistance to oppression." In time, the struggle for, and victory of, the right of liberty and security of person for many not among the elite of late eighteenth-century "man" became a reality. These rights were universalized in Article 3 of the Universal Declaration of Human Rights of December 10, 1948: "everyone has the right to life, liberty, and security of person."

V. Cross References. Life, Name, and Nationality (Civil and Political Rights); and Arrest, Detention, Due Process, Person before the Law, Privacy, and Torture (Legal Rights). *See also* annual reports of the United Nations Commission on Human Rights' Special Rapporteurs on Summary and Arbitrary Executions and Torture and the Working Groups on Arbitrary Detention and Enforced and Involuntary Disappearances.

The latter Working Group has stressed the need to enforce and supervise the General Assembly's 1992 Declaration on the Protection of All Persons from Enforced Disappearance (Res. 47/133). Article 4 of the Declaration states that "all acts of enforced disappearances shall be offenses under the criminal law punishable by the appropriate penalties which shall take into account their extreme seriousness." Article 18 has particular importance with respect to the issue of impunity (*see* Time Frames and Rights, K, in Issues and Contexts, part 1 of the dictionary, with respect to the issue of impunity). Article 18 declares that "persons who have, or are alleged to have, committed offenses referred to in Article 4, paragraph 1, shall not benefit from any special amnesty law or similar measures that might have the effect of exempting them from criminal proceedings or sanction."

Self-Incrimination

I. The Right. In the determination of any criminal charge against him or her, everyone shall be entitled . . . not to be compelled to testify against himself or herself or to confess guilt. Covenant on Civil and Political Rights, Article 14, paragraph 3-g.

II. Other Sources. ACR, 8-2-g.

III. Expanded Definition. The person who is detained by authorities of government has the right to due process of the law and to be presumed innocent unless or until the government proves otherwise. Due process precludes any attempt by officials to force the person, through any form of coercion, especially torture, to testify against himself or herself, to compel the person to incriminate himself or herself, or to alter his or her legal right of innocence by any admission of guilt.

IV. Landmarks. Throughout history, individuals have been subjected to means of compelling them to testify against themselves when charged with a violation of the rules of law. Torture has served as a compelling means to force self-incrimination, often producing testimony by the person which, while often false, was used to prosecute and condemn.

In the evolution of the common law in England, the emerging dignity of the individual led to a maxim in the sixteenth century of "nemo tenteur prodere se ipsum," or "no one should be required to accuse himself." Edward Coke apparently used this maxim as early as 1589, but judicial proceedings forcing self-incrimination continued, especially in the Star Chamber in London under the Stuart monarchy. The Star Chamber was finally abolished in 1641 when the House of Commons declared such proceedings to be "illegal and against the liberty of the subject."

The common law was conveyed in stages to the American colonies, and the proscription against self-incrimination gradually became ingrained in the American colonial state constitutions. The earliest law was Article 45 in the Massachusetts Body of Liberties of December 10, 1641, but with an important restriction: "no man shall be forced by Torture to confesse any crime against himselfe nor any other unlesse it be in some Capitall case where he is first fullie convicted by cleare and sufficient evidence to be guilty . . . then he may be tortured, yet not with such Tortures as be Barbarous and inhumane." This 1641 law clearly did not abolish torture but was a significant step toward the mitigation of torture for self incrimination. It was also still within the frame of procedure of English common law for capital crimes.

The prohibition of self-incrimination reached its full scope in the American states by 1776. Section 8, Constitution of Virginia, June 12, 1776; Article IX, Constitution of Pennsylvania, August 16, 1776; and Section 15, Delaware Declaration of Rights, September 11, 1776, declared ". . . nor can (a person) be compelled to testify against himself."

Article XII, Constitution of Massachusetts, October 25, 1780, stated that a person could not be "compelled to accuse, or furnish evidence against himself." The prohibition was incorporated into the Fifth Amendment of the United States Constitution which states that no person "shall be compelled in any criminal case to be witness against himself [or herself] . . ." The law against self-incrimination has been invoked throughout United States history and in many other nations as well.

Cross References. Appeal, Arrest, Courts/Tribunals, Double Jeopardy, Habeus Corpus, Innocence Presumption, Person before the Law, Punishment, Security of Person, Torture, Trial, and Trial Procedure (Legal Rights).

Torture

I. The Right. No one shall be subjected to torture or to cruel, inhuman, or degrading treatment or punishment. Covenant on Civil and Political Rights, Article 7.

II. Other Sources. The 1984 Convention Against Torture and Other Cruel, Inhuman, or Degrading Treatment or Punishment is the principal source for rights against torture in IHRL. Accompanying the Convention are annual reports of the Committee Against Torture, a committee of ten experts established under the Convention to monitor compliance and implementation by States Parties to the Convention.

ECR, #3; European Convention for the Prevention of Torture and Inhuman or Degrading Treatment or Punishment; ACR, #5-2; Inter-American Convention to Prevent and Punish Torture; Convention on Apartheid, #II-a (ii); Convention on Genocide, #II-b, c; Convention on Child, #37; and Supplementary Convention on the Abolition of Slavery (1956), #5.

UDHR, #5, #VII; ISLAM, #20; ASEAN, #10; Human Rights of Detained Persons (1974); Code of Conduct for Law Enforcement Officials, General Assembly Resolution, December 17, 1979, #5; Dec on Non-Nationals, #6; and "The Principles of Medical Ethics," General Assembly Resolution, December 18, 1982.

Annual Reports, United Nations Special Rapporteur on Torture, UN Commission on Human Rights. Office of Special Rapporteur established by the Commission on March 13, 1985, is another Commission mechanism for monitoring implementation of IHRL.

III. Expanded Definition. Article 1 of the Convention Against Torture has this expanded definition of torture.

Torture means any act by which severe pain or suffering, whether physical or mental, is intentionally inflicted on a person for such purposes as obtaining from him (or her) or a third person information or a confession, punishing him (or her) for an act he (or she) or a third person has committed or is suspected of having committed, or intimidating or coercing him (or her) or a third person, or for any reason based on discrimination of any kind, when such pain or suffering is inflicted by or at the instigation of or with the consent or acquiescence of a public official or other person acting in an official capacity. It does not include pain or suffering arising only from, inherent in, or incidental to lawful sanctions.

Under #4-2, ICPR, no State Party to ICPR may derogate its legal commitment not to subject anyone to torture. A United Nations Voluntary Fund for Victims of Torture was established by the General Assembly on December 16, 1981.

IV. Landmarks. The prohibition against "cruel and unusual punishment," especially torture, progressed at an extraordinarily slow pace over thousands of years. Plato and Aristotle approved of torture, and Roman law recognized torture as acceptable under its criminal procedure. However, natural law lawyers and philosophers, such as Cicero, Seneca, and Ulpian, opposed it, in keeping with their humanitarian perspective on human nature.

With the advent of more formal forms of law in medieval centuries, torture was used in judicial interrogation to decide cases of innocence or guilt and usually to inflict pain on the accused or a witness to gain a confession. "Infliction of pain" took many forms of hideous torment of the human body. Ordeal for trial was basically prohibited by the Fourth Lateran Council of the Church in 1215. Article 39 of the June 15, 1215, Magna Carta declared that "no person should in any way (be) destroyed" in a judicial process. England, in particular, then moved rapidly toward the jury as the prime means of gaining evidence in a trial, although the rites of torture continued in many forms in England and Europe. Of particular note was the use of torture against heretics, especially in the Spanish Inquisition under Torquemada in the late fifteenth and early sixteenth centuries.

The Parliament of England eventually abolished torture in the 1770s, as did Revolutionary France in 1789. Torture was employed in the Salem witch trials in 1692 but soon banned in the American colonies. The rise of democratic governance in many nations in the nineteenth century rendered torture an infamous relic, but in many parts of the world it was still used for its desired objective, to gain a confession for some civil or criminal violation. The widespread use of "cruel and unusual punishment" and torture by Nazi Germany prompted President Franklin D. Roosevelt to add another human freedom to his list of "Four Freedoms" of January 1941. He proclaimed on June 20, 1941, that "freedom from torture is a natural right." The Allies proceeded to demolish the Nazi regime and its allies by 1945 and then turned to the new United Nations and international law for universal measures against torture.

V. Cross References. Life (Civil and Political Rights); Arrest, Compensation, Detention, Due Process, Punishment, Security of Person, and Self-Incrimination (Legal Rights); and Apartheid, Genocide, and Slavery (Collective Rights).

Trial

I. The Right. In the determination of any criminal charge against him (or her), or of his (or her) rights and obligations in a suit of law, everyone shall be entitled to a fair and public hearing . . . a trial. Covenant on Civil and Political Rights, #14, paragraph 2. "Anyone arrested or detained . . . shall be entitled to a trial . . ." ICPR, #9-3.

II. Other Sources. ECR, 5-3, 6-1, and 7-2; ACR, #8-1 and #7-5 & 6; AFR, 7-1; UDHR, 10; ISLAM, #19 (e); ASEAN, #1-2 (2.03); Human Rights for Detained Persons (1974).

III. Expanded Definition. The examination before a competent tribunal according to the law of the land of the facts or law put in issue in a cause, for the purpose of determining such issue (Black, 1754). A trial is the determination of innocence or guilt of a person accused of a violation of the law of the jurisdiction, whether a sovereign state or its subordinate jurisdictions, or of international law. A trial is a procedure, taking place before a court or tribunal, following arrest and detention, administered by judges, and involving due process in the trial procedure.

In international human rights law, a trial must be fair and public. "Fair" means to provide the accused with appropriate due process of the law in the trial procedure as against any arbitrary prosecution or judgment.

"Public" means a trial that is not secret or private but one that is open to public monitoring and scrutiny. However, ICPR, #14-1, and other human rights treaties provide for exclusion of the public and press "for reasons of morals, public order, or national security . . . or when the interest of the private lives of the Parties so requires," as decided by the court.

IV. Landmarks. A trial as an authoritative procedure for determination of innocence or guilt of an accused person is rooted in the history of all civilizations. For most of that history, the "authoritative" judges of the accused were usually dominant officials of the jurisdiction in which the accused was tried. History demonstrates that the power of the jurisdiction was hardly fair to the accused, especially if guilt was presumed. Thus, through most of history trials lacked procedural due process for the accused, whose capacity to challenge the power of the state and its instruments of violence was almost completely nonexistent. Torture was often the prime inducement for the accused to confess "crimes." Unfortunately, even today, torture with or without subsequent trial remains a widespread challenge to "fair" trial and due process in many parts of the world.

The pageant of human rights is to a large extent one of emerging rights of the accused against the political community and, likewise, the duty of the state to provide and protect those developing rights. The year 1215 is remarkable in this respect. It marked the June 15th Magna Carta with its Article 39 including the right of the accused to have "legal judgment of his peers or by the law of the land" prior to a determination of his (or her) innocence or guilt. Also at the Fourth Lateran Council of the Church in 1215, trial by ordeal of fire and water to determine innocence or guilt was banned by the Church (and then by England in 1219). Over the ages, the right to a fair trial became grudgingly recognized in England and elsewhere as a limitation on the arbitrary power of government.

In the Magna Carta, "legal judgment of his peers" may mean peers as judges and/or peers as a jury. In those days, a "peer" was a man of high station, but over the centuries, a "peer" became one who had roughly the same social and economic status as the accused. A jury, which today has the authority to determine the facts of the case in common law, is not part of international human rights law. A jury in civil law is far less important than in common law and is not found in the covenants and conventions of human rights law. The history of the jury was rooted originally in Frankish law. It was brought to England by William I and was used by him and his successors in the gradual centralization of the evolving common law under the monarch. It became a viable alternative in time to trial by ordeal and a vital component of due process in the common law.

In Article 29 of the Massachusetts Body of Liberties of December 10, 1641, "it shall be the libertie of the plaintife and defendant by mutual consent to choose whether they will be tryed by the Bench [judge] or by a Jurie . . ." Trial by jury became standard procedure in due process in the colonies and led to the establishment of this right in Article III, Section 2 of the Constitution and in the Fifth and Sixth Amendments. In the latter is also found "the right to a speedy and public trial . . ." Finally, it should be added that these landmarks have not included differences between civil and criminal charges against the accused or differences between a "grand jury," making a determination of whether the accused should go to trial, and the trial jury itself.

V. Cross References. Arrest, Detention, Bail, Courts/Tribunals, Due Process, Equal Protection of the Law, Innocence Presumption, Person before the Law, Punishment, Judgment and Sentencing, Torture, and Trial Procedure (Legal Rights).

See also Stansilav Chernichenko and William Treat, The Right to a Fair Trial: Current Recognition and Measures for Its Strengthening, June 3, 1994. This is the final report by the two Special Rapporteurs to the Subcommittee on the Prevention of Discrimination and Protection of Minorities, UN Commission on Human Rights, dealing with an array of due process procedures essential to a fair trial. Previous reports by the Special Rapporteurs contain extensive material on the ingredients of a fair trial. Of particular importance is the Addendum to the Third Report, May 15, 1992: Interpretations of International Fair Trial Norms by the European Commission and Court of Human Rights.

Trial Procedure

I. The Right. Trial procedure is not a specific right but includes the rights in Trial Due Process in providing an accused person his or her "day in court" (*see* Due Process, above). Most trial procedure rights are entries in Legal Rights. Those that are not but are also in the body of IHRL are set forth below.

Following arrest, detention, and judicial decision to proceed with a trial for the accused, the following rights apply in addition to other due process rights enjoyed by the accused.

II. Sources. ICPR is listed first, followed by citations for ECR, ACR, and other sources.

A Right of the accused to be informed promptly and in detail in the language which he or she understands of the nature and cause of the charge against him or her.
   1. Nature of charge: ICPR, #14-3-a; ECR, #6-3-a
   2. Cause of charge: ICPR, #14-3-a; ECR, #6-3-a; ACR, #8-2-b
   3. Language and interpretation: ICPR, #14-3-a and #14-3-f; ECR, #6-3-a; ACR, #8-2-a

B. Right of the accused to have adequate time and facilities for the preparation of his or her defence: ICPR, #14-3-b; ECR, #6-3-b; ACR, #8-2-c; ISLAM (1990), #19-e

C. Right to be tried without undue delay: ICPR, #14-3-b; ECR, #6-1 (reasonable time); ACR, #8-1 (reasonable time); AFR, #7-1-d

D. Right to be tried in his or her (the accused) presence: ICPR, #14-3-d; ECR, #6-3-d; ACR, #8-2-d

E. Right to defend himself or herself in person: ICPR, #14-3-d; ECR, #6-3-c; ACR, #8-2-d (*see* Legal Assistance, Legal Rights)

F. Right to examine, or have examined, witnesses against him or her: ICPR, #14-3-e; ECR, #6-3-d; ACR, #8-2-f

G. Right to obtain the attendance and examination of witnesses on his or her behalf under the same conditions as witnesses against him or her: ICPR, #14-3-e; ECR, #6-3-d; ACR, #8-2-f

III. Expanded Definition. Nearly all trial procedure rights are based on the right to a fair trial or hearing. ICPR, #14-1, ECR, #6-1, and especially ACR, #8, which is quite detailed on the right of "fairness." *See* Trial, above. The right of habeus corpus (above) is closely identified with the right of the accused to be informed of the nature and cause of the charge against him (A, above). Time and facilities for defence (B, above) are associated with a fair trial and innocence (above) as are the other trial procedure rights.

IV. Landmarks. The Sixth Amendment to the Constitution of the United States of December 15, 1791, is quite explicit about trial procedure rights. "In all criminal prosecutions the accused shall enjoy the right to a speedy and public trial . . . to be informed of the nature and cause of the accusation; to be confronted with the witnesses against him; to have compulsory process for obtaining witnesses in his favor; and to have the assistance of counsel for his defence."

Witnesses have an interesting history. Article 38 of the June 15, 1215, Magna Carta states that "no bailiff for the future shall place anyone to his law on his simple affirmation, without credible witnesses brought for this purpose." Statutes in England in 1547 and 1552 permitted witnesses to testify against a defendant at trials for treason but not on behalf of a defendant. It was not until 1696 in the Trial of Treasons Act in England that the defendant gained the right to call witnesses in treason cases. This right was extended in 1702 to all defendants in England.

In the meantime, the Pennsylvania Charter of Privileges of October 28, 1701, provided in Section V "that all Criminals shall have the same Privileges of Witnesses and Council as their Prosecutors," which was an advance in the concept of a fair trial over that of the Mother country. The new constitutions of the American states including Virginia, June 12, 1776, and Pennsylvania, August 16, 1776, and the Delaware Declaration of Rights of September 11, 1776, led the pace for guarantees of witnesses for defendants and rights of examination of those testifying against him or her. These rights were confirmed in the Sixth Amendment to the Constitution.

V. Cross References. Due Process, Legal Assistance, Person before the Law, and Trial (Legal Rights).

III

Economic, Social, and Cultural Rights

Introduction

International human rights law with respect to economic, social, and cultural rights seeks to enhance the well-being and standard of living of people and to protect their interests in a wide range of human activities. The Covenant of Economic, Social, and Cultural Rights (ESCR) was approved by the General Assembly on December 19, 1966, and entered into force on January 3, 1976. The Preamble to the ESCR states that "the ideal of free human beings enjoying freedom from want and fear can be achieved only if conditions are created whereby everyone may enjoy his [or her] economic, social, and cultural rights as well as his [or her] civil and political rights." Clearly, the authors of the prime treaties intended to link closely the two sets of rights in the two treaties. The "right to life" in the Covenant on Civil and Political Rights (ICPR) and the "right to an adequate standard of living" in ESCR have an intimate association.

In the Preamble to the United States Constitution of 1787, one of the five purposes in forming "a more perfect union" is to promote "the general welfare" and ensure "domestic tranquility." In the 1789 French Declaration of the Rights of Man and the Citizen, property is an "inviolable and sacred right" of which "no individual may be deprived . . . unless some public necessity. . . clearly requires it. . ." The bond between economic rights and the civic order has a long heritage.

Civil, legal, and political rights preceded economic and social rights for many reasons, not the least of which were their roots in the historical progression of natural law. Economic and social rights grew slowly in the nineteenth and early twentieth centuries. The International Labor Organization of 1919 was the first international legal authority to recognize the right to work in its many dimensions as one to be protected under international law. The 1919 League of Nations Covenant also provided a foundation for modest achievement in economic and social rights in the 1920s and 1930s.

With the advent of World War II, President Franklin D. Roosevelt cast the purposes of the war on January 6, 1941, as a struggle for "Four Freedoms": freedom of speech and religion and freedom from want and fear, "everywhere in the world." The President thus placed civil and economic rights in one frame and proclaimed universality for these rights as well. On January 11, 1944, President Roosevelt announced a "second Bill of Rights" which included many now incorporated in ESCR such as the rights to work, health, education, home and family, and an adequate standard of living. The United States' drafts for a new world organization in the early 1940s included bills on civil, legal, political, economic, and social rights.

At the San Francisco Conference in the spring of 1945, United States Secretary of State Edward C. Stettinius pressed for full recognition of economic and social rights in observing the "disaster of the neglect of these rights" in the League era. He had strong support from many nations, which led to the affirmation of economic and social purposes in Article 55 of the new United Nations Charter in the context of "human rights and fundamental freedoms" in that Article.

Professor John Humphrey, then director of the United Nations Division of Human Rights, was the major author of what became the Universal Declaration of Human Rights of December 10, 1948. He observed that while he was composing the first draft in the spring of 1947, he included economic, social, and cultural rights along with civil, legal, and political rights because "I did not intend to be told that the former can have meaning without the latter." The Declaration, with seven substantial economic, social, and cultural rights, paved the way for the 1966 ESCR. It is also important to note that President Roosevelt's "Four Freedoms" grace the Preamble to the Universal Declaration.

A covenant on human rights law was intended to accompany the Declaration in 1948. However, the chair of the United Nations Commission on Human Rights, Mrs. Franklin D. Roosevelt, and others, considered the Declaration as a first step, to be followed by a covenant. For various reasons, including the essential differences between the two sets of rights, the Commission decided that there should be two covenants, one on civil and political and the other on economic and social. After almost twenty years of negotiations, the General Assembly approved both covenants on December 16, 1966.

Although the Preamble to both covenants proclaim the basic interdependence of the two sets of rights, Article 2 of both covenants explain in part their basic differences. ICPR, #2, calls on states to "adopt such legislative or other measures as may be necessary to give effect to the rights recognized in the present Covenant." Article 2 of ESCR recognizes that

States Parties will require time "to [achieve] progressively the full realization of the rights recognized in the present Covenant. . ."

Nearly all states had most of the rights in ICPR in their constitutional and legal systems when they ratified ICPR and thus implementing Article 2 did not impose a great difficulty. However, most states could not implement ESCR in short order because they did not have adequate resources to achieve fully such ESCR rights as "the right of everyone to the enjoyment of the highest attainable standard of physical and mental health" in #12-1 or "the right of everyone to education" in #13-1. In brief, ESCR calls for "goal" rights. It then includes means to goals such as #12-2 and "the steps to be taken by States Parties. . ." for the highest attainable standard of health or policies for "achieving the full realization" of the right of health.

ESCR makes it clear that States Parties have a duty and obligation to provide the means to the goals but adds in #2 that this should be pursued "individually and through international assistance and cooperation." Such assistance is not needed and therefore not required in #2 of ICPR.

Many specialized agencies of the United Nations have responsibilities for providing the means and resources for pursuing the goals of these rights. They include the World Health Organization for health in #12 of ESCR, the International Labor Organization for workers and trade union rights in #6, 7, and 8 of ESCR, and the United Nations Educational, Scientific, and Cultural Organization (UNESCO) for rights in #13, 14, and 15 of ESCR. The body of economic, social, and cultural rights is thus fortified by other organizations which adds to their importance and contributions to the general welfare of all humans.

Part IV of the ESCR provides for monitoring State Party compliance with obligations accepted in ratifying the Covenant. The Committee on Economic, Social, and Cultural Rights was established in 1985 to supervise and administer this section of the Covenant. In Article 16-1, states undertake to submit periodic reports on "measures which they have adopted and the progress made in achieving the observance of the rights recognized herein." The eighteen-member Committee of experts is thus similar to the Human Rights Committee of the ICPR and "treaty bodies" in other conventions, such as the Committee Against Torture in the Convention Against Torture. The Committee of the ESCR has been very active in monitoring reports and states for compliance and in assisting states in progressively meeting their obligations to realize rights in the Covenant (see *Reports* of the Committee for an accounting of its responsibilities).

Of particular importance to the ESCR are the "Limburg Principles" on the implementation of the ESCR which were negotiated and unanimously agreed to by twenty-nine leading diplomats and scholars at the University of Limburg, Maastricht, the Netherlands, in June 1986. The "Principles" interpret Part II of ESCR with emphasis in particular on #2 and its specific words on the implementation of the Covenant and the obligations of States Parties. [International Commission of Jurists, "The Limburg Principles," *The Review* (December 1986): 43–53].

In addition to the actual ESCR are the following: (1) the Protocols to the ECR which are concerned with economic and social rights; (2) the 1988 "San Salvador Protocol" of the ACR on economic, social, and cultural rights; (3) the AFR, especially #15-18; (4) the UN Declaration on Social Progress and Development, 1969; (5) the ASEAN Declaration, #5, "Social Justice," and #6; and (6) the contributions and reports of many nongovernmental organizations (NGOs) on the rights covered in ESCR.

Finally, most of the rights in the ESCR may be considered less firm as law than the historical civil, legal, and political rights, largely because their realization in many ways is more demanding than those in ICPR. However, the ESCR is an international treaty, as observed earlier, with states assuming treaty obligations as defined by the 1969 Vienna Convention on the Law of Treaties. Therefore, States Parties to the ESCR are bound to implement the Covenant in good faith and are committed to realizing expanding measures of human well-being for their peoples.

Author

I. The Right. The States Parties to the present Covenant recognize the right of everyone to benefit from the protection of the moral and material interests resulting from any scientific, literary, or artistic production of which he or she is the author. International Covenant on Economic, Social, and Cultural Rights, Article 15, paragraph 1 (c).

II. Other Sources. ACR, Protocol, 1988, #14-1 (c); UNESCO Constitution, #I-2-c;

UDHR, #27-2; ISLAM, #16; ASEAN, #7-2 & 7-4; Paris Convention for the Protection of Industrial Property, 1883; Berne Convention for the Protection of Literary and Artistic Works, 1886; the Universal Copyright Convention, 1952; Rome Convention for Protection of Performers, Producers of Phonographs, and Broadcast Organizations, 1961; and provisions and rules under current negotiation by the new World Trade Organization.

III. Expanded Definition. A "scientific, literary, or artistic production. . ." is classified as "intellectual property," which, in turn, is generally divided into "industrial property" including patents and trademarks, and "copyright property" for literary, artistic, musical, and scholarly works. The certified author or creator of such property has the right to be protected by his or her government for the exclusive production and sale of his or her product without infringement by or from others and to enjoy material and moral benefits deriving from the author's achievement, usually monetary consideration and prestige.

Industrial property protection includes the patent issued by the government to protect the author from infringement by others on producing or selling his or her invention and the trademark, a distinctive sign or mark identifying the author's production, which is also granted by the government. The copyright (author's right in most nations) is awarded by the state to the author for protection of his or her original intellectual production for a specific period of years. Protection of intel lectual property seeks to preserve the author's distinctive contribution to culture in general and to prevent piracy or other illegal reproduction of original productions for illicit monetary gain. Article 1 of the 1954 Hague Convention for Protection of Cultural Property in the Event of Armed Conflict sets forth a widely accepted definition of cultural property.

IV. Landmarks. Authors of any kind of intellectual production have always sought certification and recognition of their creations and some protection from piracy. Modest protection was afforded authors in the Roman Empire. The advent of the printing press in the mid fifteenth century, with a flourishing of printed material along with some modest inventions, required some government protection and regulation. Usually the sovereign, as in England, with the assistance of monopolistic guilds began to control and license rights to intellectual productions. However, the advent of demands for freedom of the press in the seventeenth century led to a reduction of state licensing control and to the English Statute of Anne in 1709, which as the first copyright act, both protected the author and regulated the granting of the copyright.

The United States Constitution of 1787 in Article I, Section 8, provides for promoting "the progress of science and useful arts, by securing, for limited times, to authors and inventors, the exclusive right to their respective writings and discoveries. . ." The first copyright and patent laws in the United States were passed by Congress in 1790, with progressive amendments and revisions through the years. A United States Patent Office was established for the approval and registration of patents, while legislation called for the deposit of materials for copyright with the Library of Congress. Other nations, of course, developed their own legislation for the submission, certification, registration, and protection of intellectual property.

With the heightened pace of civilization in the late nineteenth century and the flourishing of intellectual productions and inventions, the need was pressing for some international regulation to facilitate registration and regulation of creativity of all kinds. State protectionism of patents and copyrights inhibited cooperation in global sharing of intellectual productivity, and pirating of authors' creations eluded state protection of their rights to "material and moral benefits." Two major organizations based on treaties were established.

The Paris Convention for the Protection of Industrial Property was created by eleven nations in 1883 in Paris. The Union required each member to provide holders of patents from other nations the same protection as it gave its own nationals. The "Paris Union," which has been revised many times, today has a little over 100 members. The Berne Convention for the Protection of Literary and Artistic Works of 1886 established the same set of rights for holders of copyrights. The "Bern Union" also has been revised many times and today has ninety members.

The League of Nations' Committee on Intellectual Cooperation had extensive concerns for authors' rights and protection of their intellectual works.

Both Unions are administered by the World Intellectual Property Organization, founded in 1967 as one of the fifteen Specialized Agencies of the United Nations. Located in Geneva, WIPO is the principal international legal authority for the coordination and cooperation between and among states for many areas of intellectual production. WIPO also administers other treaties, including the 1971 Strasbourg Agreement on the International Classification of Patents, the 1978 Patent Cooperation Treaty, and the 1980 Trademark Registration Treaty. WIPO holds many conferences to promote cooperation and mutual assistance in areas of property and copyright piracy; counterfeiting of trademarks; protection of computer software and semiconductor (integrated circuit) designs; protection of authors and inventors in developing nations; and other concerns of intellectual property that unfold every day along with new frontiers of invention, discovery, and human creativity.

V. Cross References. Dignity, Name, Press, Property, and Speech (Civil and Political Rights); Privacy (Legal Rights); and Culture, Education, and Science (Economic, Social, and Cultural Rights.) *See also* Conferences and resources of WIPO and UNESCO with respect to authors' rights.

Culture

I. The Right. (1) The States Parties to the present Covenant recognize the right of everyone . . . [t]o take part in cultural life. (2) The steps [for] the full realization of this right shall include those necessary for the conservation, the development, and the diffusion of science and culture. (3) The States Parties undertake to respect the freedom indispensable for scientific research and creative activity. (4) The States Parties recognize the benefits to be derived from the encouragement and development of international contacts and cooperation in the scientific and cultural fields. Covenant on Economic, Social, and Cultural Rights, Article 15.

II. Other Sources. ICPR, #19; ACR, #26 and Protocol (1988), #14; AFR, #17-2, #22, and #29-7; Convention on Race, #5-e-vi; Convention on Women, #5-a; Convention on Child, #31-1; Constitution, UNESCO;

UDHR, #27-1; UNESCO Declaration of the Principles of International Cultural Cooperation (1966); Dec on Social Progress, #13-b; Dec on Non-Nationals, #5-1-f; ASEAN, #3-1; CSCE, Part III, Section 3 (Cooperation and Exchanges in the Field of Culture).

See also other UNESCO conventions and declarations.

III. Expanded Definition. Culture is the totality of socially transmitted behavior, patterns, arts, beliefs, institutions, and all other products of human work and thought characteristic of a community or population (*American Heritage Dictionary*).

In the context of IHRL

> Each culture has a dignity and value which must be respected and preserved. Every people has a right and duty to develop its culture. In their rich variety and diversity, and in reciprocal influences they exert on one another, all cultures form part of the common heritage belonging to all mankind.
>
> Nations shall endeavor to develop the various branches of culture side by side and, as far as possible, simultaneously, so as to establish a harmonious balance between technical progress and the intellectual and moral advancement of mankind.
>
> International cultural cooperation shall cover all aspects of intellectual and creative activities relating to education, science, and culture.
>
> The principles of this Declaration shall be applied with due regard for human rights and fundamental freedoms. UNESCO Declaration of the Principles of International Cultural Cooperation, #I, II, III, and XI-2. *See also* #5, UNESCO Declaration on Race and Racial Prejudice (1978).

The Constitution of UNESCO of 1945 provides a strong rationale for the right of everyone to take part in cultural life. The Preamble to the Constitution states "that since wars begin in the minds of men, it is in the minds of man that the defenses of peace must be constructed; . . . ignorance of each other's ways and lives has been a common cause, throughout the history of mankind, of that suspicion and mistrust between the peoples of the world through which their differences have all too often broken into war . . . the wide diffusion of culture (is) indispensible to the dignity of man . . ." Article 15 of ESCR also commits States Parties to "respect the freedom of scientific research and creative activity," which is also a commitment not to place any obstacles or censorship in the path of cultural authorship by means of national policy of any kind.

IV. Landmarks. The right and enjoyment of cultural freedom, both in creativity and consumption of culture, as well as protection for the international diffusion of culture and cooperation, is new to IHRL. It is stated in the 1945 Preamble and Constitution of UNESCO but enters IHRL only through the ESCR of 1966.

Culture, in all its manifestations, has been an attribute of humanity throughout history. Many rulers and philosophers sought to seal their political communities from external cultural influences which threatened their own policies and ideals for citizen beliefs and behavior. Plato advocated such a closed society for his Republic. Authority over speech and the press in England and other nations were examples of cultural protectionism. Totalitarian states such as Nazi Germany and the Soviet Union in our century imposed rigorous cultural barricades to influences they considered subversive to their respective ideologies.

Culture, however, is intangible and flows across boundaries of political communities due to its natural appeal to the emotions and sensibilities of peoples everywhere. Irrespective of patterns of state censorship, culture, such as the writings of Confucius and Beethoven's Ninth Symphony, is transnational and universal. Cultural diversity and richness among and within all states affirm the varied patterns of human dignity.

Initiative for the international protection of cultural freedom was taken by the Council of the League of Nations with the establishment in 1922 of the Committee on Intellectual Cooperation. The Committee sought to encourage and support "intellectual workers" such as authors, artists, and musicians; to advance and enhance contacts and cooperation between and among authors of creative works; and to relate these efforts to world peace. The CIC attracted some leading scholars such as Alfred Einstein and Marie Curie, but it never gained genuine support from the League despite some modest achievements. The Committee did pave the way for the authors of the United Nations Charter to consider placing cultural rights along with human rights in the Charter. They decided to defer to a French proposal to create a new organization for international intellectual policy in education, science, and culture. In less than five months, the Constitution of UNESCO was adopted in London on November 16, 1945.

V. Cross References. Dignity, Press, Religion, and Speech (Civil and Political Rights); Author and Education (Economic, Social, and Cultural Rights); Aliens, Migrant Workers, Minorities, and Refugees

(Collective Rights); and Disabled Persons and Indigenous Peoples (Declaratory Rights).

See also General Assembly proclamation of December 8, 1987, as the World Decade for Cultural Development from 1988 to 1997.

Education

I. The Right. (1) The States Parties to the present Covenant recognize the right of everyone to education. They agree that education shall be directed to the full development of the human personality and the sense of its dignity, and shall strengthen the respect for human rights and fundamental freedoms. They further agree that education shall enable all persons to participate effectively in a free society, promote understanding, tolerance, and friendship among all nations and all racial, ethnic, or religious groups, and further the activities of the United Nations for the maintenance of peace. (2) The States Parties recognize that, with a view to achieving the full realization of this right: (a) Primary education shall be compulsory and available free to all; (b) Secondary education in its different forms, including technical and vocational secondary education, shall be made generally available and accessible to all by every appropriate means, and in particular by the progressive introduction of free education; (c) Higher education shall be made equally accessible to all, on the basis of capacity, by every appropriate means, and in particular by the progressive introduction of free education; (d) Fundamental education shall be encouraged or intensified as far as possible for those persons who have not received or completed the whole period of their primary education; (e) The development of a system of schools at all levels shall be actively pursued, an adequate fellowship system shall be established, and the material conditions of the teaching staff shall be continuously improved. (3) The States Parties undertake to have respect for the liberty of parents and, when applicable, legal guardians to choose for their children schools, other than those established by the public authorities, which conform to such minimum educational standards as may be laid down or approved by the State and to ensure the religious and moral education of their children in conformity with their own convictions. (4) No part of this article shall be construed so as to interfere with the liberty of individuals and bodies to establish and direct educational institutions, subject always to the observance of the principles set forth in paragraph 1 of this article, and to the requirement that the education given in such institutions shall conform to such minimum standards as may be laid down by the State.

Each State Party (which does not as yet have free and compulsory primary education) undertakes within two years, to work out and adopt a detailed plan of action for the progressive implementation, within a reasonable number of years, to be fixed in the plan, of the principle of compulsory education free of charge for all. Covenant on Economic, Social, and Cultural Rights, Articles 13 and 14.

II. Other Sources. ICPR, #18-4; ECR, Protocol 1, #2; ACR, #12-4, Protocol (1986), #14, 15, 18; AFR, #17-1 & 3; Constitution, UNESCO, especially #1-2-b & c; Convention Against Discrimination in Education (UNESCO, 1960) and Protocol, 1962; Convention Against Racism, #5 (e) (v.); Convention on Discrimination Against Women, #10; Convention on Child, #28, 29; Convention on Refugees (1951), #22; Convention on Stateless (1954), #22; and International Labor Organization conventions relating to education and technical training.

See also UDHR, #26; European Social Charter, #I-10 & 15 and #II-10 & 15; ISLAM, #9; ASEAN, #6; Dec Social Progress, #10 (e) & 21; Declaration on Rights of Disabled Persons (1975), #8-c; CSCE, "Cooperation and Exchanges in Education," Madrid (1980); Std. Rules, Prisoners (1957 & 1977), #77; Declaration on Race and Racial Prejudice (UNESCO, 1978); and Dec on Non-Nationals (1985), #8 (c).

III. Expanded Definition. Education "refers to all types and levels of education, and includes access to education, the standard and quality of education, and conditions under which it is given." Convention Against Discrimination in Education, #1-2. To this it must be added that IHRL is concerned with formal, not informal, education and with public, not private or religious, education. ESCR covers the principal dimensions of education including the right to compulsory, free (and therefore public) education at the elementary, secondary, and higher education levels. ESCR includes fundamental or very basic education, largely for semiliterate peoples, as well as arenas for education including schools and alternatives to schools such as homes. Education also includes vocational guidance and training. ESCR and other sources specify certain goals for education, including the "full development of the human personality," which in law may be difficult to define.

IHRL is concerned with the equality of education opportunity and with nondiscrimination in education. UNESCO, "while respecting the diversity of national educational systems, has the duty not only to proscribe any form of discrimination in education but also to promote equality of opportunity and treatment for all in education" (Preamble, UNESCO). ESCR and other conventions provide for the right of parents or guardians to choose schools for their children if and when appropriate and consistent with their own convictions about the "religious and moral education of their children" (ESCR, #13-3). As IHRL considers a "child" to be a person below the age of eighteen, #13-3 may raise the question of the legal rights of the child in areas of freedom of religion, speech, and other rights.

Education is under the authority of States Parties which must consider harmonizing their laws with IHRL. This is difficult in the United States and other nations where educational law is under the authority of the states and, in fact, in the United States, under the laws of towns and cities. Most nations, however, vest legal authority for public education in their central governments.

IV. Landmarks. Theology long dominated education. The fifth- and fourth-century Greeks broke this mold with schooling in philosophy in the Athenian Academy. Parents in Rome had legal responsibility for their children's education until more formal schooling developed in the later Empire. The Church of Rome and monastic centers in early medieval Europe preserved much of that learning and expanded on it as well. New bodies of knowledge from the East, entering Europe in the era of the Crusades, joined contributions from the great centers of Arabic civilization in Spain to broaden many areas of learning. Aristotle and Cicero in particular were closely examined as church authorities and scholars explored the teachings of ancient philosophy. Peter Abelard (1079–1142) and Saint Thomas Aquinas (1225–1274), among others, introduced scholasticism in combining reason with theology. The universities evolved in this time frame, but education was mainly for the very rich and the religious, with most "learning" largely vocational and apprentice training.

The Renaissance changed all of this with a new birth of learning, followed by the Reformation and new theologies. Education now became a force for Protestant and Catholic leaders as a prime means for propogation of their theology. The advent of the printing press was of vast importance in advancing learning as well. Lower, and then higher, education evolved in England and on the European continent and spread throughout the world with European colonization.

Public schools emerged in Massachusetts fairly early in the seventeenth century, and the colonies placed great value on education and schooling. The Northwest Ordinance of July 13, 1787, proclaimed in Article III that "religion, morality, and knowledge being necessary to good government and the happiness of mankind, schools and the means of education shall forever be encouraged." In the United States, public education remained in the hands of the states and the people and was not under any central authority. In England and Europe, however, education became a centralized state function and therefore a right. This structure was adopted by most of the world's nations. These differences continue today, including the anomaly that education is not a "right" in the United States but is still free and compulsory.

The first major international frame for education was the Committee on Intellectual Cooperation (CIC) of the League of Nations, established in 1922 to further and encourage intellectual activity. The CIC was not concerned with free, compulsory, and public education. However, it did represent initial international concern for the advancement of intellectual cooperation and paved the way for the creation of UNESCO in November 1945. Education as an international right was established in the Universal Declaration of Human Rights of December 10, 1948.

V. Cross References. Child, Discrimination, and Speech (Civil and Political Rights); Equal Protection of the Law (Legal Rights); and Culture and Family (Economic, Social, and Cultural Rights). In Declaratory Rights, Education is cited in Development, Disabled Persons, and Indigenous Peoples, and it is found under Migrant Workers, Minorities, Refugees, and Stateless in Collective Rights.

See also the UNESCO Constitution and UNESCO declarations and conferences on education as well as ILO activity in vocational training and other educational programs for workers.

Family

I. The Right. (1) The family is the natural and fundamental group unit of society and is entitled to protection by society and the State. (2) The right of men and women of marriageable age to marry and to found a family shall be recognized. (3) No marriage shall be entered into without the free and full consent of the intending spouses. (4) States Parties to the present Covenant shall take appropriate steps to ensure equality of rights and responsibilities of spouses as to marriage, during marriage, and at its dissolution. In case of dissolution, provision shall be made for the necessary protection of any children. Covenant of Civil and Political Rights, Article 23.

Special protection should be accorded to mothers during a reasonable period before and after childbirth. During such period working mothers should be accorded paid leave or leave with adequate social security benefits. Covenant on Economic, Social, and Cultural Rights, Article 10-2.

II. Other Sources. ECR, #12 and Protocol 7, #5; ACR, #17 and Protocol, #15; AFR, #18-1 & 2, #27-1, #29-1; Convention on Consent to Marriage, Minimum Age for Marriage and Registration of Marriages (1962); Convention on Discrimination Against Women, #16 (with broad coverage), #11-2 & 11-1 (f); ILO Forced Labor Convention (1930), #11 (c); ILO Workers with Family Responsibilities Convention No. 156 (1981).

UDHR, #16; ISLAM, #5; ASEAN, #5-2; European Social Charter, I, #16 & 17, & II, #16 & #17; Dec on Social Progress, #4; CSCE (1975), III-I (a), (b) & (c).

III. Expanded Definition. The ICPR contains six rights of the family: (1) right of men and women of marriageable age to marry; (2) requirement of free and full consent of the intending spouses; (3) right to found a family as the result of the marriage; (4) right of the family to protection by the society and the state; (5) equal rights for both spouses during the marriage and in its dissolution; and (6) protection for children of a marriage in the event of dissolution. ESCR adds special protection for mothers before and after childbirth, including leave and social security benefits.

The law of domestic relations of each State Party to the two prime treaties defines family and terms related to the family, especially within the context of the legal culture of the state. Domestic relations law is under state law, for the most part, in the United States. In some nations, the law of the family is completely or partially under the authority of one or more religions. Considerable jurisprudence under the European Court on Human Rights and interpretations of the Covenants by their respective treaty bodies have contributed to IHRL definitions of family law. Reservations to the Covenants by some States Parties add to definitions of family law by those states.

With respect to the above rights of the family, it is clear that the intent of the provision is to limit marriage to men and women and not people of the same gender. Marriageable age is determined by each State Party. Consent may vary according to states' legal cultures but in general may not be derogated by a state. Protection by "society" includes security against individuals or groups seeking to harm a family in any way. Equal rights of spouses is tempered in many states by the legal culture. "Dissolution" was a term preferable to "divorce," which is not permitted under some legal cultures. Children are also protected by the Convention on the Rights of the Child, and mothers are generally protected by the Convention on the Elimination of All Forms of Discrimination Against Women.

IV. Landmarks. Law is ancient on the family and issues of domestic relations. Because of the historical intimate relation between marriage and the family on the one hand and the religions, cultures, and traditions in a state on the other, each state has over its history crafted its laws of domestic relations very carefully. Therefore, "international" law with respect to "domestic" relations was long a contradiction in fact.

Treaty law became necessary with problems of conflicts of law between and among states such as contentious issues arising between spouses of different citizenships. This was exemplified by the Convention for the Regulation of Conflicts of Laws and Jurisdiction in Questions of Divorce and Separation, signed at The Hague in June 1902. Other early Hague treaties dealt with conflicts of law of respective states of two spouses and their guardianship of minors (1902) and property upon dissolution of marriage (1905). Others dealt with maintenance allowances (1931), nationality of women (1933), and a variety of conflicts which could only be resolved by treaty law.

Family as an international right was first asserted in the UDHR of 1948 after protracted and sensitive negotiation. However, in many areas of family and domestic relations law, the harmonization of municipal law of many states with IHRL will progress very slowly. Exceptions are decisions on family and domestic relations law which come under authority of the European Court on Human Rights and the Inter-American Court of Human Rights. Those court decisions are binding on and must be implemented by States Parties to the European and American human rights conventions.

V. Cross References. Child, Nationality, Religion, and Women (Civil and Political Rights); Privacy and Equal Protection of the Law (Legal Rights); Social Security, Standard of Living, and Work, Conditions (Economic, Social, and Cultural Rights); family law with respect to Aliens, Migrant Workers, Minorities, Refugees, and Stateless (Collective Rights); and family law with respect to Disabled Persons and Indigenous Peoples (Declaratory Rights).

Food

I. The Right. The States Parties to the present Covenant recognize the right of everyone to an adequate standard of living for [self] and family, including adequate food. The States Parties will take appropriate steps to assure the realization of this right, recognizing to this effect the essential importance of international cooperation based on free consent.

The States Parties to the present Covenant, recognizing the fundamental right of everyone to be free from hunger, shall take, individually and through international cooperation, the measures, including specific programmes, which are needed: (a) To improve methods of production, conservation, and distribution of food by making full use of technical and scientific knowledge, by disseminating knowledge of the principles of nutrition, and by developing or reforming agrarian systems in such a way as to achieve the most efficient development and utilization of natural resources. (b) Taking into account the problems of both food-importing and food-exporting countries, to ensure an equitable distribution of world food supplies in relation to need. Covenant on Economic, Social, and Cultural Rights, Article 11-1, 2.

II. Other Sources. ACR Protocol, #12; Constitution, Food and Agricultural Organization, June 3, 1943; UDHR, #25-1; Dec on Social Progress, #10-b; Universal Declaration on the Eradication of Hunger and Malnutrition, adopted by World Food Conference, November 16, 1974, and endorsed by the General Assembly, Resolution 3348, December 17, 1974; Programme of Action on the Establishment of a New International Economic Order (1974), I-2, "Food"; General Assembly Declaration on the Right to Development, December 4, 1986; and General Assembly Resolution on the right to food as a universal human right, December 8, 1986.

III. Expanded Definition. The Preamble to the 1943 Constitution of the Food and Agricultural Organization (FAO) calls on all States Parties, through "separate and collective action," to raise "levels of nutrition and standards of living of the peoples under their respective jurisdictions; to secure improvements in the efficiency of the production and distribution of all food and agricultural products; and to better the condition of rural populations." Article I-2 elaborates on these aims and provides a fairly complete definition of "adequate food" and the right to be "free from hunger." The FAO Constitution is the principal source of IHRL on food and agriculture, in addition to ESCR, #11.

"Every man, woman, and child has the inalienable right to be free from hunger and malnutrition in order to develop fully and maintain their physical and mental facilities. Society today already possesses sufficient resources, organizational ability, and technology and hence the competence to achieve this objective. Accordingly, the eradication of hunger is a common objective of all the countries of the international community, especially of the developed countries and others in a position to help." World Food Conference Declaration, November 16, 1974.

"Food is a basic need for all human beings. Everyone requires access to food which is (a) sufficient, balanced, and safe to satisfy nutritional requirements, (b) culturally acceptable, and (c) accessible in a manner which does not destroy one's dignity as human beings." Eide, Right to Adequate Food as a Human Right, *see* Cross References.

The right to "adequate food" and the right to be "free from hunger" in Article 11, ESCR, as goal rights present enormous challenges for the means to pursue the ends. The World Food Council estimated in 1993 that there were over 550 million chronically hungry people in the developing world. Certainly this number must rise to over a billion people for the entire world. Other statistics abound, including those on starvation and the plight of starving children. Especially tragic are children so nutritionally deficient that their physical and mental well-being are being damaged beyond repair as they mature.

Articles 11-2 (a) and (b) of ESCR call on States Parties, "individually and through international cooperation," to pursue the following: (1) improve methods of production; (2) improve methods of conservation; (3) improve methods of distribution; (4) apply full use of technology and scientific knowledge of principles of nutrition; (5) develop or reform agrarian systems to achieve the most efficient development and utilization of natural resources; and (6) ensure an equitable distribution of world food supplies in relation to need (through international trade). Clearly the "right to adequate food" and the right to be "free from hunger" cut across most of the UN's operations, as well as those of a number of Specialized Agencies.

IV. Landmarks. In the *Republic,* Plato defines the state as arising "out of the needs of mankind; no one is self-sufficing, but all of us have many wants [or necessities]. . . . the first and greatest of necessities is food, which is the condition of life and existence. . ." (*Republic,* Book II, 369). As indispensable necessities for humans, food and water have not received the attention in human history they deserve. In identifying Allied goals for World War II, President Franklin D. Roosevelt called for "freedom from want" among his famous "Four Freedoms." Food certainly was a "want," as evidenced by the United States' sponsorship of the United Nations Conference on Food and Agriculture in May and June 1943. From that conference came the Constitution of the UN Food and Agricultural Organization.

Food was not considered a human right until it was included in an early draft for a Bill of Rights at the 1945 San Francisco Conference. On the basis of that draft, it finally was declared a right in Article 25 of the UDHR but within the context of the right of an "adequate" standard of living. Food thus joined many other economic, social, and cultural rights as a new human right and entered into IHRL with the ESCR in 1966.

V. Cross References. Child and Women (Civil and Political Rights); Security of Person (Legal Rights); Health, Social Security, and Standard of Living (Economic, Social, and Cultural Rights); and Peoples, Natural Resources (Collective Rights).

United Nations food organizations include the FAO as a Specialized Agency; the World Food Program of 1961 as the main food aid agency of the UN; the World Food Council of 1974 (WFC) which at the ministerial level is the highest UN body for food policy; and the International Fund for Agricultural Development (IAFD) of 1974 which supports agricultural development and reform in developing nations.

The World Food Conference of November 5 and 6, 1974, was the landmark international meeting on food and agricultural issues. It created the WFC and the IAFD, and its Universal Declaration on the Eradication of Hunger and Malnutrition called for "world food security." This led to the World Food Security Compact, adopted by the FAO on November 27, 1985, for the "development of a world food system characterized by stability and equity." Other important conferences were the FAO World Conference on Agricultural Reform and Rural Development, July 12–20, 1979; the Beijing session of the World Food Council, June 1987, and the Beijing Declaration for implementation; and the FAO-World Health Organization's International Conference on Nutrition, November 1992, which issued the World Declaration on Nutrition.

The organizations and audiences concerned with food resources, hunger, agriculture, and other dimensions of food are too numerous to include in the entry on food as a human right. They include trade organizations such as the United Nations Conference on Trade and Development, the General Agreement on Tariffs and Trade, the new World Trade Organization, and the International Trade Centre.

The International Labor Organization is concerned with minimum wages for agricultural workers; the 1982 Law of the Sea Treaty has provisions on fishing in Articles 62 and 63; and the Geneva Conventions of 1949 and the Protocols of 1977 are concerned with food needs of victims of war.

Treaties, declarations, and resolutions have provisions for food requirements for specific audiences including refugees, stateless peoples, victims of disasters, prisoners, and migrant workers. The World Health Organization, the United Nations Children's Fund, the UN Development Program, the World Bank, and the International Monetary Fund are among the many organizations and programs having international legal components and obligations which include food and agriculture among their priority interests. An official UN publication is *Right to Adequate Food as a Human Right* by Human Rights Sub-Commission Special Rapporteur Asbjorn Eide (New York: United Nations, 1989, Study Series #1).

Health

I. The Right. (1) The States Parties to the present Covenant recognize the right of everyone to the enjoyment of the highest attainable standard of physical and mental health. (2) The steps to be taken by the States Parties to the present Covenant to achieve the full realization of this right shall include those necessary for: (a) The provision for the reduction of stillbirth rate and of infant mortality and for the healthy development of the child; (b) The improvement of all aspects of environmental and industrial hygiene; (c) The prevention, treatment, and control of epidemic, endemic, occupational, and other diseases; (d) The creation of conditions which would assure to all medical service and medical attention in the event of sickness. Convention on Economic, Social, and Cultural Rights, Article 12.

The enjoyment of the highest attainable standard of health is one of the fundamental rights of every human being without distinction of race, religion, political belief, economic or social condition. Preamble, Constitution of the World Health Organization, 1946.

The objective of the World Health Organization (WHO) shall be the attainment by all peoples of the highest possible level of health. Article 1, Constitution of WHO.

II. Other Sources. ACR Protocol, #10; AFR, #16; Convention on Women, #12, 11-1 (f) & 14-2 (b); Convention on Child, #24; Constitution, WHO. *See also* ICPR, #7, ". . . no one shall be subjected without his [or her] free consent to medical or scientific experimentation," and Convention Against Torture and Other Cruel, Inhuman, or Degrading Treatment or Punishment (1984) with respect to impairing human health and well-being for malicious purposes.

UDHR, #25; ASEAN, #5-7 & 5-10; European Social Charter, I, #11 & II, #11; Dec on Social Progress, #10-d & 19 (a); Principles of Medical Ethics, General Assembly Resolution, December 12, 1982; General Assembly Declaration of the Rights of Mentally Retarded Persons, December 20, 1971, paragraph 2; General Assembly Declaration of the Rights of Disabled Persons, December 9, 1975, paragraph 6; and ILO Occupational Safety and Health Convention (No. 155), June 22, 1981.

Annual WHO Assembly decisions and resolutions (*see* in particular the Resolution of May 22, 1981, Global Strategy for Health for All by the Year 2000, and the May 1988 resolution on HIV-infected people); ILO Conference decisions, conventions, declarations and resolutions; and General Assembly resolutions and declarations for specific audiences including aliens, refugees, stateless peoples, the disabled, the mentally retarded, and prisoners.

III. Expanded Definition. "Health is a state of complete physical, mental, and social well-being and not merely the absence of disease or infirmity" (Preamble, WHO Constitution).

"The right of everyone to the enjoyment of the highest attainable standard of physical and mental health" is an end goal. Means to this end are outlined in #12-2, ESCR, and especially in Article II of the WHO Constitution which lists twenty-two functions or means for WHO to pursue its goal and human right of "the attainment by all peoples of the highest possible level of health."

The term "highest attainable standard" eludes specific definition. However, Article II of the WHO Constitution calls for the establishment of "international standards," which have been accomplished in several fields including breast milk substitutes, food safety, pharmaceuticals, and tobacco. Such standards may assume the authority of customary international law with conformance by a considerable majority of states following the adoption of such standards.

Article 2 (v) of the Constitution states that a function of WHO shall be "generally to take all necessary action to attain the objective of the Organization." An example of action with respect to a disease unknown at the time of the adoption of the WHO Constitution in 1946 is the WHO Global Programme on AIDS (Acquired Immunodeficiency Syndrome), launched in 1988, six years after WHO identified what is now a global epidemic.

See also international conventions in many areas of health, including communicable diseases and food safety, which are included in the body of world health law.

IV. Landmarks. Concerns for health and health care beyond the jurisdiction of the political community arose abruptly in the latter part of the seventeenth century due to the Great Plague of 1665 in London, which caused the deaths of thousands of people and crippling disease in many more. The plagues in the Book of Exodus and in Athens in 430 B.C. had international significance. The plague of the Black Death in 1334 is said to have caused the deaths of three quarters of the population of Europe and Asia. There was long the awareness that disease was apparently transported on ships, probably by rats. However, it was not until inspections of cargos for contamination and limited quarantines began in Alexandra in 1831 and Constantinople in 1839 that international attention was drawn to the hazards to humans caused by uninvited guests crossing state boundaries to contaminate human bodies.

The Ottoman Empire established the Counseil Superieur de Sante in 1838, which brought maritime nations together to seek to contain the spread of infectious diseases in international commerce. France in 1851 convened the first of many international sanitary conferences, and the Pan American Union established a Pan American Sanitary Bureau in 1890. Finally, an International Office of Public Health was established in Paris in 1907 to serve as a clearinghouse for cooperation on health issues, to provide research and information on public health issues, and to foster cooperation among nations' public health agencies.

The 1919 Covenant of the League of Nations in Article 23-f called for taking "steps in matters of international concern for the prevention and control of disease." In 1923, the League established a Health Section to work with the Assembly's Health Committee on a number of public health issues including means to fight epidemics, developing international biological standards, engaging in research, and providing services to national public health agencies. Specific attention was focused on health needs of women, children, and refugees. This pioneering activity formed the foundations of the WHO Constitution in 1946 with "health as one of the fundamental rights of every human being."

V. Cross References. Child, Life, and Women (Civil and Political Rights); Detention, Punishment, and Torture (Legal Rights); Family, Food, Social Security, Standard of Living, and Work, Conditions (Economic, Social, and Cultural Rights); Aliens, Migrant Workers, Minorities, Refugees, and Stateless (Collective Rights); and Disabled Persons and Indigenous Peoples (Declaratory Rights).

See also health concerns, policies, rules, and standards of Food and Agricultural Organization, International Labor Organization, United Nations Childrens' Fund, United Nations Development Program, and the United Nations Environmental Program.

Science

I. The Right. (1) The States Parties to the present Covenant recognize the right of everyone to enjoy the benefits of scientific progress and its applications. (2) The steps to be taken by the States Parties to the present Covenant to achieve full realization of this right shall include those necessary for the conservation, the development, and the diffusion of science and culture. (3) The States Parties to the present Covenant undertake to respect the freedom indispensable for scientific research and creative activity. (4) The States Parties to the present Covenant recognize the benefits to be derived from the encouragement and development of international contacts and cooperation in the scientific and cultural fields. Convention on Economic, Social, and Cultural Rights, Article 15.

II. Other Sources. Constitution, United Nations Educational, Scientific, and Cultural Organization (UNESCO); ICPR, #7; ACR, Protocol, #16; ASEAN, #3; Recommendations on Status of Scientific Researchers, UNESCO; Dec on Social Progress, #13 and #24-2; Declaration on a New International Economic Order, #4-p; Charter of Economic Rights and Duties, #13; CSCE, Part II (Cooperation in the Field of Economics, of Science and Technology); Declaration on the Use of Scientific and Technological Progress in the Interests of Peace and for the Benefit of Mankind, General Assembly Resolution, 1975.

III. Expanded Definition. In ESCR, #15-1, "the right of everyone . . . to enjoy . . ." anything depends on the value and quality of that which is to be enjoyed, a right essentially being in the eye of the beholder. "Science" is too generic a term for any fairly precise legal definition. In general, however, if the purpose of "science" is to protect and enhance the security, well-being, and rights of humans, then it is a right to be enjoyed by all humans. "Steps" to this end in ESCR, #15-2, include "conservation, development, and diffusion of science and culture," which States are also obligated to undertake in #I-2 (c) of the UNESCO Constitution. States are obligated in the provisions of ESCR, #15-3, "to respect the freedom indispensable for scientific research and creative activity," and to respect the rights of freedom of speech, press, property, author's rights, and others as set forth in the two prime United Nations Covenants.

IV. Landmarks. Over history, most states have stimulated scientific advancement for human and national well-being, although "scientific advancement" in the culture of some political communities has been tempered by the demands of theology and ideology. Article I, Section 8, of the United States Constitution of 1787 calls for promoting "the progress of science and the useful arts. . ." Scientific collaboration between and among nations has generally been pursued in treaties of friendship and commerce between nations, in agreements with respect to scientific authorship (*see* Author), and in international trade and trade agreements.

The League of Nations pioneering Committee on Intellectual Cooperation, established in 1922, had modest concerns for scientific cooperation, especially among its membership which included Alfred Einstein and Marie Curie. However, it was not until the establishment of UNESCO in 1945 that science assumed a major role in confirming fundamental freedoms and human rights.

V. Cross References. Press and Speech (Civil and Political Rights); Author, Culture, Health, and Education (Economic, Social, and Cultural Rights).

Social Security

I. The Right. The States Parties to the present Covenant recognize the right of everyone to social security, including social insurance. Covenant on Economic, Social, and Cultural Rights, Article 9.

II. Other Sources. ACR, Protocol, #9; AFR, #18-4; Convention on Racism, #5-e-iv; Convention on Women, #11-1-e, #14-2-c, #26;

Convention on Child, #26; ILO Conventions on Social Security 102 (1952) and 157 (1982); Convention on Refugees, #24; Convention on Stateless, #24;

UDHR, #22; ISLAM, #13; ASEAN, #6 (d); European Social Charter, I-#12 & II-#12; ILO Declaration of Philadelphia (1944), III (f); Dec on Social Progress, #11, #19-b; Declaration on Rights of Disabled Persons, #7; Dec on Non-Nationals, #8 (c).

III. Expanded Definition. Social security is a state policy and program to insure the security and well-being of people who for various reasons are unable to provide for their basic economic needs. Under most governments, individuals demonstrating needs for themselves and their families have a right to claim social security benefits, usually in the form of periodic cash distributions by the government.

Principal branches of social security benefits include the following: medical, sickness, maternity, invalidity, old-age, survivors (of beneficiaries), employment, injury, unemployment, and family benefits (ILO Social Security Convention, 1962, #2).

State funding for social security insurance and benefits is usually derived from deductions from wage earners' and other workers' payrolls. This is a form of insurance for the person making the obligatory contribution for future needs, as well as meeting a societal commitment to provide assistance to members of the society in economic need.

IV. Landmarks. Most societies in history have provided for their members in need, and most religions have recognized the obligation to provide some sustenance to those deprived for one reason or another. From Isaiah we are taught to "relieve the oppressed, judge the fatherless, plead for the widow. . ." "Tzedakah," or charity, in the Judaic Torah parallels "zakat" or the giving of alms to the poor in Islamic law. Similar concerns are in the religious heritage of Buddhism, Hinduism, and the writings of Confucius.

With the rise of modern socialism, first with the French Revolution and later with the "Utopian Socialists" then Karl Marx, governments were pressed to assume some role in providing assistance for the sick, the needy, and the aged. It was not, however, until 1883 that Chancellor Otto von Bismarck launched the first program for compulsory sickness insurance for workers in Germany and, six years later, compulsory old age insurance. France followed in 1905, England in 1911 with its National Insurance Act, and most of Western Europe by 1914. The new Russian Socialist Federation in 1922 instituted a broad social security program with full funding by the government. The Social Security Act of 1935 (under the leadership of President Franklin D. Roosevelt) introduced social security benefits to United States citizens, benefits which have been expanded through many amendments over the years.

On the international level, the International Labor Organization, established with the League of Nations in 1919, declared in the first sentence of the Preamble to its Constitution of 1919 that "universal and lasting peace can be established only if it is based upon social justice. . ." The Constitution called for "the protection of the worker against sickness, disease, and injury. . ." in the second paragraph of the Preamble. In Article II, the Constitution declared that "all human beings have the right to pursue . . . their material well-being . . . in conditions of freedom and dignity, of economic security and equal opportunity." In Article III (f) it called for "the extension of social security measures to provide a basic income to all in need. . ."

In their famous "Atlantic Charter" of August 14, 1941, President Franklin D. Roosevelt and Prime Minister Winston S. Churchill declared in the Fifth Article that there should be the "fullest cooperation between all nations. . .with the object of securing for all improved labor standards, economic advancement, and social security. . ." The call for universal recognition of social security was repeated in the ILO Declaration of 1944 and in Articles 22 and 25-1 of the UDHR.

V. Cross References. Child, Discrimination, and Women (Civil and Political Rights); Security of Person (Legal Rights); Family, Food, Health, Standard of Living, and entries for Work (Economic, Social, and Cultural Rights); Aliens, Migrant Workers, and Minorities, (Collective Rights); and Disabled Persons and Indigenous Peoples (Declaratory Rights).

Standard of Living

I. The Right. The States Parties to the present Covenant recognize the right of everyone to an adequate standard of living for himself or herself and his or her family, including adequate food, clothing, and housing, and to continuous improvement in living conditions. The States Parties will take appropriate steps to ensure the realization of this right, recognizing to this effect the essential importance of international cooperation based on free consent. Covenant on Economic, Social, and Cultural Rights, Article 11-1.

II. Other Sources. United Nations Charter, #55 (a); ILO Employment Policy Convention (1964), Preamble, #1; Convention on Child, #27-1.

UDHR, #25-1; ILO Declaration of Philadelphia (1944), #III a; European Social Charter, I-#4 & II-#4-1; Dec on Social Progress, #9, #10-c & #17-c; Charter of Economic Rights and Duties of States, Preamble (a) & #14.

With respect to "food," *see* entry on Food. With respect to housing, the Convention on Racism (#5-e-iii) and Convention on Women (#14-2-h) are concerned with nondiscrimination in housing. The Convention on Child (#27-3), Convention on Refugees (#21), and Convention on Stateless (#21) call for guarantees of adequate housing. For declarations concerning housing, *see* Dec on Social Progress, #10-f; UNESCO Declaration on Race and Racial Prejudice, #9-2; and ASEAN, #5-8.

See also the Vancouver Declaration on Human Settlements, United Nations Conference on Human Settlements, 1986. General Assembly resolutions on housing include establishment of UN Centre for Human Settlements, designating 1987 as the International Year for the Homeless, and the resolution of December 11, 1987, calling for a Global Strategy for Shelter to the Year 2000.

III. Expanded Definition. An "adequate standard of living" is a goal right, relative within and among nations in terms of defining basic human well-being. "Adequate" certainly means sufficient food, clothing, and housing to sustain health and basic comfort for the person and his/her family (*see* Food and Health, Economic, Social, and Cultural Rights). See Other Sources with respect to housing.

It is clear in ESCR, #11-1, that the state has the obligation to advance the realization of this right, which requires public policy and resources. Part of public policy under the European Social Charter is recognizing "the right of workers to a remuneration such as will give them and their families a decent standard of living" (#II-4-1). States lacking in such resources may be encouraged by #9 of the 1969 Declaration on Social Progress and Development, which calls for assistance from the "international community" to supplement "by concerted international action, national efforts to raise the living standards of peoples." Article 2 of ESCR also cites "international assistance and cooperation" in achieving "full realization" of the rights in ESCR.

Many General Assembly Resolutions including the 1969 Declaration on Social Progress and Development, the 1974 Declaration on a New International Economic Order, the 1974 Charter of Rights and Duties of

States, and the 1986 Declaration on the Right of Development, testify to the vast majority of United Nations members' emphatic support for "the attainment of wider prosperity among all countries and of higher standards of living for all peoples" as stated in the first "condition" in the Preamble of the 1974 Charter of Economic Rights and Duties of States. The realization of the right is, of course, subject to the provisions in #2 of the ESCR and the gaining of resources to pursue the goal right.

IV. Landmarks. Adequate standards of living for humans has been a pursuit of people and political communities throughout history. At the international level, the history of the labor movement, which led to the establishment of the International Labor Organization in 1919, reflects genuine concerns for adequate living standards. The 1919 Constitution of the ILO, with its eloquent concern for "social justice" and protection of the worker from dire conditions which erode any decent standard of living, was a stirring document on behalf of human well-being. The 1919 Constitution was also the first affirmation of an economic and social human right: "all human beings, irrespective of race, creed, or sex, have the right to pursue both their material well-being and their spiritual development in conditions of freedom and dignity, of economic security and equal opportunity." The ILO contributed significantly through conventions and machinery for state compliance to bringing the reality of the human condition closer to some of the ideals of the 1919 Constitution.

In the negotiations for provisions in the 1945 Charter of the United Nations, diplomats supportive of a strong statement on economic rights gained a remarkable provision in #55 of the Charter which states that "the United Nations shall promote: (a) higher standards of living, full employment, and conditions of economic and social progress and development. . ." In three years, these provisions were embraced in #25 of the UDHR in the promotion of the right of an adequate standard of living for everyone.

V. Cross References. Family, Food, Health, Social Security, and entries for Work (Economic, Social, and Cultural Rights).

Work, Right to

I. The Right. (1) The States Parties to the present Covenant recognize the right to work, which includes the right of everyone to the opportunity to gain his or her living by work which he or she freely chooses or accepts, and will take appropriate steps to safeguard this right. (2) The steps to be taken by a State Party to the present Covenant to achieve the full realization of this right shall include technical and vocational guidance and training programs, policies, and techniques to achieve steady economic, social, and cultural development and full and productive employment under conditions safeguarding fundamental political and economic freedoms to the individual. Covenant on Economic, Social, and Cultural Rights, Article 6.

II. Other Sources. ACR, Protocol, #6; AFR, #15 & #29-6; Convention on Racism, #5-e-i; Convention on Women, #11-a; Convention on Refugees, #17-1; Convention on Stateless, #17-1.

The International Labor Organization (ILO) is the principal legal authority with respect to right to work, conditions of work, right to form trade unions, and rights of trade unions (#6, 7, 8 of ESCR). There are at present 172 ILO Conventions on work rights and many other areas of economic, social, and cultural rights which have received over 5,500 ratifications by states. International labor law is thus the largest body of IHRL. The ILO also has effective mechanisms for supervision and implementation of its conventions, dealing with an extensive variety of labor standards and law. *See* in particular the ILO Constitutions of 1919 and the ILO Declaration of Philadelphia, 1944.

UDHR, #23-1; European Social Charter, #I-1 & II-1; ISLAM, #13; ASEAN, #5-6-b; Dec on Social Progress, #6 & #10-a; Declaration on Mentally Retarded (1971), #3; Declaration on Disabled Persons (1975), #7.

III. Expanded Definition. The right to work in #6, ESCR, includes the right to (1) gain his or her living by work and (2) work that he or she freely chooses and accepts. The goal of the right to work in ESCR 6-2 includes the State Party's "safeguarding fundamental political and economic freedoms to the individual."

The 1964 ILO Employment Policy Convention (#122) provides a significant expansion of #6-1, ESCR: (1) With a view to stimulating economic growth and development, raising levels of living, meeting manpower requirements, and overcoming unemployment and underemployment, each Member shall declare and pursue, as a major goal, an active policy designed to promote full, productive, and freely chosen employment. (2) The said policy shall aim at ensuring that: (a) There is work for all who are available for and seeking work; (b) Such work is as productive as possible; c) There is freedom of choice of employment and the fullest possible opportunity for each worker to qualify for, and to use his or her skills and endowments in a job for which he or she is well suited, irrespective of race, color, sex, religion, political opinion, natural extraction, or social origin. 3) The said policy shall take due account of the stage and level of economic development and the mutual relationships between employment objectives and other economic and social objectives and shall be pursued by methods that are appropriate to national conditions and processes.

The right to work is broadened in other conventions and declarations cited above, including the "inalienable right of all human beings" (Convention on Women); "right of productive work" (Convention on Retarded Persons); "useful, productive, and remunerative occupation (Convention on Disabled Persons); and "right to engage in wage-earning employment (Conventions on Refugees and Stateless).

Article 6-2, ESCR, sets forth the obligations of the State Party "to achieve the full realization" of the right to work. This provision is consistent with #2 of ESCR with respect to the implementation of economic, social, and cultural rights. The duty of the state with respect to the right to work is amplified in ASEAN, #6 a, b, & c, including rights for household and domestic workers (#6-c).

IV. Landmarks. "Work" was usually labor provided by the worker who had a contract or a similar agreement with the person providing the work. Throughout much of history, categories of workers were organized into guilds which specialized in specific crafts, such as the manufacture of jewelry or the building of shelters. Such organizations flourished in ancient China, India, Greece, Rome, the Islamic world, and, later, in Europe.

European guilds such as those in Flanders were economic and social enterprises which exercised tight political and production controls, determined quality standards, and prospered, as one can observe in the guild buildings in the Grand Place in Brussels. The guilds were organized into masters, apprentices, and journeymen and were powerful eco nomic forces until rising capitalism in the seventeenth and eighteenth centuries gradually replaced the guild system.

Capitalism was dominated by the owner of the production enterprise who employed workers and fully determined work conditions such as hours, wages, and the production environment. The Industrial Revolution naturally led to great expansion of production and also to demands by workers for better working conditions. Mechanical and artisan workers began to organize in a guild pattern, but as such groups expanded, they were considered criminal conspiracies under the common law in England and the American colonies. Officials in government and employers of labor thus marched together in a massive restraint of improved conditions for workers under the banner of "laissez faire."

The "Utopian Socialists" of the early nineteenth century, among others, demanded modest rights for workers. Karl Marx (1818–1883), along with Friedrich Engel, provided a historical context and theory of the exploitation of workers, or the "proletariat," by the "bourgeoise" owners and employers in the *Communist Manifesto* of 1848. In Western Europe, Marxism led to the formation of democratic socialist parties and political support for workers. In Czarist Russia, Marxism eventually led to the communism of the USSR, which subordinated workers to the dictation and command of the Communist Party.

In the industrializing democracies, workers' organizations of all kinds emerged and, although prosecuted, gradually won some victories. In Massachusetts in 1842, the Supreme Judicial Court in *Commonwealth v. Hunt* struck down the proposition that workers' combinations or "unions" were criminal conspiracies. This historic decision recognized the legality of unions. Although governments, in tandem with owners and employers, persecuted and prosecuted unions with all kinds of injunctions and often with violent anti-union tactics, the unions and workers gained strength and gradual legal recognition and protection.

In the United States, the Knights of Labor was formed in 1869, first as a secret organization and then as a thriving national union. Its rival, the Federation of Organized Trades and Labor Union, became the American Federation of Labor in 1886 and the dominant union of crafts such as housing, transportation, and apparel. The AFL gained political power with favorable judicial decisions on the rights of collective bargaining and the right to strike. The rights of individual workers were thus advanced through the collectivity and legal and political victories of the unions.

At the international level, an International Association for Labor Legislation was formed in Basel, Switzerland, in 1900. Labor leaders from many nations at that session and later in 1906 produced two conventions, one placing limits on night work by women and another on the elimination of phosphorus in the manufacture of matches. The basic idea was to seek ratification of these conventions by states which then would incorporate the body of the convention into their own national or municipal law. Only a few states ratified these conventions. However, the concept introduced in 1906 of international human rights law taking the form of a treaty to be incorporated into national law is the basic procedure through which IHRL becomes law for states today.

International labor leaders at the Paris Peace Conference in 1919, led by Samuel Gompers, President of the United States American Federation of Labor, successfully pressed for a provision in the new League of Nations Covenant, stating in Article 23 that members of the League "will endeavor to secure and maintain fair and humane conditions of labor for men, women, and children, both in their own countries and in all countries to which their commercial industrial relations extend, and for that purpose will establish and maintain the necessary international organizations."

The prime organization for labor became the ILO, which was incorporated in Part III of the Treaty of Versailles of June 28, 1919, and in the other World War I peace treaties. The 1944 ILO Declaration of Philadelphia amplified the 1919 Constitution in preparation for the post-World War II era. It states in II-a that "all human beings, irrespective of race, creed or sex... have the right to pursue both their material well-being and their spiritual development in conditions of freedom and dignity, of economic security and equal opportunity." The more than 170 ILO conventions since 1919 have brought the right to work and rights of workers to well over 100 nations ratifying ILO conventions. The ILO naturally was very influential in gaining recognition for the right to work in the UDHR, the ICPR, and especially the ESCR. The ILO with its organization, conventions, procedures for incorporating rights for workers into national law, and mechanisms for supervision, compliance, and implementation of its law established a firm foundation for the flourishing of IHRL in the twentieth century. The ILO was awarded the Nobel Peace Prize in 1969.

V. Cross References. Child, Discrimination, and Women (Civil and Political Rights); Security of Person (Legal Rights); Author, Education, Standard of Living, and entries for Work (Economic, Social, and Cultural Rights); Aliens, Migrant Workers, Minorities, Refugees, and Stateless (Collective Rights); and Disabled Persons and Indigenous Peoples (Declaratory Rights). Also, ILO Constitution, 1919, and ILO Declaration of Philadelphia, 1944, as well as ILO conventions cited above.

Work, Conditions

I. The Right. The States Parties to the present Covenant recognize the right of everyone to the enjoyment of just and favorable conditions of work. Covenant on Economic, Social, and Cultural Rights, Article 7.

II. Other Sources. ICPR, #8-3; ACR, Protocol, #7; AFR, #15; Convention on Racism, #5-e-i; Convention on Women, #11-1-b, c, d, & #11-2; Convention on Refugees, #17-3; Convention on Stateless, #17-2.

Among important ILO Conventions on conditions of work are the following: Forced Labor Convention (1930); Protection of Wages Convention (1949); Convention on Abolition of Forced Labor (1957); Equal Remuneration Convention (1951); and Discrimination (Employment and Occupation) Convention (1958). With respect to forced labor, the Slavery Convention (1926), the Protocol Amending the Slavery Convention (1953), and the Supplementary Convention on the Abolition of Slavery, the Slave Trade, and Institutions and Practices Similar to Slavery (1956) are intended to eradicate any legal justification for slave or bonded labor as a condition of work.

UDHR, #23-2; European Social Charter, I #3, 4, 8, 9, 10, & II #3, 4, 8, 9, 10; ISLAM (1990), #13; ASEAN, #6-a, d; Dec on Social Progress, #10-a & #20-b; Dec on Non-Nationals, #8-1 (a).

III. Expanded Definition. A basic condition for the worker is "the right to just and favorable remuneration ensuring for himself [or herself] and his [or her] family an existence worthy of human dignity, and supplemented, if necessary, by other means of social protection."

"Just and favorable conditions of work" are set forth in Article 7, ESCR. They include the following: (a) Remuneration that provides all workers, as a minimum with: (i) Fair wages and equal remuneration for work of equal value without distinction of any kind, in particular women being guaranteed conditions of work not inferior to those enjoyed by men, with equal pay for equal work; (ii) A decent living for themselves and their families in accordance with the provisions of the present Covenant; (b) Safe and healthy working conditions; (c) Equal opportunity for everyone to be promoted in his or her employment to an appropriate higher level, subject to no considerations other than those of seniority and competence; (d) Rest, leisure, and reasonable limitation of working hours and periodic holidays with pay, as well as remuneration for public holidays.

For workers in labor unions, the contract between union and management or employer usually dictates most working conditions along with legislation of States Parties on labor conditions and policy. *See also* the ILO conventions on working conditions that stress nondiscrimination in all areas, including provisions on nondiscrimination in ESCR.

IV. Landmarks. *See* Landmarks, Work, Right to.

V. Cross References. Child, Discrimination, and Women (Civil and Political Rights); Security of Person (Legal Rights); Education, Health, Social Security, Standard of Living, and entries for Work (Economic, Social, and Cultural Rights); Aliens, Migrant Workers, Minorities, Refugees, Slavery, and Stateless (Collective Rights); and Disabled Persons and Indigenous Peoples (Declaratory Rights).

Work, Trade Unions

I. The Right. (1) The States Parties to the Covenant undertake to ensure: (a) The right of everyone to form trade unions and join the trade union of his or her choice, subject only to the rules of the organization concerned, and for the promotion and protection of his or her economic and social interests. No restrictions may be placed on the exercise of this right other than those prescribed by law and which are necessary in a democratic society in the interests of national security or public order or for the protection of the rights and freedoms of others. (2) This article shall not prejudice the imposition of lawful restrictions on the exercise of these rights by members of the armed forces or of the police or the administration of the State. (3) Nothing in this article shall authorize the States Parties to the International Labor Organization Convention of 1948 concerning Freedom of Association and Protection of the Right to Organize to take legislative measures which would prejudice, or apply the law in such a manner as would prejudice, the guarantees provided for in that Convention. Covenant on Economic, Social, and Cultural Rights, Article 8-1-a, 2, 3. Everyone shall have the right to freedom of association with others, including the right to form and join trade unions for the protection of his or her interests. Convention on Civil and Political Rights, Article 22-1. Article 22-2, ICPR, is basically the same as ESCR, #8-1-a, with respect to "no restrictions. . ." although ICPR, #22-1, adds the "interests of public safety and the protection of public health or morals. . ." However, these additions refer largely to "freedom of association." ICPR, #22-3, is the same as ESCR, #8-3.

II. Other Sources. ACR, Protocol, #8; ACR, #16-1; ECR, #11; Convention on Racism, #5-e-ii.

Among the important ILO Conventions on forming and joining trade unions are the following: Convention on Freedom of Association and

Protection of the Right to Organize (1948); Right to Organize and Collective Bargaining Convention (1949); Workers Representations Convention (1971); Rural Workers Convention (1975); and Collective Bargaining Convention (1981).

UDHR, #23-4; European Social Charter, #I, #5, 6 & #II, #5, 6; Dec on Social Progress, #10-a & #20-a; ASEAN, #6-b, c; CSCE, #I-13; Declaration on Rights of Disabled Persons, #7; Dec on Non-Nationals, #8-1-b.

III. Expanded Definition. The ILO and its international conventions have long defined the right of everyone to form and join trade unions, the conditions of work (*see* Work, Conditions of) which generally are guaranteed by trade union membership, and workers' rights, including collective bargaining and the right to strike. These rights are confirmed in ESCR, #8. The ILO was instrumental in incorporating in ESCR the basic tenets of international labor law to reinforce its own impressive authority.

Restrictions on the right of everyone to form and join a trade union in ESCR, #8-1-a, as well as in ICPR, #22-2, provide the state with broad authority over unions and union activity. The restriction with respect to the "rights and freedoms of others," which protects non-union members' own right to work in the event of a strike, boycott, or other union activity, is considered by unions to be detrimental to union solidarity.

ESCR, #8-2, with respect to possible limitations on union activity by public employees, is largely the concern of the State Party and its judgment on the "right to strike" by a union of public employees (see Work, Trade Union Rights). Public employees' rights to organize are protected in the ILO Labor Relations (Public Service) Convention (1978), which requires States Parties to ensure public employees' organizations complete independence from state officials and protects such organizations from anti-union discrimination. These provisions present possibilities for conflicts between States Parties to these conventions and public employee rights and unions.

ESCR, #8-3, emphasizes the ILO 1948 Freedom of Association Convention, which provides protection on many fronts for union members from anti-union discrimination.

IV. Landmarks. *See* Work, Right to.

V. Cross References. Assembly, Association, Political and Women (Civil and Political Rights); Security of Person (Legal Rights); and entries for Work (Economic, Social, and Cultural Rights).

Work, Trade Union Rights

I. The Right. (1) The States Parties to the present Covenant undertake to ensure: (a) The right of trade unions to establish national federations or confederations and the rights of the latter to form or join international trade-union organizations; (b) The right of trade unions to function freely subject to no limitations other than those prescribed by law and which are necessary in a democratic society in the interests of national security or public order or for the protection of the rights and freedoms of others; (c) The right to strike, provided that it is exercised in conformity with the laws of the particular country. (2) This article shall not prevent the imposition of lawful restrictions on the exercise of these rights by members of the armed forces or of the police or of the administration of the State. (3) Nothing in this article shall authorize States Parties in the International Labor Organization Convention of 1948 concerning Freedom of Association and Protection of the Right to Organize to take legislative measures that would prejudice, or apply the law in such a manner as would prejudice, the guarantees provided for in that Convention. Covenant on Economic, Social, and Cultural Rights, Article 8-1-b, c, d & Article 8-2, 3.

II. Other Sources. ACR, Protocol, #8 and #9; International Labor Organization: Conventions, Resolutions, and Decisions, ASEAN, #5-c; CSCE, #I-13; Dec on Social Progress, #20.

III. Expanded Definition. The provisions in ESCR, #7-b and c, require little added definition. The basic ILO Freedom of Association and Protection of the Right to Organize Convention of 1948 defines many rights of trade unions, as do other ILO conventions and laws of each State Party. The right to strike is guaranteed in ESCR, #7-1-d, as well as ACR, Protocol, #9. *See also* European Social Charter, II, #5 & 6.

IV. Landmarks. *See* Work, Right to.

V. Cross References. Assembly, Association, and Political (Civil and Political Rights); Education and entries for Work (Economic, Social, and Cultural Rights).

IV

Collective Rights

Introduction

International human rights law, with respect to collective rights, is concerned with the rights of specific categories of people as well as the individual rights of people in those categories. The first collective right in the dictionary deals with the rights of aliens, or non-nationals, people present in a state other than the state of their own nationality. This right applies to the category of aliens as a whole and to individual aliens as well.

Article 1 of the two prime treaties declares in the first sentence, "All peoples have the right of self-determination." "Peoples" is a category or collectivity and "person" a member of that category. The African Charter on Human and Peoples' Rights includes rights for "every individual" in most articles, but Articles 19 through 24 are for "all peoples" as collective rights.

The dictionary has included collective rights in other categories such as Women in Civil and Political Rights, Juvenile Due Process in Legal Rights, and Family in Economic, Social, and Cultural Rights. These, however, are somewhat different in that women comprise about fifty-two percent of the world's population, juveniles as people under the age of eighteen about forty percent, and the family encompasses most of the people of the world.

In terms of history, minorities were the first collectivity to have some basic rights with the rights of religious minorities in the 1555 Peace of Augsburg and later in the Peace of Westphalia of 1648. Minorities were also pioneer beneficiaries of human rights under the World War I peace treaties and enjoy collective and individual rights under contemporary IHRL. Other collective rights include those for victims of severe human rights violations including apartheid, genocide, and slavery. Refugees, stateless persons, and migratory workers are categories of non-nationals.

Collective rights may be viewed as incompatible with individual human rights. The latter focuses on the right of the person to be free of constraint by government in many areas such as religious freedom but also to have the protection of government in other areas such as due process.

However, if we view the collective right as a category of people who share certain individual rights with others in that category, then collective rights become a convenient way to identify clusters of rights. It should not be forgotten that the United States Constitution and the United Nations Charter both begin with "We the people" ("peoples" for the Charter), which identifies a collectivity enjoying common as well as individual rights.

Aliens

I. The Right. An alien lawfully in the territory of a State Party to the present Covenant may be expelled therefrom only in pursuance of a decision reached in accordance with law and shall, except where compelling reasons of national security otherwise require, be allowed to submit the reasons against his or her expulsion and to have his or her case reviewed by, and be represented for the purpose before, the competent authority or a person or persons especially designated by the competent authority. Covenant on Civil and Political Rights, Article 13.

II. Other Sources. Convention on Women, #9-1, Protocol 4, #3 & Protocol 7, #1-1, 2; ACR, #22-6 & 8; AFR, #12-4;

UDHR, #9; Declaration on the Human Rights of Individuals who are not Nationals of the Country in which They Live (General Assembly, 1985).

III. Expanded Definition. An alien is "any individual who is not a national of a State in which he or she is present," Dec on Non-Nationals, #1. Because of the global mobility of people and the necessary temporary or even permanent presence of people in countries of which they are not nationals, aliens have always held legal rights in jurisdictions other than their own. They generally enjoy the same rights as do nationals of the country in which they are present, rights based on reciprocity between nations and the doctrine of "national treatment." This doctrine asserts that an alien should have the same rights and treatment as nationals of the country in which the alien is present and is usually covered in the standard Treaty of Friendship and Commerce between two states.

However, the alien must enter the country legally (Dec on Non-Nationals, #2), fully accept the host state's regulations and conditions of presence, and observe the same laws as are required of the nationals of the host state (Dec on Non-Nationals, #2, 3). For its part, the host state may not discriminate against the alien on the ground of the alien's national origin (*see* Discrimination in nearly all treaty entries including "national origin" in provisions for nondiscrimination). An extensive statement of alien rights is in Articles 5 and 8 of the Dec on Non-Nationals as well as in #9 and 10.

IHRL (in ICPR, #13) is very concerned about state expulsion of the alien. The alien has full access to due process of the host state. Expulsion is forbidden unless the alien has full access to due process of the host state or grounds of national security or some other compelling reason for expulsion is set forth, as in ECR Protocol 7, #1-1, 2 (including "public order"). *See also* ACR, #22-6, 8; AFR, #12-4; and Dec on Non-Nationals, #4. Article 16 of ECR provides for "restrictions on the political activity of aliens." Collective expulsion is specifically forbidden in ECR, Protocol 4, #4; ACR, #22-9; AFR, #12-5; and Dec on Non-Nationals, #7. Article 1-2 of the Convention on Racism states that the "Convention shall not apply to distinctions, exclusions, restrictions or preferences made by a State Party to this Convention between citizens and non-citizens." As "non-citizens" includes aliens, refugees, stateless persons, or others, this provision may be in contradiction to provisions of other conventions and declarations above.

International law on aliens and alien rights includes provisions regarding alien property in another state, alien corporations, and the extensive law of expropriation of alien property by a host state, including the right of the state to eminent domain with respect to any property. Immigration law and the rights of non-nationals in nations where they seek refuge and/or asylum are also distinct issues in IHRL. Extradition law and extraditable offenses of aliens are also of concern in alien rights law, as are the rights of alien prisoners in Standard Minimum Rules for the Treatment of Prisoners (1957 & 1977), #38. *See* Cross References, below.

IV. Landmarks. Throughout history, political communities had either short- or long-term aliens or permanent resident aliens. They were treated in various ways depending upon the governing authority of the community which always claimed—and still does—the right to say who may enter the community's jurisdiction, the rights and duties of the alien who may become a citizen of the community, and who must leave. The rights and duties of the alien were generally based on reciprocal understandings between the state hosting the alien and the alien's home state. The metic, or alien, in ancient Athens was often a prominent person, engaged in commerce and trading. The metic was either transient or a permanent resident but could not be a citizen, a right enjoyed only by male, native Athenians with property and education.

In the modern state system, the state continues to remain dominant over alien rights as well as immigration and asylum law. Bilateral treaties and other agreements between states on reciprocal rights and duties of aliens in each other's jurisdictions modify any exclusive state authority. This was particularly true with the extensive network of bilateral treaties of friendship and commerce between states. The League of Nations began to deal with significant flows of refugees after 1919. Legal rights and international law became further developed with respect to alien property and corporation rights, expropriation, and rights and duties of states with respect to non-nationals. The Hitler era and its racial policies led to vast discrimination of people on racial and non-national grounds, which resulted in the crime of genocide and the Holocaust.

For these and other reasons, provisions on human rights entered into the 1945 United Nations Charter and led to the 1948 Universal Declaration of Human Rights. However, states retained the protection of domestic jurisdiction from intervention by the United Nations under Article 2-7 of the Charter. This led to classic contentions over authority for alleged human rights violations between a state claiming domestic jurisdiction and the IHRL claim for international authority to intervene in that domestic jurisdiction.

A tragic case study of such a contention was that of Uganda, which on August 4, 1972, issued an order for the expulsion of over 50,000 Ugandans holding United Kingdom passports and several days later for about 10,000 holding Indian, Pakistani, and Bangladeshi passports. The order was signed by President Idi Amin Dada who took over the office from the first President, Dr. Milton Obote, in early February 1971. Another decree by President Amin on October 4, 1972, called for confiscation of the expelled Asians' property.

The outraged public condemnation, especially from the United Kingdom, pointed to the blatant racist orders in violation of the United Nations Charter, the UDHR, and especially the 1965 Convention Against Racism, legally in force and ratified by many states including Uganda. Under international law, the state of the national, the United Kingdom in this case, has the right of diplomatic protest on behalf of nationals arbitrarily expelled from another state and the right to protect such nationals. However, both the United Kingdom and the United Nations, while protesting, did little on behalf of the expelled Asians, and Uganda made an extensive argument for its right of domestic jurisdiction. The Organization of African Unity was more impressed with the domestic jurisdiction argument than with protection of the Asians' rights in an African state.

The Economic and Social Council did call for a study of rights of aliens in a resolution of May 18, 1973, and the Human Rights Sub-Commission appointed Special Rapporteur Baroness Elles to study the issue. Her final report was finished in 1976 and finally reached the General Assembly in 1980. In the meantime, much wrangling took place, but the expulsions and confiscations in Uganda became disgraceful pages on the downside of protection of human rights. On the upside was a United States embargo against Ugandan coffee instituted by Congress on October 10, 1978. This was followed with an intervention by Tanzanian troops in March 1979, a new government in Kampala, Uganda, on April 13, 1979, and the rapid departure of General Amin, eventually to asylum in Saudi Arabia.

The report and recommendations of Baroness Elles did lead to the appointment by the General Assembly in 1980 of a Working Group on rights of aliens. After five years of further study and negotiation, the General Assembly approved the 1985 Declaration of the Rights of Non-Nationals, or aliens, cited above. All the events of this case study suggest an unacceptable period of time for IHRL to respond to the 1972 Amin expulsions and the Amin regime which led to over 300,000 deaths attributable to his murderous tenure of office. However, it does reflect the weakness of IHRL in dealing with expulsions and other human rights violations that are protected in part by the domestic jurisdiction provision #2-7 of the UN Charter and the lack of even declaratory authority of the UN in areas jealously guarded by sovereign states. The 1985 Declaration remedies this in part. Events of the last fifteen years have also largely eroded "domestic jurisdiction" as against a state's claim of immunity to violations and the protection of human rights.

V. Cross References. Asylum, Discrimination, and Property (Civil and Political Rights); Due Process, Equal Protection of the Law, and Person before the Law (Legal Rights); Migrant Workers, Minorities, Refugees, and Stateless (Collective Rights); and Indigenous Peoples (Declaratory Rights).

Apartheid

I. The Right. Inhuman acts committed for the purpose of establishing and maintaining domination by one racial group of persons over another racial group of persons and systematically oppressing them. International Convention on the Suppression and Punishment of the Crime of Apartheid (1973), Article II.

II. Other Sources. Convention on the Prevention and Punishment of the Crime of Genocide (1948); International Convention on the Elimination of All Forms of Racial Discrimination (1965), Preamble & #3; Convention on the Non-Applicability of Statue of Limitations on War Crimes and Crimes Against Humanity (1968); Convention on the Elimination of Apartheid in Sports (1985).

Lusaka Manifesto on Southern Africa (1969); Dec Social Progress, #2-a; UN Commission on Human Rights Sub-Commission Resolution 1 (XXIV) on Implementation of Economic and Social Council Resolution 1503 (on communications procedure), #1-b; Charter of Economic Rights and Duties (1974), #16-1; Universal Declaration on the Eradication of Hunger and Malnutrition, Preamble-c (1974); Declaration on Fundamental Principles of Mass Media, UNESCO (1978), Preamble & #1; Declaration on Race and Racial Prejudice, UNESCO (1978), #1-2, #4-2, #6-2, #10.

III. Expanded Definition. As an extreme form of racism, apartheid (Afrikaner for "apartness") includes in the definition in #II of the Apartheid Convention (in part) inhuman acts of (1) denial to a member or members of a racial group or groups the right of life and liberty of person; (2) deliberate imposition on a racial group or groups of destruction in whole or in part; (3) legislative measures or other measures calculated to prevent a racial group from participation in the active life of a country and to deny any group basic human rights and freedoms; (4) measures, especially legislative, designed to divide the population along racial lines; (5) exploitation of labor of members of the group; and (6) persecution of organizations and persons denying them fundamental rights and freedoms because they oppose apartheid. Under Article I of the Convention, apartheid is a "crime against humanity" and a "serious threat to international peace and security . . ." Under Article III, international criminal responsibility "shall apply" to perpetrators of apartheid.

IV. Landmarks. The indigenous Bantu peoples met Dutch traders settling the Cape area of Southern Africa early in the seventeenth century. England annexed the territory in 1806, and South Africa was progressively settled in the nineteenth century. England and the Dutch (Afrikaners) fought the intense Boer War, 1899–1902, with England gaining victory and establishing the Union of South Africa in 1910. Laws for progressive and harsh racial segregation were passed, beginning in 1911 and continuing with severity in scope and punishment. The Afrikanar Nationalist Party was elected in 1948 and immediately accelerated the pace of segregation legislation for apartheid. The United Nations General Assembly protested apartheid in a series of resolutions with emphasis on denial of human rights for the non-white population of South Africa which exceeded the white Afrikaner and British by a ratio of 5 to 1.

A major massacre of blacks by Union troops at Sharpeville in March 1960 led to the Security Council condemnation of the violence as endangering international peace and security. The Union withdrew from the British Commonwealth and became the Republic of South Africa. Progressive crises and the Republic's acceleration of racist measures led to the Security Council's call for a mandatory arms embargo on the Republic in 1963.

The United Nations Commission on Human Rights and other UN organs repeatedly passed resolutions condemning apartheid, and the Republic was banned from representation in the General Assembly. International outrage over the Republic's arrest of African National Congress leader Nelson Mandela in 1963 and his protracted imprisonment led to continuing General Assembly and Security Council condemnations and international isolation of the Republic. The United Kingdom and the United States continued flourishing economic relations with the Republic throughout the 1960s and 1970s. Finally, protests from other governments, many nongovernmental organizations, corporations, universities, and others demanded increased measures and pressures against apartheid.

Key Security Council resolutions followed. Council Resolution 418 of November 4, 1977, under Chapter VII of the UN Charter unanimously imposed a mandatory embargo on military and nuclear collaboration with the Republic. Resolution 418 was reaffirmed and strengthened by Resolution 558 of December 13, 1984, and Resolution 591 of November 28, 1986. The United Kingdom and the United States, however, consistently opposed strong economic sanctions.

Over President Ronald Reagan's veto of congressional legislation, the United States finally launched its Comprehensive Anti-Apartheid Act of 1986 with substantial economic sanctions, and many Western corporations progressively divested their holdings in the Republic. Following massive strikes, Frederik W. de Klerk was elected President of the Republic on August 14, 1989. He immediately began the dismantlement of apartheid and released Mandela in February 1990. A broadly democratic constitution was written by representatives from the major parties in 1992 and 1993, which included a Charter on Rights of South Africans. The national elections in April 1994 elevated Mandela to the presidency and de Klerk became Vice President. Both de Klerk and Mandela were awarded the 1993 Nobel Peace Prize. Apartheid is now history in the Republic of South Africa, but its crushing impact on generations of South Africans must not be forgotten: its manifestation in any form must be prosecuted with the instruments of IHRL.

V. Cross References. Discrimination and Life (Civil and Political Rights). Practically all other human rights were denied to most Republic of South Africa non-whites. See Reports of the eighteen-member Special Committee Against Apartheid, established by the General Assembly in 1962 and responsible for the review of apartheid practices and for annual reports to General Assembly and Security Council. *See also* Reports of "Group of Three" appointed by the Chair, UN Commission on Human Rights, under #IX of Convention Against Apartheid to receive reports from States Parties on implementation of Convention. *See also* annual resolutions on apartheid by the General Assembly as well as Security Council resolutions on condemnations and sanctions with respect to apartheid. *See UN Action,* pp. 170–92.

Genocide

I. The Right. The Contracting Parties confirm that genocide, whether committed in time of peace or in time of war, is a crime under international law which they undertake to prevent and to punish. Convention on the Prevention and Punishment of the Crime of Genocide, Article I.

II. Other Sources. ICPR, #6-3; Convention on the Non-Applicability of Statuatory Limitations to War Crimes and Crimes Against Humanity (1968), #1.

Advisory Opinion on Reservations to the Convention on the Prevention and Punishment of the Crime of Genocide, 1951, International Court of Justice.

General Assembly Resolution on War Crimes, December 3, 1973; Declaration on Race and Racial Prejudice, UNESCO (1978), 34-2, 10; ISLAM (1990), #2-b.

III. Expanded Definition. Genocide is from "genus" (group) and "caedre" (to kill) and is a term coined by Professor Raphael Lemkin in 1944.

In the present Convention, genocide means any of the following acts committed with intent to destroy, in whole or in part, a national, ethnic, racial or religious group, as such: (a) Killing members of the group; (b) Causing serious bodily or mental harm to members of the group; (c) Deliberately inflicting on the group conditions of life calculated to bring about its physical destruction in whole or in part; (d) Imposing measures intended to prevent births within the group; (e) Forcibly transferring children of the group to another group. Article II, Genocide Convention. The following acts shall be punishable: (a) Genocide; (b) Conspiracy to commit genocide; (c) Direct and public incitement to commit genocide; (d) Attempt to commit genocide; (e) Complicity in genocide. Article III, Genocide Convention.

IV. Landmarks. The crime of genocide as defined in the Convention on Genocide has been committed by officials of political communities and states throughout history. The measures taken by Spain and other nations in North and South America against the indigenous populations from 1492 onward, slavery and the slave trade, countless massacres, the extermination of over one million Armenians by the Ottoman Empire from 1915 to 1918, Stalin's condemnation of millions of kulaks to death in the 1930s, and the horrors of the Nazi Holocaust are red pages on man's inhumanity to man in the books of history.

Raphael Lemkin survived the Holocaust, which destroyed about fifty members of his family, by fleeing his native Poland and gaining asylum in the United States. A legal scholar, he became a member of the law faculties of Duke and Yale Universities and authored a remarkable book, *Axis Rule in Occupied Europe* (New York: Carnegie Endowment for International Peace, 1944), in which he coined the word "genocide."

The Nuremberg War Crimes Trial of Nazi perpetrators produced abundant evidence of genocidal crimes. The trial concluded in September 1946 with the conviction of the leading Nazi officials for crimes of war, crimes against the peace, and crimes against humanity. In a resolution of December 11, 1946, the General Assembly affirmed the principles of international law recognized by the Charter of the Nuremberg Tribunal. The Assembly called for the codification "of the principles recognized in the Charter of the Nuremberg Tribunal and in the judgment of the Tribunal."

In a second resolution on the same day, the Assembly affirmed that "genocide is a denial of the right of existence of entire human groups, as homicide is the denial of the right to live of individual human beings . . ." The Assembly affirmed that "genocide is a crime under international law which the civilized world condemns . . ." and called on the Economic and Social Council to draft a convention for the prevention and punishment of the crime of genocide. The International Law Commission of the United Nations began drafts on codification of a treaty on genocide for which Professor Lemkin lobbied with great zeal at the United Nations. Fluent in eleven languages, Professor Lemkin without doubt was the most influential person in gaining an international treaty on genocide.

The Economic and Social Council drafted a brief convention on genocide on August 26, 1948, and forwarded it to the General Assembly. The draft was examined and approved by the Assembly's Fifth Committee (Legal) in the fall of 1948 and was approved by the General Assembly on December 9, 1948. The Genocide Convention went into force on January 12, 1951.

It took many years for the United States to ratify the Genocide Convention. The United States signed the Convention on December 11, 1948, and President Truman sent it to the Senate for advice and consent on June 16, 1949. The Convention was held up in the Senate for thirty-seven years until that body finally gave it its constitutional advice and consent on February 19, 1986. It took another two years for Congress to pass legislation implementing and incorporating the Convention into the national law of the United States. President Reagan formally ratified the Convention on November 4, 1988, when he signed the Genocide Implementation Act of 1987. About 110 states today have ratified or acceded to the Genocide Convention.

Although hundreds of genocidal acts have been policy instruments of states and others against national, ethnical, racial, and religious groups since 1951, the Genocide Convention has never been applied in any trial or punishment of any state official or other person or group. The crime of genocide is included in the list of crimes allegedly committed in former Yugoslavia in Security Council Resolution 808 of February 22, 1993, and the Secretary General's report on the implementation of the Council's resolution of May 3, 1993. In October 1994, genocide was also ascribed to crimes against humanity in Rwanda. The crime of genocide is among the crimes in the case of *Jane Doe I and II, Plaintiffs v. Radovan Karadzic, Defendant,* U.S. District Court, Southern District of New York, February 11, 1993.

V. Cross References. Life (Civil and Political Rights); Death Penalty, Due Process, Equal Protection of the Law, Security of Person, and Torture (Legal Rights); and Apartheid and Slavery (Collective Rights).

See also Annual Reports, Working Group, Enforced or Involuntary

Disappearances; Special Rapporteur on Torture; Special Rapporteur on Summary and Arbitrary Executions, Commission on Human Rights.

Migrant Workers

I. The Right. The term "migrant worker" refers to a person who is to be engaged, is engaged, or has been engaged in a remunerated activity in a state of which he or she is not a national. International Convention on the Protection of the Rights of All Migrant Workers and Their Families, 1990, Article 2, Paragraph 1. The present Convention is applicable to all migrant workers without distinction of any kind (#1-1). The present Convention shall apply during the entire migration process of migrant workers and members of their families, which comprises preparation for migration, departure, transit, and the entire period of stay and remunerated activity in the state of employment as well as return to the state of origin or the state of habitual residence (#1-2).

II. Other Sources. International Labor Conventions: No. 97, Migration for Employment; No. 143, Migrations in Abusive Conditions and the Promotion of Equality of Opportunity and Treatment of Migrant Workers, 1975; No. 29, Convention on Forced Labor; and No. 105, Convention on the Abolition of Forced Labor. Also, Recommendations concerning Migration for Employment, No. 86, and Recommendation on Migrant Workers, No. 151.

Dec Social Progress, #19-c; Dec on Non-Nationals; European Social Charter, #18 & #19.

"Migrant Women," Forward-Looking Strategies, #m, Nairobi World Conference on Women, 1985.

III. Expanded Definition. The Migrant Workers' Convention includes definitions of specific terms. Article 2-2 defines categories of migrant workers including (a) frontier worker; (b) seasonal worker; (c) seafarer worker; (d) worker on offshore installation; (e) itinerant worker; (f) project worker; (g) specified-employment worker; and (h) self-employed worker. Article 4 defines "members of the family." Part III includes articles on human rights for all migrant workers and their families including due process (#18, 19, 20). Part IV contains other rights for documented workers. The 1990 Convention elaborates on rights for migrant workers who are also protected along with workers in other conventions such as ICPR, ESCR, and in United Nations' Conventions on Racism, Women, and the Child.

IV. Landmarks. Humans have always migrated, usually in search of better sustenance, living conditions, and gainful employment, and also to depart from harsh conditions and threats to their security and well-being. Ancient migrations in Africa and Asia, migrations to the Western Hemisphere beginning over 20,000 years ago, and migratory patterns throughout history gradually led to more permanent settlements and the formation of political communities and to states over the past 400 years. Migrations have continued for various reasons, especially due to masses of people fleeing areas of war and civil strife. In the early and mid-1990s, the world witnessed the migration tragedies in Rwanda, Haiti, Cambodia, and former Yugoslavia.

Migratory workers and their families have sought employment and better living conditions in other states for centuries. However, it was not until the post–World War II period that the demands for workers to meet the needs of industrial recovery and expansion in Western Europe led to migrations of workers to the thriving industrial centers. Many industrial states were signatories to ILO conventions on migration for employment. However, non-national workers were often subjected to broader violations of human rights, which resulted in United Nations concern for the security and well-being of the migrants.

Documented mistreatment, exploitation, illicit trafficking, and other abuses of migrants and their families in Europe, Africa, and Asia led to the Economic and Social Council action in 1972 seeking protection of migrants and an attack on adverse conditions affecting their right to seek employment in other states. The Council and the UN Commission on Human Rights Sub-Commission, in a series of resolutions and studies, called for states to ratify and implement ILO conventions on migrant workers and to negotiate a convention on rights of migrant workers. Although it took many years due to the complexities of legal issues on migrant workers, the Convention was finally completed and opened for signature and ratification by states in 1990.

V. Cross References. Child, Discrimination, Territory, Movement in, Nationality, Property, and Women (Civil and Political Rights); Due Process and Torture (Legal Rights); Family, Standard of Living, and entries for Work (Economic, Social, and Cultural Rights); Aliens,

Refugees, Stateless, and Slavery (Collective Rights); and Indigenous Peoples (Declaratory Rights).

Minorities

I. The Right. In those states in which ethnic, religious, or linguistic minorities exist, persons belonging to such minorities shall not be denied the right, in community with other members of their group, to enjoy their own culture, to profess and practice their own religion, or to use their own language. Covenant on Civil and Political Rights, Article 27.

II. Other Sources. Declaration of the Principles of International Cultural Cooperation, UNESCO (1966); Declaration on the Rights of Persons Belonging to National or Ethnic, Religious, and Linguistic Minorities (approved by the Commission on Human Rights, 1992).

Sub-Commission on Prevention of Discrimination and Protection of Minorities of the UN Commission on Human Rights.

III. Expanded Definition. A minority is a collectivity of people in a state sharing a common characteristic, usually one of nationality, religion, ethnicity, language, or other identifiable property. The United Nations' organs which have devoted decades of negotiation on a draft for minority rights have been in continuous disagreement on the definition of a minority. However, the UN Sub-Commission on the Prevention of Discrimination and Protection of Minorities did provisionally decide in 1954 that for the purpose of a study, a minority would include "only those non-dominant groups in a population which possess and wish to preserve ethnic, religious, or linguistic traditions or characteristics markedly different from those of the rest of the population" (Sub-Commission, Sixth Session, 1954, Resolution F). The Draft Declaration on Minorities (*see* above) has been delayed for many years, in part over the inability of states to agree on a definition of a minority.

IV. Landmarks. Political communities have always had within their jurisdictions people who are not full members of the community (including nationality and citizenship) and who possess common characteristics that differ in various ways from the mainstream body politic. Often, minority groups presented threats to the security and well-being of the political community and were subjected to persecution and/or banishment. That condition persists today.

In the vast range of history, minorities have played important roles and have in many instances become majorities. A significant minority presence in a political community over history has been the religious minority, often persecuted by the governance, especially when the governance is identified with a state religion. This mold was broken in part with very modest religious minority rights guaranteed in the Treaty of Augsburg of 1555 and later in the Peace of Westphalia of 1648 (*see* Religion, Civil and Political Rights).

In Africa, Asia, and other parts of the world, each political community and, later, colony had to deal with its own minority configuration. The ethnic structure of African communities was (and is) particularly complex, and each society had to determine how to relate to both the minority groups and dominant governance. As democratic governance evolved in the eighteenth and nineteenth centuries in Europe and North America in particular, human rights came to include rights for members of minorities as individuals but not for minorities as groups of people. The latter category was often viewed as a challenge to the authority of the dominant governance. However, each government developed its own minority policy in many areas such as worship, education, commerce, housing, leisure, and political participation.

The minority issue gained international prominence at the peace negotiations after World War I. United States President Woodrow Wilson had proclaimed a doctrine of national self-determination in 1918 which was designed to facilitate the creation of new states from the territories of defeated powers, especially Austria-Hungary and the Ottoman Empire. Among these, Poland, Czechoslovakia, and Yugoslavia had significant minority populations, thus presenting the problem as to the rights of minorities in the new states. This was particularly the case with many Germans who lost their citizenship with the territorial deprivations of the former German Empire.

The issue was debated and resolved in part with the inclusion of Articles 86 and 93 in the 1919 Treaty of Versailles, which provided for the protection of minorities in the new states. Poland and the other states committed themselves to give all rights as were enjoyed by Polish citizens to the minorities and to engage in no discrimination against them. The impressive German-Polish Convention on Upper Silesia of 1922 guaranteed to Polish minorities the right to life, liberty, free exercise of religion, and equal treatment before the law. In this treaty, the rights of Polish nationals in Upper Silesia were the first guarantees by treaty of the enjoyment and protection of human rights of individuals. Peace treaties for Austria, Bulgaria, Czechoslovakia, Greece, Hungary, Romania, and Turkey provided for protection of minorities.

The treaties compelled the signatories to agree that the League of Nations should be authorized to guarantee minority rights. The Council of the League established a Minorities Committee to which states were obliged to submit reports on treatment of minorities in their jurisdictions along with other information. Minorities were also entitled to report to the Committee and to send petitions of complaints with respect to alleged violations of their rights. This pioneering human rights procedure for due process of the law gained momentum in the 1920s but unravelled in the 1930s as nations moved toward war.

It is most significant to observe that the treaty, as the prime source of international law, became the principle mechanism for the first commitment to and guarantee of protection of international human rights by the designated states. The League was the international legal authority designated to manage the protection and enhancement procedures for the protection of the rights of humans.

Provisions against discrimination are abundant in the 1945 United Nations Charter and the 1948 Universal Declaration of Human Rights. However, neither the Charter nor the Declaration mention minorities as such because of substantial disagreement on the definition of a minority. Some states pressed hard for inclusion of minority rights, while others felt that a specific definition might create an entity within the state claiming more rights—especially political—than the state wished to accept, let alone guarantee. The debate over what became Article 27 in the ICPR was extensive in the years before its inclusion when the ICPR was adopted in 1966. Much remains to be done to advance minority rights in IHRL.

V. Cross References. Association, Asylum, Territory, Movement in, Nationality, and Religion (Civil and Political Rights); Due Process, Equal Protection of the Law, Person before the Law, and Security of Person (Legal Rights); Culture, Education, Family, and entries for Work (Economic, Social, and Cultural Rights); Aliens, Migrant Workers, Refugees, and Stateless (Collective Rights); and Indigenous Peoples (Declaratory Rights).

Refugees

I. The Right. The term "refugee" shall apply to any person who "as a result of events occurring before January 1, 1951, and owing to well-founded fear of being persecuted for reasons of race, religion, nationality, membership of a particular social group, or political opinion, is outside the country of his or her nationality and is unable, or owing to such fear, is unwilling to avail himself or herself of the protection of that country; or, who, not having a nationality and being outside the country of his or her former habitual residence as a result of such events, is unable or, owing to such fear, is unwilling to return to it. Convention Relating to the Status of Refugees, 1951, Article 1, paragraph A-2. (Note: The 1967 Protocol Relating to the Status of Refugees extended the application of the Convention to the situation of "new refugees" or persons who, while meeting the Convention definition, had become refugees as the result of events that took place after January 1, 1951. Also, see below on the addition of "internally displaced persons" as qualifying as "refugees").

The Organization on African Unity Convention on Refugees (1969) defines the refugee in #1-2 as "every person who, owing to external aggression, occupation, foreign domination, or events seriously disturbing public order in either part or the whole of his [or her] country of origin or nationality, is compelled to leave his [or her] place of habitual residence in order to seek refuge in another place outside his [or her] country of origin or nationality."

II. Other Sources. In addition to the 1951 Convention and the 1967 Protocol is the Statute of the Office of the United Nations High Commissioner for Refugees, 1950. *See also* the Organization on African Unity Convention on Refugees, 1969, and the Council of Europe agreements on refugees. Article 44 of the 1949 Fourth Geneva Convention Relative to the Protection of Civilian Persons in Time of War and #73 of the 1977 Additional Protocol provide for protection of refugees and stateless persons. *See also* Annual Reports, United Nations Relief and Works Agency for Palestine Refugees in the Near East (established by General Assembly in 1949 for relief, education, training, health, and other services for Arab refugees from Palestine).

UNDR, #14; The Cartagena Declaration on Refugees (Inter-America, 1984); and International Conference on Central American Refugees (CIREFCA, 1989).

III. Extended Definition. The 1951 Convention includes the above definition of a refugee as well as definitions of refugees under previous "Arrangements" under the League of Nations, the Conventions of 1933 and 1938, the Protocol of 1939, and the Constitution of the post–World War II International Refugee Organization (1946–1951). Article 1 (C, D, E, and F) of the 1951 Convention sets forth provisions and conditions of nonapplicability to people for refugee status.

The 1951 Convention includes specific rights for refugees which affirm their protection under ICPR and ESCR. The basic rights of refugees include registration, assistance for basic human needs, protection in the state of refuge, opportunity to return to the home state if possible, and settlement in state of refugee if possible and/or repatriation to a third state. Under #33-1 of the Convention, "no Contracting State shall expel or return ("refouler") a refugee in any manner whatsoever to the frontiers of territories where his [or her] life or freedom would be threatened on account of his [or her] race, religion, nationality, membership of a particular social group, or political opinion."

Perhaps the most difficult problem in the definition of a refugee is whether the person left his/her home state because of fear of persecution on the grounds specified in #1-A-2 of the Convention or whether the person is in reality an economic migrant. An economic category is not included in the legal definition. However, many people seek refuge in another state because of economic deprivation in their home state and then claim other legal grounds for seeking official refugee status.

Another major problem is the legal status of the internally displaced person. There is no legal definition of such a person, although a resolution of the Commission on Human Rights of March 5, 1991, states that internally displaced persons are people "who have been forced to flee their homes and seek shelter and safety in other parts of their own country."

Further, the burden placed on the country of refuge for large numbers of refugees has often reduced the capacity of those states and the UN High Commissioner for Refugees and the Commissioner's staff to provide legal rights and protection for refugees. The receiving state itself is protected by its right of derogation on the grounds of national security, public order, and other conditions as set forth in the ICPR with respect to many rights. (*see* E,"Limitations on Rights" in part 2, Issues and Contexts).

It was estimated in the 1991 Cuenod Report (*see* Cross References) that there are about 17,000,000 legal refugees and about 24,000,000 internally displaced persons. These numbers have substantially grown in the succeeding years. The principal causes of people seeking refuge, as well as of mass exoduses and migrations, are constant persecution and violations of human rights in the home state, armed conflict and internal strife, forced relocation, and natural disasters.

IV. Landmarks. People have sought refuge in lands other than their own for many reasons, even before political communities evolved over 7,000 years ago. The English settling in Virginia and New England early in the seventeenth century were refugees, as were the millions who sought and gained new homes in North America and many other nations in the hundreds of years since the 1600s.

It was not until after World War I that "international refugees" became a concern to the international legal community, particularly to the new League of Nations. The League established the Office of the High Commissioner for Refugees in 1921, largely to respond to the millions of people, especially Russians, who were seeking refuge from persecution in their native lands and were flooding into other states. Dr. Fridtjof Nansen of Norway was appointed High Commissioner and immediately organized a small but dedicated staff to assist Russian refugees and those from Greece and Armenia fleeing Turkey in 1922.

A major contribution to the League's international protection of the refugee was the "Nansen Passport," which was a certification by the High Commissioner for legal entitlement by the refugee to cross national borders in flight from persecution and in search of a new home. The Nansen office provided modest support to people fleeing Nazi Germany, but limited political and financial support from the League prevented the Office from adequately meeting the many demands on it.

During World War II, the International Committee of the Red Cross provided considerable assistance and protection for many refugees. The United Nations Relief and Rehabilitation Organization (UNRRA) was established in 1943 to extend emergency relief for millions of war-torn refugees and displaced persons. The United Nations established the International Relief Organization in 1946 to meet the unprecedented postwar need for refugee protection and resettlement. However, the task grew to such proportions that a more extensive organizational structure was required, and the IRO was terminated on June 30, 1950. It was replaced by the Office of the United Nations High Commissioner, established by the General Assembly on December 3, 1949, with the Statute for the High Commissioner approved by the Assembly on December 14, 1950. The Office of the High Commissioner, under the aegis of the Assembly, serves refugee needs today as best it can with ever increasing demands under the 1951 Convention and the 1967 Protocol. The Office was awarded the Nobel Peace Prize in 1954 and 1981.

V. Cross References. Asylum, Life, Territory, Movement in, Name, Nationality, and Women (Civil and Political Rights); Detention, Due Process, Person before the Law, Security of Person (Legal Rights); Family (Economic, Social, and Cultural Rights); Aliens, Migrant Workers, and Slavery (Collective Rights); and Indigenous Persons (Declaratory Rights).

See also Annual Reports, United Nations High Commissioner for Refugees; "Human Rights and Massive Exoduses," Study by Special Rapporteur Sadruddin Aga Khan for Commission on Human Rights, March 3, 1982, and Report by Secretary General, "Massive Exoduses," with General Assembly Resolution, December 7, 1987; Study by Jacques Cuenod, "Refugees, Displaced Persons and Returnees," Economic and Social Council, 1991, with "Analytical Report of Secretary General on Internally Displaced Persons," Commission on Human Rights, February 14, 1992.

Peoples, Self-Determination

I. The Right. 1. All peoples have the right of self-determination. By virtue of that right, they freely determine their political status and freely pursue their economic, social, and cultural development.

3. The States Parties to the present Covenant, including those having responsibility for the administration of Non-Self-Governing and Trust Territories, shall promote the realization of the right of self-determination, and shall respect that right, in conformity with the provisions of the Charter of the United Nations. Covenant on Economic, Social, and Cultural Rights and Covenant on Civil and Political Rights, Article 1, paragraphs 1 and 3.

II. Other Sources. AFR, #20; United Nations Charter, #1-2 and #55; ISLAM, #11 b.

Declaration on Granting of Independence to Colonial Countries and Peoples, General Assembly, 1960; Declaration on Principles of International Law Concerning Friendly Relations and Cooperation Among States in Accordance with the Charter of the United Nations (The Principles of Equal Rights and Self-Determination of Peoples), General Assembly, 1970; Declaration on the Establishment of a New International

Economic Order, General Assembly, 1974; Charter of Economic Rights and Duties of States, General Assembly, 1974; Dec Social Progress, #3-a; Declaration on Race and Racial Prejudice, UNESCO, 1978, #3.

III. Expanded Definition. "Self-determination of peoples" entered international law with its incorporation in the United Nations Charter of June 26, 1945. In Landmarks, below, it is clear that "self-determination" has significant roots in the founding of states and the aspirations of peoples for national sovereignty. "Peoples," however, has always been an ambiguous term and remains so today, irrespective of "peoples right of self-determination" in the two prime United Nations treaties.

The intent of the inclusion of self-determination for peoples in the 1945 Charter, a proposal championed by the USSR, was to support the right of peoples under colonial authority to gain independence which was identified with "self-determination." However, the link between self-determination and a sovereign, independent state never has been clear. AFR, #20-1, does not clarify this important dilemma. It states that "all peoples shall have the right to existence. They shall have the unquestionable and inalienable right to self-determination. They shall freely determine their political status and shall pursue their economic and social development according to the policy they have freely chosen."

This is a provision in treaty law, but even treaty law includes some questionable rhetoric which lacks the clarity essential to law. One may question whether self-determination of peoples is an "inalienable right." However, the words of the United States Declaration of Independence cited below support #20 in AFR.

It can be argued that self-determination of peoples is actually "national self-determination" or the right of a people to declare and establish a sovereign nation-state. Once the state is established, the right of peoples within the state for self-determination is foreclosed. If not, the state itself will suffer constant fragmentation with constant demands by categories of peoples for their own self-determination.

This interpretation is in accord with the 1960 General Assembly Declaration on the Granting of Independence to Colonial Countries and Peoples cited in Other Sources. The Declaration hails peoples' right to self-determination in #2 and moves to independence in #3, 4, and 5. It then declares in #6 that "any attempt aimed at partial or total disruption of the national unity and territorial integrity of a country is incompatible with the purposes and principles of the Charter of the United Nations." As a member of the United Nations, the new nation now has sovereign equality with other nations, the right to political independence and territorial integrity, and is immune from intervention by the United Nations in its domestic jurisdiction (Article 2, paragraphs 1, 4, and 7, United Nations Charter). Article 73 of the UN Charter on Non-Self-Governing Territories makes no mention of self-determination of peoples and deals only with "self-government" in the area of political goals.

In brief, "self-determination of peoples" may be viewed as a proclaimed right of peoples to aspire to and achieve sovereign independence, join the United Nations, secure the rights and duties as members of the UN, and protect itself from claims by any category of peoples within the new state for their own self-determination if those claims aspire toward sovereign independence. However, minorities in the new state or in any state have specific rights under #27, ICPR, and under other international law protecting minority rights.

IV. Landmarks. Self-determination of peoples is the aspiration of a people for their own sovereign authority, free from control over them by others. The United States Declaration of Independence of July 4, 1776, is a supreme statement on this aspiration which begins with these stirring words: "When in the course of human events, it becomes necessary for one people to dissolve the political bands which have connected them with another, and to assume, among the powers of the earth, the separate and equal station to which the laws of nature and of nature's God entitle them . . ." The link between people and the identity of their nationality with the sovereign state is the heart of self-determination. The 1787 United States Constitution begins with "We the people . . ."

Goethe observed at the battle of Valmy of September 20, 1792, the dogged determination of the French soldiers fighting for the national pride of France and not for their deposed King Louis XVI; they managed to reach a standoff with the Prussian army. The great German poet, with an incisive sense of history, declared, "In this place and on this day there commences a new epoch in the history of the world." The new epoch was that of the nation-state.

The pageant of nationalism was vigorous in the nineteenth century and was usually linked with the belief that the national sovereign state would usher in self-determination for its peoples. The opposite was the case, of course, with the flourishing of imperialism and colonialism in this era, the antithesis of self-determination. President Woodrow Wilson preached the gospel of national self-determination in his famous "Fourteen Points" address of January 8, 1918. The final peace treaties of World

War I led to national self-determination and independence for Albania, Czechoslovakia, Estonia, Finland, Latvia, Lithuania, Poland, Romania, and Yugoslavia. The League of Nations Mandate system, which anticipated independence for at least some of these colonies under Article 22 of the League's Covenant, was established for colonies of enemy states in World War I. However, "self-determination" for the vast colonial domains in Africa and Asia was never contemplated in the 1919 Treaty of Versailles.

President Franklin D. Roosevelt assumed leadership for the cause of independence and self-determination with some ambiguity. The President and British Prime Minister Winston Churchill promised in their Atlantic Charter of August 14, 1941, that at the end of the war, there would be "no territorial changes without the freely expressed wishes of the people concerned" and that "they respect[ed] the right of all peoples to choose the form of government under which they will live . . ." The January 1, 1942, Declaration of the United Nations included a commitment by the twenty-six signatories to subscribe to the provisions of the Atlantic Charter. Prime Minister Churchill was quite specific about excluding colonial domains from any right to self-determination.

The 1944 Dumbarton Oaks Proposals, which became the draft for the 1945 United Nations Charter, made no mention of self-determination. However, at the San Francisco Conference, the Soviet Union pressed hard for self-determination of peoples which was incorporated in #1-2 and #55 of the Charter. Clearly, the USSR was championing the goals of colonial peoples, which were also on the agenda of President Roosevelt. However, the President died on April 12, 1945, thirteen days before the San Francisco Conference began, and with him, a strong United States policy on independence for most people then under colonial rule.

Self-determination is not in the Universal Declaration of Human Rights of December 10, 1948. In a resolution of December 4, 1950, however, the General Assembly recognized the right of peoples and nations to self-determination as a fundamental human right. The Assembly then declared on February 5, 1952, that the proposed covenants on human rights should contain an article affirming "the right of all peoples and nations to self-determination . . ." This was buttressed by an Assembly resolution on December 16, 1952, that "the right of peoples and nations to self-determination is a prerequisite to the full enjoyment of all fundamental human rights . . ." By 1955, self-determination of peoples (but not of nations) was confirmed as inclusion in a draft article for both of the emerging prime human rights covenants, with most of the Western states in opposition to the draft article. They were joined by Professor John Humphrey, Director of the UN Division of Human Rights, who considered the concept of self-determination to be a political goal rather than a legal right.

It was during this time frame that the march toward self-determination by peoples under Western colonial control accelerated their demands for state sovereignty. The nationalist leader of the British Gold Coast Colony, Kwame Nkrumah, proclaimed in a speech in the Gold Coast Legislative Assembly in 1953 that "the right of a people to decide their own destiny . . . was an inalienable right of peoples . . ." The Gold Coast, as Ghana, became the first post–World War II independent African state on March 6, 1957. Within a few short years, well over fifty former colonies and their peoples achieved self-determination and sovereign statehood. The Assembly as noted above adopted its historic Declaration on the Granting of Independence to Colonial Peoples and Nations on December 14, 1960. On November 27, 1961, the Assembly established the Special Committee on the Situation with Regard to the Implementation of the Declaration on Granting of Independence to Colonial Countries and Peoples which is now known as the Special Committee on Decolonization or the Committee of Twenty-four.

Self-determination of peoples was incorporated in #1-1 of both prime covenants when they were adopted by the General Assembly on December 16, 1966. In a resolution of November 22, 1988, the Assembly proclaimed the period 1990–2000 as the International Decade for the Eradication of Colonialism. The Assembly continues to call each year for the implementation of resolutions and decisions on the right of self-determination. In the 1995 annual report by the Committee of Twenty-four, self-determination for the remaining seventeen "colonial" territories was urged, although most of these territories, such as those under the United States and the British Virgin Islands, are hardly pressing for independence and the British possession of Pitcairn Island with its sixty-five people is hardly a solid candidate for sovereign independence. On the other hand, armed force in the cause of independence continues to be waged by East Timor from Indonesia and by the Polisario guerrillas against Morocco.

V. Cross References. Association, Nationality, and Political (Civil and Political Rights); Aliens, Minorities, and Peoples, Natural Resources (Collective Rights); and Development (Declaratory Rights).

See also United Nations Action, pp. 247–68.

Peoples, Natural Resources

I. The Right. All peoples may, for their own ends, freely dispose of their natural wealth and resources, without prejudice to any obligations arising out of international economic cooperation, based on the principle of mutual benefit, and international law. In no case may a people be deprived of its own means of subsistence. Covenant on Economic, Social, and Cultural Rights and Covenant on Civil and Political Rights, Article 1, paragraph 2.

II. Other Sources. AFR, #21;

ISLAM, #11-b; ASEAN, #3-2 and #3-3.

Declaration on the Granting of Independence to Colonial Countries and Peoples, General Assembly, 1960; Permanent Sovereignty over Natural Resources, General Assembly Resolution, 1962; Dec Social Progress, #3-d and #16; Declaration on the Establishment of a New International Economic Order, General Assembly, 1974; Programme of Action on the Establishment of a New International Economic Order, #7 (Assistance in the Exercise of Permanent Sovereignty over Natural Resources), General Assembly, 1974; and Charter of Economic Rights and Duties of States, General Assembly, 1974.

III. Expanded Definition. The right of peoples freely to dispose or to distribute their natural resources as they so determine is a declared right of sovereignty since control over natural resources is under the jurisdiction of the state. Therefore, it is a claim by the state over the possession, property, and/or control of such resources by any other state or by any external corporation or other foreign interest. The right, which is a major issue with many developing states, is well defined in Article 2 of the 1974 General Assembly Resolution, the Charter of Economic Rights and Duties of States. The Article declares that each state has authority over foreign investment and the activities of transnational corporations within its jurisdiction. It claims the right "to nationalize, expropriate, or transfer ownership of foreign property" with "appropriate compensation." If there is a question about compensation, the issue "shall be settled under the domestic law of the nationalizing State and by its tribunals" unless there are other peaceful means to settle the issue.

This right has presented a major problem to states which have substantial investments and property in developing states. Expropriation of foreign interests or property is a standard procedure in international law, provided there is adequate, fair, and prompt compensation by the nationalizing state (*see* Property, Civil and Political Rights). The right of use and disposal of natural resources is a political plank of developing states. They became particularly assertive at the time of the 1973–1974 oil crisis when the New International Economic Order was proclaimed along with the Charter of Economic Rights and Duties of States. Since that time, negotiations between the industrial and the developing states have led to negotiations for mutually satisfactory agreements and arrangements for industrialized state and transnational corporate activity in most developing states. Mutually beneficial economic relations have thus diluted the rather intimidating vocabulary of the mid-1970s General Assembly declarations. In brief, the right in #1-2 of both Covenants has not been pressed or implemented.

IV. Landmarks. Peoples' rights with respect to their natural resources was first stated in the 1960 General Assembly Declaration on Independence for Colonial Peoples. Paragraph 8 of the 1960 Declaration's Preamble is the same as the first sentence in ESCR and ICPR, #1-2. However, states which have hosted foreign investment, external ownership of property, and activity by international corporations have long sought to exercise authority over such entities if and when the host state has claimed exploitation by the external enterprises. The most common means of seeking control has been expropriation by the host state of the property or investments of the external enterprise, which has usually been accompanied by fair, prompt, and adequate compensation to the foreign state or corporation. The first six decades of the twentieth century witnessed extensive expropriations by host states of foreign ownership with appropriate compensation to the foreign enterprise. Mexico's expropirations in 1913, the Russian government's seizures after the 1917 Bolshevik Revolution, and the oil expropriations of the 1950s and 1960s were major structural changes in ownership of valued property and resources. Cuban expropriations after 1960, especially of United States enterprises, remain unresolved.

Peoples' rights to dispose freely of their natural wealth and resources go beyond expropriation. They include the demand by developing states to control in large part the international market conditions for the sale and distribution of such resources. In particular, they seek to influence the price and supply of natural resources to generate capital for their economic development. The substantial control by the oil producing states over the price and supply of oil during and after the Mideast crisis in 1973 became a model for the developing states to seek similar controls over their own natural resources.

The demands by the developing states for "peoples' rights" led to the 1974 General Assembly Declaration for a New International Economic Order. This Declaration and the accompanying 1974 Charter of Economic Rights and Duties of States do not have the standing of law. They served as the basis for global bargaining between the developing and the industrialized states during the remainder of the 1970s. Some agreements were reached on economic relations between the two blocs, especially under the aegis of the United Nations Conference on Trade and Development (UNCTAD). However, the central thrust of peoples' rights with respect to their natural resources is conducted under traditional procedures of international law and relations and is not viewed, in general, as an international human right.

V. Cross References. Political and Property (Civil and Political Rights); Peoples, Self-Determination (Collective Rights); and Development (Declaratory Rights).

Slavery

I. The Right. (1) No one shall be held in slavery; slavery and the slave trade in all their forms shall be prohibited. (2) No one shall be held in servitude. (3) (a) No one shall be required to perform forced or compulsory labor. (b) Exceptions to #8-3 (a). Covenant on Civil and Political Rights, Article 8, paragraphs 1, 2, and 3.

II. Other Sources. Convention on Slavery, 1926; Protocol on the Slavery Convention, 1953; and the Supplementary Convention on the Abolition of Slavery, the Slave Trade, and Institutions and Practices Similar to Slavery, 1956.

ECR, #4; ACR, #6; AFR, #5; Genocide Convention; Convention for the Suppression of the Traffic in Persons and of the Exploitation of the Prostitution of Others, 1949; Convention on Apartheid, #II-e; Convention on Women, #6; Convention on Child, #19, 32, 34, 35, and 36; International Labor Conventions on Forced Labor, 1930 (No. 29) and 1956 (No. 105).

UDHR, #4; Reports and Studies, Working Group on Contemporary Forms of Slavery, Subcommission, UN Commission on Human Rights, and reports, Special Rapporteur on the Child (sale, prostitution, pornography, etc.), Subcommission, UN Commission on Human Rights.

III. Expanded Definition. Article 1 of the 1926 Convention on Slavery includes the following definitions of slavery and the slave trade:

Slavery is the status or condition of a person over whom any or all of the powers attaching to the right of ownership are exercised.

The slave trade includes all acts involved in the capture, acquisition, or disposal of a person with intent to reduce him to slavery; all acts involved in the acquisition of a slave with a view to selling or exchanging him; all acts of disposal by sale or exchange of a slave acquired with a view to being sold or exchanged, and, in general, every act of trade or transport in slaves.

The word "slavery" today covers a wide variety of human rights violations. In addition to traditional slavery and the slave trade, these abuses include the sale of children, child prostitution, child pornography, the exploitation of child labor, the sexual mutilation of female children, the use of children in armed conflicts, debt bondage, the traffic in persons and the sale of human organs, adult prostitution, and certain practices under apartheid and colonial regimes ("Contemporary Forms of Slavery," UN Centre for Human Rights, 1991).

Clearly, the definition of slavery has broadened considerably since the 1926 League of Nations Convention to include "Institutions and Practices Similar to Slavery" in the title of the 1956 Supplementary Convention. Abuses to children, in particular, are the most extensive increases in the crime of slavery. The ILO recently estimated that over 100 million children are the victims of labor exploitation.

IV. Landmarks. Slavery has existed throughout history and continues today in many and varied forms. "Everyone was born free under the law of nature," wrote the great Roman jurist Ulpian (d. 226 A.D.), but the Jus Gentium, or law of Rome, held just the opposite. Slavery rose to new heights after the sixteenth century with the importation into the Western Hemisphere of millions of Africans who provided enormous economic return to the slave traders and slave owners in the Hemisphere. The gross exploitation and degradation of humans called slaves can never be measured.

In England, the Anti-Slavery Committee, formed in 1787, was probably the first nongovernmental organization in the cause of human rights. Beginning in 1789 the Committee's leader, William Wilberforce (1759–1833), introduced legislative proposals in the House of Commons which demanded the abolishment of the slave trade. Although concerted opposition on economic grounds slammed the door on ending the trade,

Wilberforce and his associates had a major influence on public opinion. England followed Denmark's 1792 lead in banning the slave trade with its own act outlawing slave trading in 1808. The antislavery movement also won the endorsement of Viscount Castlereagh (1769–1822), who took up the banner against slavery.

At the Congress of Vienna in 1814 and 1815, Castlereagh pressed hard for agreement among the great powers to end slave trading. In spite of his intensive lobbying, Castlereagh gained only a weak declaration at Vienna which called for "prompt suppression" of the trade but left it to each nation to make its own determination for "the definitive abolition of Slave Trade." Nevertheless, nations progressively banned slave trading in the years after 1815 and then slavery as well, with England taking the lead in 1833. The United States Constitution outlawed slavery in the 1865 Thirteenth Amendment after a long war fought in large part over the institution of slavery in the Southern states.

International momentum for outlawing slave trading accelerated with the 1885 Congress of Berlin's General Act declaring "trading in slavery" to be "forbidden in conformity with the principles of international law." The Act, indeed, was one of the first international legal measures condemning a violation of human rights. Berlin was followed by the General Act of the Brussels Conference of 1889–1890, which confirmed the outlawing of slave trading and the Treaty of Saint-Germain-en-Laye of 1919, which revised and expanded the Brussels Act.

The League of Nations Council established the Temporary Slavery Commission in 1924, which negotiated the League's Slavery Convention of 1926. This remains the basic treaty outlawing slavery and the slave trade. The League then constituted a Committee on Slavery which had authority to review and report on continued practices. In 1953 the United Nations became the successor to the League in the implementation of the 1926 Convention. It then negotiated the 1956 Supplementary Convention on Slavery and Institutions and Practices Similar to Slavery which substantially broadened the scope of human rights abuses associated with enslavement. The UN Commission on Human Rights and its Subcommission were delegated authority to continue international action in all areas of slavery including monitoring practices, reports, studies, and implementation of treaties and provisions in United Nations covenants and conventions on slavery.

V. Cross References. Child, Life, Property, and Women (Civil and Political Rights); Due Process, Person before the Law, and Security of Person (Legal Rights); Family and Work, Conditions (Economic, Social, and Cultural Rights); and Apartheid and Genocide (Collective Rights).

See also the activities of the World Health Organization, UNESCO, UNICEF, the Food and Agricultural Organization, the UN High Commissioner for Refugees, and the Commission on the Status of Women among other organizations for their contributions to ending human rights abuses associated with slavery, especially those affecting children.

Stateless

I. The Right. Every stateless person has duties to the country in which he or she finds himself or herself, which require in particular that he or she conform to its laws and regulations as well as to measures taken for the maintenance of public order.

II. Other Sources. Convention on the Reduction of Statelessness, 1961; Convention on the Taking of Hostages (1979), #5-1 (b).

III. Expanded Definition. For the purpose of this Convention [The Status of Stateless Persons], the term "stateless person" means a person who is not considered to be a national by any state under the operation of its law (#1-1). Article 1-2 sets forth conditions of persons to whom the Convention does not apply. Refugees may include stateless persons. However, the legal definition of the refugee excludes many stateless persons who do not qualify as refugees (Refugees, Collective Rights). A de jure stateless person is fairly rare.

The Convention on the Status of Stateless Persons does not provide for rights of such persons but rather for protection, treatment, and other means of stability for the stateless person. Only thirty-seven states have ratified the Convention. The Convention on the Reduction of Statelessness is largely designed to harmonize nationality laws of states, including those for stateless persons. Only fifteen states have ratified this convention.

IV. Landmarks. Landmarks for Refugees (Collective Rights) have many parallels to the problems of stateless persons. After the Bolshevik Revolution of 1917 millions of Russians were stripped of their citizenship and became refugees, later under the protection of the League of Nations. The German Nazi regime likewise washed away the citizenship of millions, who in time became refugees or "Displaced Persons."

In defining the legal status of a refugee the Convention on Refugees of 1951 did not include any provisions for a person who did not have or never had a legal title to a nationality or citizenship. The 1954 United Nations Conference on the Status of Stateless Persons developed the Convention on Stateless Persons, which, along with the Convention on the Reduction of Statelessness, has not enjoyed wide popularity among the world's states. This reflects a desire by most states to exercise sovereign control over stateless people in their jurisdictions.

V. Cross References. Asylum, Dignity, Life, and Territory, Movement in (Civil and Political Rights); Due Process and Security of Person (Legal Rights); Aliens, Apartheid, Migrant Workers, and Refugees (Collective Rights); and Indigenous Peoples (Declaratory Rights).

V

Declaratory Rights

Introduction

International human rights law, with respect to declaratory rights, is concerned with rights that are expressed in declarations and resolutions of the General Assembly and by authoritative organs of other major international organizations. These are rights that are declared but are not law. An exception in the rights in part 5 is the Assembly's 1989 Convention on Mercenaries. This Convention is clearly a treaty but has not attracted sufficient ratifications by the required number of states to have the authority of treaty law.

Most of the international human rights treaties emerged from declarations, including the Universal Declaration of Human Rights. A declaration is usually a necessary step toward a right or set of rights becoming treaty law. A declaration is the result of considerable political negotiation in the General Assembly or other organ and is adopted by a majority vote of states. The declaration then serves as the basic draft for further negotiation for a treaty on a human right or rights.

Some declarations on human rights may succeed in securing a majority of votes in the Assembly or other organ but may fail to gain the support of a significant number of states. Some states may be opposed for one reason or another to viewing the declaration as a statement of a human right and therefore to elevating the right or rights to the status of international law. Such is the case with the 1986 Assembly's Declaration on the Right to Development. Most industrial states do not consider development as a legal human right. Others may oppose declarations of some rights on the grounds that the inventory of legal human rights is extensive and that priority should be given to their implementation before more rights are added to the agenda of IHRL.

Development

I. The Right. All peoples shall have the right to their economic, social, and cultural development with due regard for their freedom and identity and in the enjoyment of the common heritage of mankind. States shall have the duty, individually and collectively, to ensure the exercise of the right to development. African Charter on Human and Peoples' Rights, Article 22.

II. Other Sources. Declaration on the Right to Development, General Assembly Resolution 41/128, December 4, 1986.

III. Expanded Definition. Development is a comprehensive economic, social, cultural, and political process, which aims at the constant improvement of the well-being of the entire population and of all individuals on the basis of their active, free, and meaningful participation in development and in the fair distribution of benefits resulting therefrom. Preamble, Declaration on the Right to Development.

The right to development is an inalienable human right by virtue of which every human person and all peoples are entitled to participate in, contribute to, and enjoy economic, social, cultural, and political development, in which all human rights and fundamental freedoms can be fully realized.

The human right to development also implies the full realization of the right of peoples to self-determination, which includes, subject to the relevant provisions of both International Covenants on Human Rights, the exercise of their inalienable right to full sovereignty over all their natural wealth and resources. Article 1, Declaration on Development, General Assembly, December 4, 1986.

The human person is the central subject of development and should be the active participant and beneficiary of the right to development. Declaration on Development, #2-1.

Development should be understood as a process designed progressively to create conditions in which every person can enjoy, exercise, and utilize under the Rule of Law all his or her human rights, whether economic, social, cultural, civil, or political (International Commission of Jurists, Development, Human Rights and the Rule of Law. Oxford: Pergamon, 1981).

"The common heritage of mankind" in AFR, #22-1, was first articulated by Ambassador Prado from Malta in the General Assembly of the

United Nations on November 1, 1967. At that time, he declared that the bed under the high seas is the "common heritage of mankind." The sea bed, which has rich mineral resources, was thus claimed to be a common area to be enjoyed and exploited by all nations and not just by nations which have the technology to mine the sea bed under the December 10, 1982 Law of the Sea Treaty. The "common heritage" concept was incorporated into this Treaty with respect to sea bed resources. However, its legal status is very unclear and is considered at best a declaratory right.

IV. Landmarks. "Development" is a term with extensive use at the national and international levels to refer to the progressive improvement of the economic, social, and political conditions in the world's less advantaged countries, often referred to as the developing nations. In January 1941, President Roosevelt framed one of the goals of World War II as "freedom from want." The United States was the principal nation to incorporate economic and social well-being in the United Nations Charter, especially in Article 55 and the establishment of the Economic and Social Council. Article 73 (d) of the Charter calls for the promotion of "constructive measures of development . . ." The United Nations Covenant on Economic, Social, and Cultural Rights of 1966 has become the principal legal authority for advancing the development of human well-being.

Aid for development from many nations and the United Nations to the new nations was extensive after 1950. The United Nations Development Program, established in 1966, has been the leading force for international development programs. The UNDP has not only promoted development on a national scale in over a hundred nations but also stressed human development which it defines as follows.

Human development is a process whereby people are given better opportunities, notably for a longer life and better health, education, and access to the resources needed for a decent standard of living, along with political freedom, human rights guarantees, and self-respect. Commission on Human Rights, Report of the Secretary-General, November 29, 1991. Clearly, development is intended to enhance the well being both of nations and individuals.

Ambassador Keba M'Baye of Senegal was the first to deem development a human right in a lecture at Strasbourg in 1972. From that time on, the right to development was viewed by many as a right under IHRL. However, the ambiguity of the meaning of right to development continues to render this right declaratory and not of legal status.

The demands for a New International Economic Order in the General Assembly Resolution of May 1974 and Assembly's Resolution, the Charter of Economic Rights and Duties of States of December 1974 pressed in a rather strident manner for extensive development assistance from the industrialized states to the developing states. This quest for a major restructuring of the international economic architecture did produce some modest arrangements for expanded assistance from the Western states to the developing nations. However, these demands of the mid-1970s did not advance the concept of right to development except to introduce considerable rhetoric and debate in the diplomatic conference rooms of the United Nations and especially in the Commission on Human Rights for over five years.

Finally, a fifteen-member Working Group of Governmental Experts on the Right to Development was appointed by the UN Commission on Human Rights in March 1981 to make an extensive study of the right and to report back to the Commission. The Working Group's report was submitted to the Commission in 1984 and after considerable review and revisions was completed by 1986. The report, which recommended a declaration on the right, was approved by the General Assembly which adopted the Declaration on the Right to Development on December 4, 1986.

In March 1989 the Commission on Human Rights launched a "Global Consultation on the Realization of the Right to Development as a Human Right." A broadly based conference met in Geneva in January 8–12, 1990, under the auspices of the Secretary General to explore the human rights issues of development. Follow-up reports on Global Consultation in January 1991 and November 1991 are of considerable interest, especially the November 1991 Report by the Secretary-General on Effective Implementation of the Declaration on the Right to Development.

Problems remain, however, with the status and meaning of right to development. Professor Philip Alston writes that "while the Declaration on the Right to Development reflects a range of political compromises hammered out over a five year period, it has succeeded more in restating and enshrining the competing and often contradictory visions of the different groups [of interpretation of development] than in resolving them." He adds that the observer cannot "help but be struck by the paucity of specific proposals which have been put forward as means by which the right to development could be given operational substance. This may be an inevitable by-product of the continuing absence of a genuine consensus as to the core meaning of the concept . . ."

The right to development means different things to different people and nations. There is no question of the right of people and nations to develop toward progressively higher levels of well-being and social justice. There is no question that there should be a more equitable distribution of valued national and international economic and social resources toward those ends. However, the "right to development" as an entitlement of a state or a person has yet to be defined in a genuinely meaningful manner.

V. Cross References. Standard of Living and other Economic, Social, and Cultural Rights and Peoples, Self-Determination, and Peoples, Natural Resources (Collective Rights).

Disabled Persons

I. The Right. Everyone affected by a diminution of his or her physical or mental capacities is entitled to receive special attention designed to help him or her achieve the greatest possible development of his or her personality. The States Parties agree to adopt such measures as may be necessary for this purpose. American Convention on Human Rights, Additional Protocol, 1988, Article 18.

II. Other Sources. Covenant on Child, #23;

Declaration on the Rights of Disabled Persons, General Assembly Resolution 3447, 1975; Declaration on the Rights of Mentally Retarded Persons, General Assembly Resolution 2856, 1971; ASEAN, #5-11; Dec Social Progress, #11 (c).

III. Expanded Definition. A disabled person means any person unable to ensure by himself or herself, wholly or partly, the necessities of a normal individual and/or social life, as a result of deficiency, either congenital or not, in his or her physical or mental capabilities. Declaration on the Rights of Disabled Persons, #1. A mentally retarded person is a disabled person.

Disabled persons have the inherent right to respect for their human dignity. Disabled persons, whatever the origin, nature, and seriousness of their handicaps and disabilities, have the same fundamental rights as their fellow citizens of the same age, which implies first and foremost the right to enjoy a decent life as normal and as full as possible. "All disabled persons have the same civil and political rights as other human beings . . . " Declaration on the Rights of Disabled Persons, #3 and 4. "The mentally retarded person has, to the maximum degree of feasibility, the same rights as other human beings." #1, Declaration on the Rights of Mentally Retarded Persons.

The precariousness of the disabled person's physical situation is compounded by the degree of precariousness of his or her legal position, with respect to specific rights granted to him or her and the lack of precision as to the extent to which rights already established are guaranteed. In addition, disabled persons are often subjected to serious de facto violations, which must be prevented and eliminated through the strengthening of legal instruments and the establishment of control mechanisms to stop such violations. The United Nations must pay particular attention to human rights violations causing disability, such as military conflicts, torture, cruel and inhuman treatment, and others. Report, Special Rapporteur on Disabled Persons (Leandro Despouy) to Subcommission, UN Commission on Human Rights, 1985.

IV. Landmarks. Disabled and other handicapped persons have enjoyed rights under laws in many nations, but international rights and protection are fairly new. The Declaration on Social Progress of 1969 briefly mentioned concerns for the disabled. Extensive discussion at the General Assembly, buttressed by significant contributions from nongovernmental organizations, led to the Declaration of the Rights of Mentally Retarded Persons in December 1971 and the Declaration on the Rights of Disabled Persons of December 9, 1975. Both of these Declarations pioneered the international recognition of the plight and legal needs of the disabled.

In December 1976 the General Assembly called on all states to implement the Declaration on Disabled Persons and also designated 1981 as the International Year for the Disabled. A World Program of Action Concerning Disabled Persons was announced by the Assembly on December 3, 1982. At the same time, the Assembly declared 1983–1992 as the United Nations Decade of Disabled Persons with emphasis on international implementation of the World Program. A UN Voluntary Fund on Disability was also established. In 1984, the Subcommission of the Commission on Human Rights designated Leandro Despouy, whose studies and reports contributed much to literature and research on the disabled, as Special Rapporteur on the Disabled.

The Center for Social Development and Humanitarian Affairs, under the UN Commission for Social Development at the UN Office in Vienna, had administrative responsibilities for the Decade's programs, which included the development of international classification of impairment, disability, and handicap. A working group addressed itself to the development of standard rules on equalization of opportunities for disabled persons, among many other activities and programs during the Decade.

At the international legal level, Article 18 of the 1988 Protocol to the American Convention on Human Rights pioneered legal rights of the disabled, following the extensive provisions in #23 of the 1989 Convention on the Child.

V. Cross References. Child, Dignity, and Life (Civil and Political Rights) and Family and Health (Economic, Social, and Cultural Rights). *See also* the extensive programs and activities for the disabled and mentally ill persons of the World Health Organization as well as similar programs of the United Nations Children's Fund.

See also the Tallinn Guidelines for Action on Human Resources Development in the Field of Disability, General Assembly Resolution, December 8, 1989; Annual Reports of Special Rapporteur on the Disabled, Leandro Despouy; and Principles for the Protection of Persons with Mental Illness and for the Improvement of Mental Health Care, General Assembly Resolution, December 17, 1991.

Indigenous Peoples

I. The Right. Indigenous and tribal peoples shall enjoy the full measure of human rights and fundamental freedoms without hinderance or discrimination. Convention Concerning Indigenous and Tribal Peoples in Independent Countries, Article 3 (International Labor Convention 169, 1989).

Indigenous peoples have the right to full and effective enjoyment of all the human rights and fundamental freedoms which are recognized in the Charter of the United Nations and in international human rights law. Draft United Nations Declaration on the Rights of Indigenous Peoples (1994), Article 2.

II. Other Sources. Indigenous and Tribal Populations, ILO Convention 107, 1957.

III. Expanded Definition. This Convention (ILO, #169) applies to tribal peoples in independent countries whose social, cultural, and economic conditions distinguish them from other sections of the national community, and whose status is regulated wholly or partly by their own customs, traditions, by special laws or regulations. It also refers to peoples in independent countries who are regarded as indigenous on account of their descent from the populations which inhibited the country, or a geographical region to which the country belongs, at the time of conquest, colonization, or the establishment of present state boundaries and who, irrespective of their legal status, retain some or all of their own social, economic, cultural, and political institutions. #1, ILO Convention 169.

Indigenous populations, communities, peoples, and nations are those that, having a historical continuity with preinvasion and precolonial societies that developed on their territories, consider themselves distinct from other sections of the societies now prevailing on those territories or in parts of them. They form at present nondominant sectors of society and are determined to preserve, further develop, and transmit to future generations their ancestral territories and their ethnic identity as the basis of their continued existence as peoples, in accordance with their own cultural patterns, social institutions, and legal systems. United Nations Working Group on Indigenous Populations, Subcommission, UN Commission on Human Rights, interim definition of "Indigenous Peoples."

IV. Landmarks. Beginning in the sixteenth century, the crushing imperialism and colonialism of the Western European states for the most part dismantled or destroyed the governing, social, economic, and legal systems of the indigenous peoples they conquered. Indigenous peoples suffered the degradation of virtual or actual slavery, if not extinction, and without any recourse except responding with force where and when they could. The Spanish Dominican Francisco de Vitoria (1480–1546) claimed that the native peoples were as free under the law of nature as were their conquerors. He denied any proclaimed right by any religious or governing authority of any right over native peoples. de Vitoria, a renowned lawyer and professor at the University of Salamanca, was the first champion of the conquered indigenous peoples. Roger Williams (1603–1683) made the same argument a hundred years later in Massachusetts and departed to found a new colony in Rhode Island in 1636.

Nevertheless, the native populations of most conquered countries or areas were partially or totally subordinated to the control and subjection of the Western colonists in varying measures in the Americas, Africa, and Asia. Western colonialism reached its peak about 1910 and then the League of Nations, through its Mandate System and minority treaties, began to reverse many patterns of Western domination. Native populations in independent states, however, had very few champions. Their aspirations for improved living and working conditions, as well as some civil and political rights independent of the dominant governing authority, were totally absent in the United Nations Charter and the 1948 Universal Declaration of Human Rights. They had practically no unity or organization to express their views. Further, the doctrine of state sovereignty in Article 2 of the United Nations Charter erected a wall between the indigenous peoples in independent states and aspirations and demands for enhanced rights and the legal authority of the sovereign state. The two prime United Nations Covenants on Human Rights also offered little to indigenous populations, with the exception of #27 of ICPR on rights of minorities, a category which may or may not include indigenous peoples.

The International Labor Organization, the first organization to sponsor human rights and their implementation, also pioneered legal rights for indigenous peoples. The ILO sponsored a major study of indigenous peoples' rights in 1952 and developed an innovative "Andean Program" in the northwest Southern Hemisphere in 1954. The ILO 1957 Convention on Indigenous and Tribal Populations cited above was the first international treaty for the protection of indigenous peoples' rights.

At the United Nations level, the Subcommission of the Commission on Human Rights appointed Jose R. Martinez Cobo of Equador as Special Rapporteur to make a study and recommendations on rights of indigenous peoples. His "Study of the Problem of Discrimination against Indigenous Populations" was adopted by the Economic and Social Council in August 1984 and was widely circulated within the UN and among UN members.

The United Nations Working Group on Indigenous Populations was established by the Economic and Social Council in May 1982. Working under the Subcommittee of the Commission on Human Rights, the Working Group was delegated to undertake two tasks. First, it was asked to review national developments pertaining to the promotion and protection of the human rights of indigenous peoples. Second, it assigned the development of international standards concerning the rights of indigenous peoples. The Working Group sponsored a study (by Special Rapporteur Miguel Alfonso Martinez) of universal standards and the treaty rights of indigenous peoples under agreements they may have with the state in which they live. Further, the Working Group, under Chair and Special Rapporteur Ms. Erica-Irene Daes of Greece, voted in 1985 to prepare a Draft Declaration of the Rights of Indigenous Peoples which is undergoing further stages of negotiation. In 1985, the General Assembly established a Voluntary Fund for Indigenous Populations.

It is estimated today that there are about 300 million indigenous peoples in hundreds of groupings around the world. They are represented in part by the World Council of Indigenous Peoples. The Council and many nongovernmental organizations have played a very influential role in the negotiations on the Draft Declaration. Nineteen-ninety-three was the International Year of the World's Indigenous People. The United Nations Goodwill Ambassador for the Year was Rigoberta Menchu Tum, an indigenous Quiche woman from Guatemala and recipient of the 1992 Nobel Peace Prize for her work in the cause of indigenous populations.

V. Cross References. Association, Asylum, Dignity, Life, Territory, Movement in, Nationality, Political, Property, and Religion (Civil and Political Rights); Due Process and Security of Person (Legal Rights); Culture, Education, Family, and entries for Work (Economic, Social, and Cultural Rights); Aliens, Apartheid, Genocide, Migrant Workers, Minorities, Refugees, Peoples, Self-Determination, Peoples, Natural Resources, and Stateless (Collective Rights); and Development (Declaratory Rights).

Mercenaries

I. The Right. Any person who recruits, uses, finances, or trains mercenaries . . . commits an offense for the purposes of this Convention. A mercenary who participates directly in the hostilities or in a concerted act of violence, as the case may be, commits an offense for the purpose of the Convention. International Convention Against the Recruitment, Use, Financing, and Training of Mercenaries, General Assembly, 1989, Articles 2 and 3.

II. Other Sources. Condemnation of use of mercenaries as a means to violate human rights and to impede this exercise of the right of peoples to self-determination (Annual Resolution by the General Assembly); Draft Code of Crimes Against the Peace and Security of Mankind, United Nations International Law Commission, #18.

III. Expanded Definition. A mercenary is any person who (a) is specially recruited locally or abroad in order to fight in an armed conflict;

(b) is motivated to take part in the hostilities essentially by the desire for private gain and, in fact, is promised, by or on behalf of a party to the conflict, material compensation substantially in excess of that promised or paid to combatants of similar rank and functions in the armed forces of that party; (c) is neither a national of a party to the conflict nor a resident of territory controlled by a party to the conflict; (d) is not a member of the armed forces of a party to the conflict; and (e) has not been sent by a state which is not a party to the conflict on official duty as a member of its armed forces. Article 1-1, Convention on Mercenaries. *See also* #1-2, Convention on Mercenaries.

IV. Landmarks. Mercenaries and war have been intertwined throughout history. The Hessian soldiers fighting on the payroll of England are well-known to any student of the American Revolutionary War. Niccolo Machiavelli (1469–1527) condemned mercenaries in *The Prince* and declared that the best warriors are those fighting with conviction for their native lands. His main target was the famous condottieri, Italian city-state mercenaries of the fourteenth and fifteenth centuries. In the sixteenth century, the soldiers of Holland fought Spain in this spirit, and nationalism in due course produced the national soldier in preference to the mercenary.

Mercenaries never went out of business. They found new opportunities with the post–World War II clashes between the colonial status quo and national self-determination, especially in Southern Africa, and were often condemned by the UN General Assembly and occasionally by the Security Council. In a resolution of December 14, 1979, the Assembly urged all states to prohibit any involvement of mercenaries in their territories and also voted to prepare a convention outlawing mercenaries. In 1980, the Assembly established an Ad Hoc Committee to draft a convention which, after years of difficult negotiation, was adopted by the Assembly on December 4, 1989. The Convention is not yet in force because of insufficient ratifications.

In 1986 the Commission on Human Rights condemned mercenaries as a means of impeding the right of peoples to self-determination, especially in Southern Africa and Central America. The Commission appointed a Special Rapporteur to examine the question of mercenaries violating human rights and the exercise of self-determination on March 9, 1987. As Special Rapporteur, Enrique Bernales Ballesteros of Peru has submitted to the Commission and the General Assembly a series of annual reports, which, joined with the 1989 Convention, have added a new dimension to the inventory of human rights.

V. Cross References. Life and Nationality (Civil and Political Rights); Aliens, Apartheid, Genocide, and Peoples, Self-Determination (Collective Rights); and Indigenous Peoples (Declaratory Rights).

Bibliography

It is only natural that fifty years after the founding of the United Nations in 1945 the bibliography for international human rights has become a vast collection of primary and secondary resources. The bibliographical entries for the dictionary are thus limited to those which provide the reader with additional resources to amplify and illuminate the more than sixty entries for international human rights law found here. Nevertheless, they also lead to most of the material published in the past fifteen or twenty years, providing a comprehensive reference guide for human rights law.

The nine sections of the bibliography include the following: basic references and resources; general resources; historical resources including the Universal Declaration of Human Rights; civil and political rights; legal rights; economic, social, and cultural rights; collective and declaratory rights; regional human rights regimes; and miscellaneous resources including publications, annual volumes, and nongovernmental organizations.

Five volumes were of particular value to the author in the preparation of the dictionary: Blaustein, Albert P., Roger S. Clark, and Jay A. Sigler, eds., *Human Rights Sourcebook* (New York: Paragon House Publishers, 1987); Brownlie, Ian, ed., *Basic Documents on Human Rights* (Oxford: Clarendon Press, 1992, 3rd ed.); Newman, Frank, and David Weissbrodt, *International Human Rights* (Cincinnati, Ohio: Anderson Publishing Company, 1990); Perry, Richard L., and John C. Cooper, eds., *Sources of Our Liberties* (Chicago: American Bar Foundation, 1978); and *United Nations Action in the Field of Human Rights* (New York: United Nations, 1994). The extensive bibliography section in Newman and Weissbrodt was of particular value.

I. Basic References and Resources

A. Principal Human Rights Resources

Human Rights: A Compilation of International Instruments. 5th ed. New York: United Nations, 1988.

Human Rights, Status of International Instruments. New York: United Nations, 1987.

Sohn, Louis B., ed. *International Organization and Integration: Annotated Basic Documents of International Organizations and Arrangements*. Boston: Martinus Nijhoff Publishers, 1986.

Twenty-four Human Rights Documents. New York: Columbia Center for the Study of Human Rights, 1992.

B. Secondary Resources

Andrews, J., and W. Hines. *Key Guide to Information Sources on International Protection of Human Rights*. New York: Facts on File Publications, 1987.

Black's Law Dictionary. 5th ed. St. Paul, Minnesota: West Publishing Company.

Encyclopaedia Britannica. 15th ed. Chicago: Encyclopaedia Britannica, 1995.

Friedman, Julian, and Sherman Marc. *Human Rights: An International and Comparative Law Bibliography*. Westport, Connecticut: Greenwood Press, 1985.

Hannum, Hurst, ed. *Guide to International Human Rights Practice*. Philadelphia: University of Pennsylvania Press, 1992.

Human Rights Internet. Human Rights Center, University of Ottawa, 57 Avenue Louis Pasteur, Ottawa, Ontario KIN 6N5 Canada (613) 564-3492.

Humana, Charles, ed. *World Human Rights Guide*. New York: Oxford University Press, 1992.

Lawson, Edward, ed. *Encyclopedia of Human Rights*. New York: Taylor and Francis, Inc., 1991.

Tessitore, John, and Susan Woolfson. *A Global Agenda: Issues Before the 50th General Assembly of the United Nations*. Lanham: University Press of America, 1995. (Published each year by the United Nations Association of the United States with review in depth of UN human rights activities.)

United Nations Publications and Information on UN Primary and Secondary Resources on Human Rights: Centre for Human Rights, United Nations, New York, NY 10017 & Centre for Human Rights, United Nations Office at Geneva, 8–14 avenue de la Paix, 1211 Geneva 10, Switzerland.

II. General Resources

Alston, Philip, ed. *The United Nations and Human Rights: A Critical Appraisal.* Oxford: Clarendon Press, 1992.

An-Na'im, ed. *Human Rights in Cross Cultural Perspectives.* Philadelphia: University of Pennsylvania Press, 1991.

Baxi, Upendra, ed. *The Right To Be Human.* Delhi: India International Centre, 1987.

Claude, Richard Pierre, and Burns H. Weston, eds. *Human Rights in the World Community: Issues and Action.* 2nd ed. Philadelphia: University of Pennsylvania Press, 1992.

Donnelly, Jack. *Universal Human Rights in Theory and Practice.* Ithaca, New York: Cornell University Press, 1989.

Forsythe, David P. *Human Rights and World Politics.* Lincoln, Nebraska: University of Nebraska Press, 1988.

———. *Internationalization of Human Rights.* New York: Lexington Books, 1991.

Friedman, Lawrence M. *The Republic of Choice; Law, Authority, and Culture.* Cambridge, Massachusetts: Harvard University Press, 1990.

Gibson, John S. *International Organization, Constitutional Law and Human Rights.* New York: Praeger, 1992.

Henkin, Louis, ed. *The International Bill of Rights, The Covenant on Civil and Political Rights.* New York: Columbia University Press, 1981.

Juviler, Peter, et al. *Human Rights for the 21st Century.* Armonk, New York: E. Sharpe, 1992.

Kamminga, Menno T. *Inter-state Accountability for Violations of Human Rights.* Philadelphia: University of Pennsylvania Press, 1992.

Kothari, Smitu, and Harsh Sethi, eds. *Rethinking Human Rights: Challenges for Theory and Action.* Delhi: New Horizons Press, 1989.

Lauterpacht, Hersch. *International Law and Human Rights.* London: Archon Books, 1968.

Lillich, Richard B. *International Human Rights: Problems of Law, Policy and Practice.* Boston: Little, Brown & Co., 1991.

Livezey, Lowell. *Non-Governmental Organizations and the Ideas of Human Rights.* Princeton: Princeton University Center of International Studies, 1989.

McDougal, Myres, Harold D. Lasswell, and Lung-chu Chen. *Human Rights and World Public Order: The Basic Principles of International Law of Human Dignity*. New Haven, Connecticut: Yale University Press, 1980.

McWhinney, Edward. *United Nations Law Making*. New York & London: Holmes & Meier Publishers, 1984.

Meron, Theodor, ed. *Human Rights and Humanitarian Norms in Customary Law*. Oxford: Clarendon Press, 1989.

———. *Human Rights in International Law: Legal and Policy Issues*. Oxford: Clarendon Press, 1984.

———. *Human Rights Law Making in the United Nations*. Oxford: Oxford University Press, 1986.

Newman, Frank, and David Weissbrodt. *International Human Rights*. Cincinnati, Ohio: Anderson Publishing Company, 1990.

Nino, Carlos Santiago. *The Ethics of Human Rights*. New York: Oxford University Press, 1991.

Ramcharan, B. G. *The Concept and Present Status of the International Protection of Human Rights*. Boston: Martinus Nijhoff Publishers, 1989.

———. *Humanitarian Good Offices in International Law*. Boston: Martinus Nijhoff Publishers, 1983.

Renteln, Alison Dundes. *International Human Rights: Universalism versus Regionalism*. Newbury Park, California: Sage, 1990.

Robertson, A. H. Revised by J. G. Merrills. *Human Rights in the World: An Introduction to the Study of the International Protection of Human Rights*. 3rd ed. New York: St. Martin's Press, 1990.

Sieghart, Paul. *The International Law of Human Rights*. Oxford: Clarendon Press, 1983.

Teson, Fernando. *Humanitarian Intervention: An Inquiry into Law and Morality*. Dobbs Ferry, New York: Transnational Publishers, Inc., 1988.

Tolley, Howard. *The United Nations Commission on Human Rights*. Boulder, Colorado: Westview Press, 1987.

van Boven, Theo. *People Matter: Views on International Human Rights Policy*. Amsterdam: Muelenhoff, 1982.

von Glahn, Gerhard. *Law Among Nations*. 6th ed. New York: Macmillan Publishing Company, 1992.

Winston, Morton. *The Philosophy of Human Rights*. Belmont, California: Wadsworth, 1989.

III. Historical Resources Including Universal Declaration of Human Rights

Note: Many of the volumes cited in General Resources include historical material and references on human rights. The following resources, along with Perry, cited above, were invaluable for the Landmarks section of entries in the dictionary.

Burns, James MacGregor, and Stewart Burns. *The Pursuit of Rights in America: A People's Charter*. New York: Random House, 1993.

Chandler, Ralph C., et al. *The Constitutional Law Dictionary. Volume One: Institutional Rights*. Oxford: ABC-CLIO, 1985.

Daes, Erica-Irene A. *Freedom of the Individual Under Law: A Study of Duties and Limitations on Rights in Article 29 of the Universal Declaration of Human Rights*. New York: United Nations, 1990.

Durant, Will. *The Story of Civilization*. Eight vol. New York: Simon & Schuster, 1935–1963.

Eide, Asbjorn, et al., eds., *The Universal Declaration of Human Rights: A Commentary*. Oslo: Scandinavian University Press, 1992. Also, Oxford: Oxford University Press, 1992.

Encyclopaedia Britannica. 15th ed. Chicago: Encyclopaedia Britannica, 1995.

Great Books of the Western World. Chicago: Encyclopaedia Britannica, Inc., 1952.

Henkin, Louis. *The Age of Rights*. New York: Columbia University Press, 1990.

Humphrey, John P. *Human Rights and the United Nations: A Great Adventure*. Dobbs Ferry, New York: Transnational Publishers, Inc., 1984.

Lacey, Michael, and Knud Haakonsen, eds. *A Culture of Rights: The Bill of Rights in Philosophy, Politics and Law, 1791 and 1991*. New York: Cambridge University Press, 1991.

Laqueur, Walter, and Barry Rubin, eds. *The Human Rights Reader*. New York: Penguin, USA, 1990.

Levy, Leonard W. *Original Intent and the Framers of the Constitution*. New York: Macmillan Publishing Company, 1988.

Nickel, James W. *Making Sense of Human Rights*. Berkeley, California: University of California Press, 1987.

Sabine, George H., and Thomas L. Thorson. *A History of Political Theory*. Hinsdale, Illinois: Dryden Press, 1973.

Seagle, William. *Men of Law: From Hammurabi to Holmes*. New York: The Macmillan Company, 1947.

———. *The Quest for Law*. New York: Alfred A. Knopf, 1941.

Strauss, Leo. *Natural Right and History*. Chicago: University of Chicago Press, 1965.

The Universal Declaration of Human Rights, 1948–1988: Human Rights, The United Nations and Amnesty International. New York: Amnesty International USA, 1988.

IV. Civil and Political Rights

Alston, Philip, et al. *Children, Rights and the Law*. New York: Oxford University Press, 1992.

Arat, Zehra F. *Democracy and Human Rights in Developing Countries*. Boulder, Colorado: Lynne Rienner Publishers, 1991.

Benito, Elizabeth Odio. *Elimination of All Forms of Intolerance and Discrimination Based on Religion or Belief*. New York: United Nations Study Series Number Two, 1989.

Bossuyt, M. *Guide to the "Travaux Preparatoires" of the International Convention on Civil and Political Rights*. Boston: Martinus Nijhoff Publishers, 1987.

Flanz, G. H. *Comparative Women's Rights and Political Participation in Europe*. Dobbs Ferry, New York: Transnational Publishers, 1983.

Goodwin-Gill, Guy S., and Ilele Cohn. *Child Soldiers*. New York: Oxford University Press, 1994.

Hannum, Hurst. *The Right to Leave and Return in International Law and Practice*. Boston: Martinus Nijhoff Publishers, 1987.

Hazon, Winnie. *The Social and Legal Status of Women: A Global Perspective*. Westport, Connecticut: Greenwood Press, 1990.

Hevener, Natalie Kaufman. *International Law and the Status of Women*. Boulder, Colorado: Westview Press, 1983.

McKean, W. *Equality and Discrimination Under International Law*. Oxford: Clarendon Press, 1983.

Ramcharan, B. G., ed. *The Right To Life in International Law*. Boston: Martinus Nijhoff Publishers, 1985.

van Dyke, Vernon. *Human Rights, Ethnicity and Discrimination*. Westport, Connecticut: Greenwood Press, 1985.

Weissbrodt, David, et al. *Human Rights and Pre-trial Detention*. New

York: United Nations (Centre for Human Rights and Crime Prevention and Criminal Justice Branch), 1994.

Zuijdwijk, T. J. M. *Petitioning the United Nations: A Study in Human Rights*. New York: St. Martin's Press, 1982.

V. Legal Rights

Andrews, J. A., ed. *Human Rights in Criminal Procedure: A Comparative Study*. Boston: Martinus Nijhoff Publishers, 1982.

Gray, Ian, and Moira Stanley. *A Punishment in Search of a Crime*. New York: Amnesty International USA, 1990.

Guest, Ian. *Behind the Disappearances: Argentina's Dirty War Against Human Rights and the United Nations*. Philadelphia: University of Pennsylvania Press, 1990.

Hixon, Richard F. *Privacy in a Public Society: Human Rights in Conflict*. New York: Oxford University Press, 1989.

Hood, Roger. *The Death Penalty: A World-wide Perspective*. Oxford: Clarendon Press, 1989.

Lauterpacht, E. *Aspects of the Administration of International Justice*. Cambridge: Cambridge University Press, 1991.

Ramcharan, B. G. *International Law and Fact-finding in the Field of Human Rights*. Boston: Martinus Nijhoff Publishers, 1982.

Rodley, Nigel R. *The Treatment of Prisoners Under International Law*. Oxford: Clarendon Press, 1986.

Stover, Eric, and Elena Nightengale, eds. *The Breaking of Bodies and Minds: Torture, Psychiatric Abuse and the Health Professions*. New York: W. H. Freeman, 1985.

VI. Economic, Social, and Cultural Rights

Alston, Philip, and Katarina Tomasevski. *The Right To Food*. Boston: Martinus Nijhoff Publishers, 1984.

Breum, Martin, and Art Hendriks, eds. *AIDS and Human Rights: An International Perspective*. Copenhagen: Akademisk Forlag, 1988.

Crahan, Margaret E., ed. *Human Rights and Basic Needs in the Americas*. Washington, D.C.: Georgetown University Press, 1982.

Eide, Asbjorn, et al. *Food as a Human Right*. Tokyo: United Nations University Press, 1984.

VII. Collective and Declaratory Rights

Berting, Jan, et al. *Human Rights in a Pluralistic World.* London: Meckler Corporation (with UNESCO), 1991.

Capotorti, Francesco. *Study on the Rights of Persons Belonging to Ethnic, Religious and Linguistic Minorities.* New York: United Nations (Center for Human Rights Study Series Number Five), 1991.

Crawford, James, and Hans Kruck. *The Rights of Peoples.* New York: Oxford University Press, 1988.

Cristescu, Alfredo. *The Right to Self-determination.* New York: United Nations, 1981.

Fein, Helen. *Accounting for Genocide: National Responses and Jewish Victimization During the Holocast.* New York: Free Press, 1979.

Franck, Thomas M. *Human Rights in the Third World.* 3 vols. New York: Oceana Publishers, Inc., 1982.

Gurr, Ted Robert. *Minorities at Risk: A Global View of Ethnopolitical Conflicts.* Washington, D.C.: United States Institute of Peace Press, 1993.

Hannum, Hurst. *Autonomy, Sovereignty and Self-determination: The Accommodation of Conflicting Rights.* Philadelphia: University of Pennsylvania Press, 1990.

———. *The Right to Leave and Return in International Law.* Boston: Martinus Nijhoff Publishers, 1987.

Horowitz, Donald L. *Ethnic Groups in Conflict.* Berkeley, California: University of California Press, 1985.

International Commission of Jurists. *Development, Human Rights and the Rule of Law.* Oxford: Pergamon Press, 1981.

Janke, Peter. *Guerrilla and Terrorist Organizations: A World Dictionary and Bibliography.* New York: Macmillan Publishing Company, 1983.

Lerner, Nathan. *Group Rights and Discrimination in International Law.* Boston: Martinus Nijhoff Publishers, 1991.

Lillich, Richard B. *The Human Rights of Aliens.* Manchester, UK: Manchester University Press, 1984.

Mendelsohn, Oliver, and Upendra Baxi. *The Rights of Subordinated Peoples.* New York: Oxford University Press, 1994.

Shepherd, George W., and Ved P. Nanda. *Human Rights and Third World Development.* Westport, Connecticut: Greenwood Press, 1985.

Thornberry, Patrick. *International Law and the Rights of Minorities.* New York: Oxford University Press, 1991.

UNESCO. *Human Rights in Urban Areas.* Paris: UNESCO, 1983.

Welch, Claude, and Ronald I. Merltzer. *Human Rights and Development in Africa: Domestic, Regional and International Dilemmas*. Albany, New York: State University of New York Press, 1984.

VIII. Regional Human Rights Regimes

Buergenthal,Thomas A., et al. *Protecting Human Rights in the Americas*. Arlington, Virginia: Engel, 1986.

Fawcett, J. E. S. *The Application of the European Convention on Human Rights*. Oxford: Oxford University Press, 1987.

Hamalengwa, C., C. Flinterman, and E. V. O. Dankwa. *The International Law of Human Rights in Africa*. Boston: Martinus Nijhoff Publishers, 1988.

Hennelly, Alfred, and John Langan. *Human Rights in the Americas: The Struggle for Consensus*. Washington, D.C.: Georgetown University Press, 1982.

Howard, Rhoda E. *Human Rights in Commonwealth Africa*. Totowa, New Jersey: Rowman and Littlefield, 1986.

Janis, Mark, and Richard S. Kay. *European Human Rights Law*. Hartford, Connecticut: University of Connecticut Law School Foundation Press, 1991.

Mastny, Vojtech, and Jan Zielonka. *Human Rights and Security: Europe on the Eve of a New Era*. Boulder, Colorado: Westview Press, 1991.

Merrills, J. G. *The Development of International Law by the European Court of Human Rights*. Manchester: Manchester University Press (with St. Martin's Press), 1988.

Mower, A. Glenn. *Regional Human Rights: A Comparative Study of the West European and Inter-american Systems*. Westport, Connecticut: Greenwood Press, 1991.

Peter, Chris Maina. *Human Rights in Africa*. Westport, Connecticut: Greenwood Press, 1990.

van Dijk, Pieter, and G. J. H. van Hoof. *Theory and Practice of the European Convention on Human Rights*. Deventer: Kluwer Law and Taxation Publishers, 1990.

Catalogues of primary and other resources of regional regimes, including reports of proceedings, commissions, and courts, may be obtained from the following addresses of the three principal regimes:

The European Convention for the Protection of Human Rights and

Fundamental Freedoms—Directorate of Human Rights, Council of Europe, Strasbourg, France

The American Convention on Human Rights—General Secretariat, Human Rights, Organization of American States, Washington, D.C.

The African (Banjul) Charter of Human and Peoples' Rights—The Secretariat, African Commission on Human and Peoples' Rights, Banjul, The Gambia. Also, The African Centre for Democracy and Human Rights Studies, OAU, Banjul, The Gambia

IX. Miscellaneous Resources

Human rights periodicals, especially quarterlies, annual publications, and yearbooks, and information on selected nongovernmental organizations are further resources for inquiry, research, and complementary information on entries in the dictionary. The three categories below are hardly complete collections but rather some principal resources highly esteemed by scholars and practitioners of international human rights law.

A. Periodicals

American Journal of International Law. Washington, D.C.: American Society of International Law (quarterly).

Amnesty International Newsletter. New York: Amnesty International (monthly).

Amnesty International USA Legal Support Newsletter (quarterly).

Bulletin of Human Rights. Geneva: UN Centre for Human Rights (quarterly).

Columbia Human Rights Law Review. New York: Columbia Law School (semi-annual).

Cornell Journal on Human Rights. Ithaca, New York: Cornell Law School (quarterly).

Harvard Human Rights Journal. Cambridge, Massachusetts: Harvard Law School (annual).

Human Rights Internet Reporter. Ottawa: University of Ottawa Human Rights Center.

Human Rights Law Journal. Kiel: Engel & with International Institute of Human Rights, Strasbourg, France (quarterly).

Human Rights Monitor. Geneva: International Service for Human Rights (quarterly).

Human Rights Newsletter. Geneva: UN Centre for Human Rights (quarterly).

Human Rights Quarterly. Cincinnati, Ohio: Morgan Institute for Human Rights, University of Cincinnati (quarterly).

Netherlands Quarterly of Human Rights. Utrecht: Netherlands Institute of Human Rights (quarterly).

New York Law School Journal of Human Rights. New York: New York Law School (annual).

Nordic Journal on Human Rights. Oslo: Norwegian Institute of Human Rights (quarterly).

Review. Geneva: International Commission of Jurists (quarterly).

South African Journal on Human Rights. Johannesburg: Centre for Applied Legal Studies at the University of Witwatersrand.

B. Annual Reports and Yearbooks

Amnesty International. New York (322 Eighth Avenue): Amnesty International Publications (annual country report).

Country Reports on Human Rights Practices. Washington, D.C.: US Government Printing Office (US State Department annual country reports).

Human Rights in Developing Countries. Oslo: Norwegian University Press, Nowak & Swinehart, eds. under Danish Center for Human Rights.

Human Rights Watch World Report. New York: Human Rights Watch (485 5th Avenue).

Harvard Human Rights Yearbook. Cambridge, Massachusetts: Harvard Law School.

Israel Yearbook on Human Rights. Tel Aviv: Faculty of Law at Tel Aviv University.

Yearbook of the United Nations. New York: United Nations.

Yearbook on Human Rights. New York: United Nations.

Yearbook of the Human Rights Committee. New York: United Nations

(Committee under aegis of UN International Covenant on Civil and Political Rights).

C. Nongovernmental Organizations

Amnesty International, USA. 322 Eighth Avenue, New York, New York 10001.

Danish Center for Human Rights. Copenhagen, Denmark.

Helsinki Watch Committee. 485 Fifth Avenue, New York, New York 10017-6104 & 1522 K Street, NW, #910, Washington, D.C. 20005.

Human Rights Internet Reporter (Master List of Human Rights Organizations and Serial Publications). Human Rights Center, University of Ottawa, 57 Avenue Louis Pasteur, Ottawa, Ontario KIN 6N5 Canada.

Human Rights Watch. 485 Fifth Avenue, New York, New York 10017-6104 & 1522 K Street, NW, #910, Washington, D.C. 20005-1202.

International Commission of Jurists. P.O. Box 145, CH-1224, Geneva, Switzerland (American Association, ICJ, 777 UN Plaza, New York, New York 10017).

International Human Rights Law Group. 1601 Connecticut Avenue, NW, Suite 700, Washington, D.C. 20009.

International Institute of Human Rights. Strasbourg, France.

Minnesota Lawyers International Human Rights Committee. University of Minnesota Law School, Minneapolis, Minnesota.

Norway Institute of Human Rights. Oslo, Norway.

Physicians for Human Rights. 100 Boylston Street, Suite 620, Boston, Massachusetts 02116.

About the Author

John S. Gibson (B.A., Oberlin College; M.A., Case-Western Reserve University; and Ph.D, Columbia University, 1956) is professor emeritus, Tufts University, having served as professor of political science at Tufts since 1963. During that period, he was an adjunct professor, Fletcher School of Law and Diplomacy; director of the Tufts Program in International Relations; and director of the Tufts Lincoln Filene Center. He has authored or co-authored ten books, including *International Organizations, Constitutional Law and Human Rights* (Praeger, 1992). Professor Gibson has held a wide range of consultantships to the United States government and has served as president of the National Council of International Visitors in cooperation with the United States Information Agency. He has conducted annual Tufts seminars in Geneva on international law and human rights and has had extensive associations with the UN Commission on Human Rights and the Centre for Human Rights where he was a scholar-in-residence in 1992.